The Gospel In Nature: A Series Of Popular Discourses On Scripture Truths Derived From Facts In Nature... - Primary Source Edition

Henry Christopher McCook

THE GOSPEL IN NATURE

A SERIES OF POPULAR DISCOURSES ON SCRIPTURE
TRUTHS DERIVED FROM

FACTS IN NATURE

BY HENRY C. MCCOOK, D. D.

AUTHOR OF "THE AGRICULTURAL ANT OF TEXAS"
"THE HONEY AND OCCIDENT ANTS"
"TENANTS OF AN OLD FARM"
ETC., ETC., ETC.

PUBLISHED BY
ALLEN, LANE & SCOTT
229–233 South Fifth Street
PHILADELPHIA

Entered, according to Act of Congress, A. D. 1887, by

HENRY CHRISTOPHER McCOOK,

In the Office of the Librarian of Congress, at Washington.

Allen, Lane & Scott, Prs., Phila.

TO MY WIFE,

EMMA HERTER McCOOK,

WHO HAS SHARED WITH ME

ALIKE THE LIGHTS AND SHADOWS

OF A QUARTER CENTURY

OF MARRIED LIFE,

THIS BOOK

IS LOVINGLY DEDICATED

AS A MEMORIAL OF OUR COMMON

JUBILEE BIRTH-YEAR.

PREFACE.

FOR many years it has been the author's custom to preach a series of Sunday afternoon discourses on special themes. In the selection and treatment of these subjects he has used a larger liberty, and taken a wider range than is usually allowed in the ordinary sermon. The following book is the outgrowth of this custom, as was also the writer's last work, "The Women Friends of Jesus." The church which he serves happens to be located in the neighborhood of the University of Pennsylvania, and is therefore within easy reach of a great number of students, especially in the departments of medicine, biology, dental and veterinary surgery. With a view in great part to attract and influence for good this company of young men, the discourses on the "Gospel in Nature" were preached.

It will be observed that they are based almost entirely upon atmospheric phenomena, and the lessons presented are largely illustrated by natural imagery. Every lecture was introduced by a prelude giving a simple explanation of the natural facts or phenomena chosen as a symbol. This treatment in itself proved not only attractive to many who are eager to obtain such knowledge of nature, but was calculated to give all hearers a more intelligent understanding of the spiritual truths conveyed; for it is obvious that a parable or metaphor drawn from nature cannot be fully apprehended without a knowledge of the natural drapery of the thought. A popular style of presenting the matter in hand was, of course, necessary before a popular audience; and this style has been preserved in the printed lectures.

In the course of the twenty lectures here published many of the living questions of this era are introduced and more or less freely considered. They are not treated in a controversial spirit; indeed, at times they are barely alluded to in direct terms; but those truths and arguments are presented which have been thought best calculated to prevent or clear away doubts engendered by misleading lights of science, literature or art. In short, the author has sought to avoid that treatment which, in dealing with the religious difficulties that earnest, candid and thoughtful minds are required to

(5)

meet, so magnifies the statement of the difficulty in order to answer it, that the objection rather than the explanation remains,
and doubt is crystallized rather than dissolved.

Ten of these lectures were issued, one every week as delivered,
under the auspices of the Young Men's Church Association of the
Tabernacle Church.   The enterprise was attempted with a view of
furnishing religious reading especially to invalids, the aged, and
others detained from Sunday worship and instruction, as well as
to persons who do not habitually attend church services.   It was
successful beyond expectation, as a large number of copies was
thus distributed as current literature.   It is hoped that readers
who have fallen in with those occasional issues may wish to possess
the entire series in this book form.

The Bible approves itself a creation of the Divine Spirit by the
profound sympathy which it has with physical nature.   On the
other hand Nature shows the traces of her Creator's touch by the
readiness with which she yields up her every form and force to be
the drapery and sign of spiritual truths.   Nature is God's great
book of parables.   The undevout eye may read the title, finger
the covers, scan the title-page, the frontispiece, the pictures, may
even con some of the broader script; but it needs a devout mind
to so read the book as to drink in the hidden meanings, to come
into very spiritual communion with the Divine Author's most holy,
vital and vitalizing thoughts.

That is why those holy men of old, who spake as they were
moved by the Holy Ghost in their moments of inspiration, read
religious lessons in the sky, the sea, the earth, stars, flowers and
birds, in leaf, cloud and murmuring brook, in mountain, storm
and snow-crystal; "found books in the running brooks, sermons
in stones, and good in everything."   There is no nature-book so
sweet, pure, and true as the Bible of God.   The author sends
forth this volume with the earnest wish that it may bring to a few
of his fellow-men some measure of confirmation of this truth or
the sweet surprise of its revelation.

THE MANSE,
TABERNACLE PRESBYTERIAN CHURCH,
    Philadelphia, July 3d, A. D. 1887.

CONTENTS.

LECTURE I.

_____

God as Force.

_"The blessed and Only Potentate,   *   *   *   *
to whom be power eternal."_—I. TIM. vi. 15.

GOD AS FORCE.

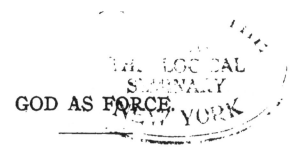

A CRITICAL study of the New Testament uncovers evidence of the existence of hymns in the primitive church. The Magnificat, the Benedictus, the Gloria in Excelsis, the Nunc Dimittis of Simeon were outbursts of song which mark the very beginning of the Christian era. The new spirit of praise thus manifest doubtless expressed itself at an early period in new forms, although we know that the ancient Psalms which had voiced the worship of the Church through so many ages were by no means set aside. Among the indications of early hymns presented by the New Testament is the passage of which our text forms a part. It is thought to be an ancient doxology used separately or attached to some hymn. We can better perceive the justice of this opinion, perhaps, by presenting the passage in this form:—

The blessed and only Potentate
The King of kings and Lord of lords,
Who only hath immortality,
Dwelling in light unapproachable,
Whom no man hath seen nor can see,
To whom be honor and power eternal.
Amen!

This ancient hymn or confession expresses a truth which when illustrated by the facts of Nature transcends the utmost flight of fancy. I can therefore hope to be only partially successful in the purpose thus to present it.

I. God is the supreme Force of the universe, the sovereign Potentate.

Jehovah is the supreme Lord. Such is the voice of Scripture. God is the Almighty One; "a mighty fortress is our God."* The Pagans were not unmindful of

---

* "Ein feste Burg ist Unser Gott."—*Luther's Hymn.*

this fact, for the Jupiter or Jove of ancient Latins and Greeks, the Thor of the Norseman with his mighty thunder hammer, were expressions to the men of past ages of the truth that there is above all gods and all forces and forms of Nature some one being, some one power who is entitled to the supreme place.

The truth thus dimly seen by the Gentiles, the Jews discerned fully. Their Lord was the Almighty. Their theology is transmitted to the Christian Church which equally believes in the all-potency of the Divine Being, and puts at the very front of its creed the article "I believe in God the Father Almighty."

1. Our first natural illustration of this truth we shall take from one of the most familiar objects—water. This element consists of two permanent gases condensed by the force of chemical affinity to the liquid condition. One of the gases is oxygen; the other united with it in double proportion is hydrogen. Hydrogen is a combustible gas fourteen and a half times lighter than air— one of the lightest forms of matter known. A cubic foot of water is equal to eighteen hundred cubic feet of a mixture of these gases. How has that mixture been accomplished and how is it maintained? The answer to these questions introduces us to the fact that these two constituents of water so persistently retain their aerial condition that it requires a pressure of twenty tons to the square inch to reduce them to the liquid state. Can you conceive of so immense a force as this —forty thousand pounds to the square inch? It requires all the mechanical skill possessed by man to apply it. Yet every drop of water upon the face of the earth is held in the liquid state by such a pressure as this. How is it held? What—WHO holds it? To strengthen our illustration let us compare force with force.

Water is easily decomposed by electricity. What amount of this agency would be equal to force apart the constituent gases of water?

The distinguished philosopher (and he was a Christian philosopher), Prof. Michael Faraday, proved that it requires more electricity to decompose a single drop of water than to charge a thunderbolt. If we reverse the proposition, therefore, we shall see that the pressure required to hold the gaseous constituents of water in their liquid state is equal to as many times the force of electricity contained within a thunderbolt as there are drops in the water itself.* In the face of this fact think of the ocean reaching to great depths and covering three-fourths of the surface of the globe. Think of that atmospheric ocean—the water contained in vapor forever held in suspense in the air above us. Think of the water which goes to make up in large proportion all living things in the animal and vegetable world. So thinking, will you stop to raise the question—nay, our question must be simply an exclamation—what power, what infinite power is here expressed!

2. Our second illustration is the atmosphere, or rather the play of forces by which its physical condition is compelled. Two mighty forces are continually acting thereon. The one is heat, which tends to expand it and force it like an unbent coil into surrounding space. The other force is gravitation, which grasps the atmosphere and holds it to the surface of the earth. These two opposing forces are so balanced that they may be said to be held in equilibrium, and few persons would suspect the vastness of either one.

Let us take the simple experiment which most students have made or seen made with Torricelli's tube, and from its results make these calculations. The pressure of the atmosphere on one man is equal to sixteen tons—thirty-two thousand pounds.† The pressure of the atmosphere upon this church is much more than the weight of the building itself. The pressure of the atmosphere upon one square mile of the earth's surface is over twenty-six millions of tons. The pressure of the atmosphere on the entire State of Pennsylvania with its forty-six thousand square miles is equal to two million three hundred and ninety-two thousand millions of pounds, or in other

---

*Cooke—"Religion and Chemistry," page 159. †Fourteen tons, A. Buchan—Encyclopædia Britannica, art. *Atmosphere.*

words two quadrillions three hundred and ninety-two trillions of pounds.

This is the work that gravity does in the whole world upon the elements of the atmosphere alone.

Now consider the power that balances all this. What is it? The sun's heat; the force that is lodged in sun-beams. How softly they fall! How they brighten the face of Nature! How gladly we welcome them as they steal gently through the window glass to sweeten and cheer the frosty brow of winter, or flood the fields and hills to gladden and enrich the soft days of spring. What gentle things they are! How noiselessly they fall! Yet all this force is lodged within their touch.

Attempt now to bring together in imagination all the energies acting at one moment on the earth, and unite them in one tremendous aggregate. Begin with the power of the air expressed in all its motions from the tornado to the zephyr. Next think of the force of electricity with its phenomena of lightning and thunder, and those heretofore hidden stores which modern physical science has brought to light and enlisted in the service of man. Think next of the mechanical power expressed in the flow of waters, in streams and rivers, in cascades, and Falls of Niagara, in ocean currents, in the sluggish creeping of the glacier and the swift crash of the avalanche.

Think again of those forces at work in vegetable and animal life; such for example as lift up mighty forests above the earth and hold them there. Think again of the force of fire, so terrible in our experience when it seizes upon our homes or business places, or sweeps unrestrained through vast cities. Think of the force of powder, or steam, or dynamite, which, however, are but insignificant things compared with the rest. Think of every other known and conceivable power, then make all the allowance that you choose for discount of your closest calculations and sum them all up. Let us see what part of the whole by reasonable calculation and estimate they may express.

This—one two thousand three hundred millionth of the force which the sun is every moment pouring into space.*   In other words, divide the force of the sun into two thousand three hundred million parts—all these vast powers which you have attempted to set in array before your imagination would be equal simply to one of those parts.

That would seem to be enough.   Imagination falters. Thought staggers in vain endeavor to conceive of such power.   But we must not stop here.   We have but placed our feet upon the outer steps leading to the threshold of the realm of facts that lie beyond.   For, what is the sun? A small star in the infinitude of space !   Yet the grand total of the powers streaming from all the suns seen in our night sky and undiscovered in its stellar deeps alone represents the active energy of the universe.

What is that energy?   GOD,—The very Power of God acting in all action.†   GOD—the Will of GOD.‡

There is now present in this country a welcome visitor, one of the most distinguished of British naturalists, Mr. Alfred Russel Wallace.   He enjoys the unique distinction of being, jointly with the late Mr. Darwin, the inventor of the theory of natural selection as applied to the evolution of species.   He differs from Mr. Darwin, however, in one exception which he makes to the law of natural selection. That exception is the most notable of all objects in the universe, the crown, the head of all—even man himself. Man, Mr. Wallace thinks, never could have been produced by those evolutionary laws which he believes to operate in the production of all the lower creatures. In one of his works,§ while speaking on the limits of natural selection as applied to man, he uses these words: "All force is probably will-force."   "Force is the product of mind."   In leading his readers up to the thought that the mind, out of which all force is originated, is the supreme intelligence whom we call God, he alludes to the operation of the human will.   "If will is anything," he says, "it is a power that *directs* the action of forces stored up in the body, and it is not conceivable that this

---

*COOKE—"Religion and Chemistry," page 304. †McCOSH— "Christianity and Positivism," page 15. ‡PROF. FLINT—"Theism," page 112. § On Natural Selection, page 366, Sqq.

direction can take place without the exercise of some force in some part of the organism. In the animal machine, however minute may be the changes required in the cells or fibres of the brain to set in motion the nerve currents which loosen or excite the pent-up forces of certain muscles, *some force* must be required to effect those changes."

In other words, you bend your arm. The supreme and ultimate power which compels that action is the human will. You flex your arm, and throw it out with such vigor as to fell to the ground the enemy, beast or man, who would assail your life. The ultimate power compelling that action is the human will. From such analogy Mr. Wallace rises to the lesson which it seems to me, by fair implication, is taught in our text. I quote his words :—

"If, therefore, we have traced one force, however minute, to an origin in our will, while we have no knowledge of any other primary cause of force, it does not seem an improbable conclusion that all force may be will-force; and thus that the whole universe is not merely dependent on, but actually is, the will of higher intelligences or of one Supreme Intelligence. It has been often said that the true poet is a seer; and in the noble verse of an American poetess, we find expressed what may prove to be the highest fact of science, the noblest truth of philosophy:"

> God of the granite and the rose !
>   Soul of the sparrow and the bee !
> The mighty tide of being flows
>   Through countless channels, Lord, from thee.
> It leaps to life in grass and flowers,
>   Through every grade of being runs,
> While from creation's radiant towers
>   Its glory flames in stars and suns.

II. Our text asserts yet another truth, viz., that God is the blessed as well as the only Potentate. The almighty is the Father Almighty! The supreme power in whose hands we all lie is a power of supreme benevolence.

It is certain that study of Nature's works opens up to us from many quarters the truth that the divine

Overmind and controlling Will is one of benevolence. God's creatures are, for the most part, blessed. But the perfect lesson of the supreme goodness of God must come to us from other sources than Nature. The truth is, Nature, in some of its phases, fills man and lower creatures with terror, and justly so. Storm, tornado, lightning, the wild lashing of sea waves, floods, fire, hail, and frost —these are in the aggregate benevolent forces, but alas! to multitudes of individuals they bring suffering and death. We do not wonder that they have raised in the minds of untutored man, and men without a complete revelation of the character of God, the suggestion of hostility and malignity in the character of Deity.

This thought has had and still has expression in the deities of pagan nations. Those gods are gods of cruelty and revenge too often, and their unhappy devotees are the victims of terror, which through all their lives they seek to remove by placating the angry powers above and around them. Men who have derived their theology from no source but Nature, have personified and deified the sternest and cruelest forces, rather than the gentlest and most benevolent. At least such gods have been most honored because most feared. To know God as he is we must turn from Nature to the revealed Word. The Bible supplements the book of creation. When we can read the mighty works of the Supreme Power as interpreted by words of Hebrew prophets and the life of the Son of God, then and only then can we see the force of the apostle's title, "the *blessed* Potentate."

Travelers inform us that those who live upon the equator command at night a view of both the stellar hemispheres. In our latitude we see the northern constellations led by the "Great Bear" as he swings upon his ceaseless rounds about the polar star. In the southern hemisphere men gaze upon the "Southern Cross." But standing at the equator midway between the two, the eye glances northward and southward alike, sweeping over the whole dome of heaven from the Great Bear to the Southern Cross. Even thus it is that we may come to that line in the history of human redemption that marks for us the advent and the sacrifice of Christ.

With our thought upon the infinite love of God as expressed in the life and death of Jesus, we are enabled to sweep that undivided dome of truth concerning the character of God which leaves him upon his throne an object of love.   Nature's teachings give us one view of the hemisphere.   The Old Testament Scriptures and human theology give us another view of the hemisphere. But when we stand with Jesus the Christ at the altar of Golgotha our eye covers the whole expanse, and we know that the dome of truth is one.   The LAMB is "in the midst of the Throne!"   Benevolence is sovereign still!

1. Turning then to the inspired word for lessons which we would associate with our natural facts, we learn, *first,* that the power of God is in subjection to his goodness. There is no more significant text in all Scripture, as it seems to me, than the saying of St. Paul, "We preach Christ crucified—Christ the power of God."[*]
Wonderful as are the applications of power in nature, as we have just briefly reviewed them, the manifestation of power that appears in the life and death of Jesus is more wonderful still.   Take your seat with his disciples on the Mount of Beatitudes, and listen to the words of Him who spake as never man spake.   The scene in itself seems insignificant enough, an assemblage of humble people in a remote spot of a remote land, a conquered province.   Yet these words, falling softly like drops of water, have carried within them a potency beyond the thought of man to estimate.   They have subdued and held the nations of mightiest force.   They have regenerated the state, have permeated the race.   Their inherent power has borne them and those who believed them over all oppositions of society; all persecutions of kings and priests; all trials, suffering, and terrors of death. The power of God has been in them, the very mightiest manifestation of his power, that which lies under the spiritual realm.
Once more, take your stand upon the summit of Mount Calvary. Lift your eyes to the central cross of those three

---

[*] I. Corinthians i. 23, 24.

standing there in the midst of mailed soldiers of iron
Rome, mocking priests of Israel's temple, and howling
citizens of Judah's town. Look upon the pale figure
hanging there! His thorn-crowned head is bowed upon
his pierced breast; his hands and feet are bleeding and
distorted with wounds of nails driven by hireling soldiers.
Could any one seem more helpless than he? He is dead!
Yet that silent figure, issuing from the tomb in which
loving hands had laid him, stands to-day regnant over
those nations of the world who are mightiest in all elements of human force, and lifts aloft the emblem of the
accursed tree on which he died as the sign of the faith
of millions. This is "Christ crucified—Christ the power
of God."

Reasoning from any standpoint of human philosophy, I do not know how it is that a life and death such
as this should have had results so wonderful. But when
I turn to the blessed book of God, and reverently accept
the lesson written there that he who thus lived, spoke,
and died was not man simply, but bore within himself
the power of the invisible God; when I read that he sits
now in glory at the right hand of the majesty on high,
to command in behalf of his Church and people every
force among men, and if need be, every force in nature,
I can understand the secret of his triumph. It issues
from the source of infinite power, for he who controls it
is Christ—the power of God. Great as are the marvels
which divine force in nature accomplishes, greater still
are those which in the name of Jesus are won from erring
hearts, and blinded minds, and perverted spirits, and
wayward passions, and wicked intents of the race of
men.

2. A second lesson which we derive from our subject
is that the noblest use of power is the rescue of the
weak and support of the true. What an inspiring view
of divine character is that uncovered to us through the
words of Isaiah! (lvii. 15.) "For thus saith the High and
Lofty One that inhabiteth eternity, whose name is Holy:
I dwell in the high and holy place, with him also that is
of a contrite and humble spirit, to revive the spirit of

the humble, and to revive the heart of the contrite ones."
This God, whose infinitude of power we have dimly
pictured to our thought by its manifestations in the
natural world, who inhabiteth immensity and through
all his lofty seats exerts his eternal strength, this is He
who stoops from the throne of his power to dwell in
the humblest seat of human weakness, the heart of a
penitent sinner.

The same truth is no less significantly revealed to us
in the fortieth chapter of Isaiah, where the divine strength
is depicted in words of striking beauty and faithfulness.
"Who hath measured the waters in the hollow of his
hand and meted out heaven with a span, and comprehended the dust of the earth in scales, and weighed the
mountains in scales and the hills in a balance?"   "It is
he who sitteth upon the circle of the earth and the inhabitants thereof are as grasshoppers; that stretcheth
out the heavens as a curtain and spreadeth them out as
a tent to dwell in.   Lift up your eyes on high and see
who hath created these, that bringeth out their host by
number : He calleth them all by name; by the greatness
of his might, and for that he is strong in power, not one
is lacking."   Think of that!   God likened to a shepherd
leading out the stars as one would lead forth his sheep,
tamed to subjection and every one known and named!

What is the purpose of this sublime picturing of the
infinite power of the Creator?   It is this, and mark the
lesson well! (verse 29): " He giveth power to the faint,
and to him that hath no might he increaseth strength.
Even the youths shall faint and be weary and the young
men shall utterly fall, but they that wait upon the Lord
shall renew their strength; they shall mount up with
wings as eagles, they shall run and not weary, they shall
walk and not faint."

Well may the feeble ones, the faint-hearted and weak-
lings of this our world of sorrows, rejoice that He who is
almighty has pledged his power to a purpose such as this.
Would that I could persuade all such to come this day
with their burdens and lay them down at his feet!

" Come unto me, all ye that labor and are heavy laden,
and I will give you rest."

What a lesson in practical duty is suggested to us by these teachings! Do you possess strength in any of its many forms? Strength of body, financial strength, social strength, intellectual power? What is the noblest use to which you can put it?

The learned Egyptologist, Eber,* puts these noble words upon the lips of Rameses, the ancient Pharaoh: "The only real divine attribute of our royal condition is that it is so easy for a king to make men happy." The men and women of strength are the kings and queens of this modern world of ours. Let them see to it that they are not wanting in that divine element of strength which brings to the sorrowful and weak the boon of happiness and the gift of help. Thus shall they enter into the life of and be yoke-fellows together with him who is the blessed Potentate.

3. Again, it is within the boundary of this thought to suggest that in all the exercise of divine power of which we have spoken there is no waste of energy. Economy in the use of forces is certainly a law of nature. Would that man might learn this lesson! Much human energy in Church, in philanthropic endeavor, in political life is simply wasted. It is wasted not merely because misdirected, but because it is without direction and regulation. There is scarce a gift of Nature, so lavish of noblest resources to this young land, that we do not use like the veriest spendthrifts. We foolishly and mercilessly hew down our forests, wasting far more than we use. We exhaust our fat soils with reckless disregard of the future. Thus it is through all the circle of our national domain. It is true as well in the domain of intellectual and religious forces. We are prodigal in their expenditure to a fault. Our social life is so ordered that we drink up the streams of vitality as "Behemoth" the rivers. We spend young lives by scores of thousands, casting them away as freely as the Canaanites of old offered them in sacrifice to Moloch. This is a deplorable condition of society! Is there no remedy for it? Will

---

*Uarda, By Geo. Eber.

we never learn to treasure the noblest gifts of nature, those high faculties and forces which beat within the breast of man himself? We deplore the waste of forests and fields, and it is sad enough. But sadder far than this is the waste of which I speak, because utterly irreparable. We must learn to distinguish between wise activity and wasteful action. We must learn that hurry is not always haste; that bustle is not business. That the ceaseless go, and run, and racing over life's highway; the grinding of our faculties in the noisy mills of human excitement and occupations, do not necessarily add to the force of our character or the effectiveness of our toil. Men may be forceful without being fussy.

God, who is always self-poised, for the most part is silent; his mightiest forces are voiceless. Work! work all you can, but learn from God the lesson to work without waste.

How shall I speak of that mournful waste of life's best powers which goes on daily among the victims of intemperance and lust? The heart grows heavy with grief as one passes by the numerous tippling-shops in this great city, and remembers that those doors which swing outward into our streets, open inward upon the gates of hell. And through them are continually drawn into the fires of death the noblest force of our fair town—our youth and strong men. Oh, how pitiful! Mighty God, have mercy! Make bare thine arm and stay this awful waste!

4. There is a final lesson which we associate with the teaching of our text. A lesson without which all others will avail nothing. We know the almighty power of God. We know the willingness of God both in the physical and spiritual world to extend that power to help man. Let us know also that that help is extended through channels which are fixed by immutable law.

He who would sail his ships across the sea calls to his aid in one form or another the forces of nature. If he would spread his snowy sails to the winds of heaven that their force may bear his cargo to a desired haven, he must seek those parallels along which the trade winds blow. In other words, he must conform his human machinery and action to the laws which regulate the forces which he would utilize for his good. If he would sail his vessel by steam he must conform his machinery to the laws which regulate the force and the application of force expressed by that mighty motor.

You have heard men speak of chaining lightning and making it a servant to man's will. The figure is based in part upon a truth; but it is equally true that he who would chain lightnings must first chain himself. In other words, if electricity is to be made a servant of man, man must conform himself to those laws imposed by the almighty Will-force upon that physical force which man seeks to utilize for his advantage. Men never think otherwise in their relations to natural forces in all lines of mechanics and commerce. Should they not remember this also when they enter the domain of spiritual forces? Are there no laws fixed for the moral direction of man? Are there no laws imposed upon man for the accomplishment of salvation? Surely there are! They are written for us in the holy pages of the inspired Scripture, and to these we must bow ourselves if we would be lifted by the hand of God into the immortality of the blessed.

It is the law of the spiritual kingdom that without holiness no man shall see God. It is a law of the spiritual kingdom that whosoever believeth in the Lord Jesus Christ shall be saved. Faith and righteousness, these are channels along which runs for man that almighty power which shall bear him in the end to eternal glory. Outside of these channels no man dare hope for redemption. Though he stand upon the very brink, and be able to dip his finger in the full flowing stream of saving help, if he step not in and yield himself to the power appointed for his rescue, he must stand in his chosen place—unsaved! Sinful man, step into the channel! Yield thee to God's laws of grace. Believe! Obey!—and thou shalt be saved.

LECTURE II.

———

Mist, or Vapor of Water.

"For what is your life? It is even a vapor, that appeareth for a little while, and then vanisheth away." —JAMES iv. 14.

MIST, OR VAPOR OF WATER.

VAPOR of water, mist or fog are common names for the natural phenomenon which supplies the symbolism for the spiritual lessons of this discourse.

A determined volume of air—a cubic foot, for example, at a given temperature has the property of receiving certain quantities of vapor of water in an invisible state, or as it is called, humidity. When it contains all the humidity it is capable of receiving it is said to be saturated. If then the temperature be increased the atmosphere will hold more vapor. If the temperature be lowered, the capacity for containing vapor is diminished and a part thereof will be condensed, appearing within the atmosphere in the form of fog or mist, or will be precipitated as dew, rain, or frost, according to the degree of cold and consequent condensation. The moist air is, in fact, like a sponge filled with water, which if it be squeezed by pressure of any sort will yield up a portion of its contents.* This pressure upon the atmosphere is supplied by various causes, principally the presence and absence of heat.

The air surrounding the earth is continually charged more or less freely with the vapor of water. In the aggregate the amount of moisture contained is immense. Under ordinary circumstances it is so expanded by heat of the sun's rays that it is invisible, but when the two conditions of a moisture-charged atmosphere and a reduced temperature come together this invisible vapor is condensed and becomes visible. As the earth is commonly cooler at nights, mist or fogs are more likely to prevail during that season, or in the early morning when the earth is most chilled by radiation. Since the air which rests immediately over beds of water, running

---

* GUYOT—"Earth and Man," page 152.

streams, and moist bits of earth is apt to be most freely charged with vapor, we see mist or fog more commonly in such situations.

The great source of the aqueous atmosphere is the torrid zone, where the heat of the sun converts water into vapor in large quantities, and sets in play the currents by which humid air is distributed throughout the earth. The general aqueous or vapor circulation has well been compared to a great steam-heating apparatus with its boilers in the tropics and the condensers all over the globe.* Any large building heated by steam will therefore afford an object lesson by which this phenomenon may be explained. The heat of furnaces converts the water within the boilers into steam. Water, when changed into vapor, absorbs more heat probably than any other liquid. The steam-pipes charged with this heated steam are coiled within chambers, or distributed in series of variously folded and interfolded loops throughout the building. These iron pipes or condensers come in contact with the cold air, whereupon the steam is cooled, and in the process of condensation yields up its latent heat. In some buildings, as in this church, cold, pure air from the outside is blown through the condensing chamber across iron pipes, and after being thus heated, is forced still further through long ducts which empty their heated contents through the registers into the audience room.

Now, the cold earth, or a colder stratum of atmosphere, form conductors which come in contact with the vapor-charged atmosphere and cause it to give up its heat. Thus the invisible vapor being cooled is condensed and is yielded, as has already been stated, in the form of rain, snow, dew, and mist or fog. Mist is simply a coarser form of invisible vapor or a finer form of dew. It is caused by a degree of cold which is just enough to condense the vapor, but not enough to break up its vaporous form and cause precipitation in dew.

Another, and perhaps even more familiar and simpler, illustration of this atmospheric phenomenon may be given. Have you noticed your bed-room windows,

---

* COOKE—"Religion and Chemistry," page 140.

when the weather is cold, covered with a fine mist upon which you may write your name with your finger, or which you may wipe off with your handkerchief, leaving the latter moist? It is the aqueous vapor from your own lungs which has been condensed into mist by contact with the cold window-glass. Go out into the air on a frosty morning, and as you breathe you observe a little mist-cloud issuing from your mouth, which is the result of the same process. If the doors or windows be suddenly opened upon a heated and crowded room, the atmosphere within the place will at once become dim, a fact which is produced by the aqueous vapor from the multitude of lungs, previously invisible on account of its greatly-rarefied condition, being suddenly precipitated in the form of mist. If the weather be intensely cold the entrance of fresh air may even cause snow to fall. This has been observed in Russian ball-rooms, and also in the subterranean stables at Erzeroom when the doors are opened and the cold morning air is permitted to enter.* Having thus explained the origin and character of the natural phenomenon of mist or fog or aqueous vapor, let us turn to the lessons which the inspired writers have associated therewith.

I. Our first lesson is drawn from the ephemeral nature of vapor. "What is your life? It is a vapor, that appeareth for a little while and then vanisheth away." How apt a description is this of even the longest life!

"Like mist on the mountain, like waves of the sea,
So quickly the years of our pilgrimage flee."

The time allotted to us here is none too long to fulfill the duties assigned us and make preparation for the life which lies beyond. It is strange, indeed, that men should be so careless of the fact, even while they are profoundly convinced that there is a future for the soul, and that beyond the mists of this life there shall open an eternal day.

I once stood upon the highest peak of the Allegheny hills in the vicinity of Pittsburgh and looked eastward upon a beautiful landscape. Before me were rolling

---

* TYNDALL—"Forms of Water," page 5.

hills dotted with farm-house, cottage, and wood ; beyond was the valley of the Monongahela, and beyond that still the landscape stretched in more impressive beauty until it grew dim in the distant horizon.   An hour there-after I looked again.   A dense mist had risen from the ríver, and the lovely scene on which I had gazed with such delight was hidden.   Only hidden! for I knew that the landscape still remained, and that the morrow's sun would chase away the fog and reveal once more the woods, cottages, farm-houses, and rolling hills.

It is not strange that those who are overwhelmed with the cares and pressing engagements and hard con-flicts of this life, should at times permit these things to dim their views of God, of coming judgment, and the Heaven of the redeemed.   But certain it is that the fact of these obscuring earth-born mists does not blot out the more substantial facts of God and eternity.   Behind them all, beyond them all, above them all, is that life which shall be, and which shall open upon our vision and enjoyment when the mists of death have fallen from our mortal eyes forever, and our spirits have passed into the sunlight of immortality.   This life hides heaven, but it comes out again with the vanishing mists.   Knowing that this is so, is it not becoming that our energies should be addressed to prepare for the certainties that await us after death ?   The vapor vanishes, but the day remains.   Let us so live that we shall remain within the precincts of the eternal day.

It is the duty of man to think of his life in this its larger outlook.   Even here, if he will, he may have visions of himself, of his larger self as projected through the lens of faith upon the years of futurity.   The high-est summit of the Hartz mountains of Saxony is the Blocksberg or Brocken.   It is frequently veiled in mist and cloud strata, and is celebrated for the phenomenon known as the Spectre of the Brocken (" Brockenge-spenst "), which is nothing more than the shadow of men, houses, or other objects thrown upon the misty eastern horizon by the light of sunset.*

---

* Chambers' Encyclopædia, art. *Brocken.*

A scientific man thus describes his experience of his first sight of this spectre. In descending from one of the summits he came into a region of mist, when suddenly turning a corner he saw standing before him two immense human forms. For a moment he was startled. A strange feeling as of superstition crept through his frame. He stopped, and the figures stopped. He made a motion, and the figures met it with a corresponding movement. He lifted both hands, and the figures lifted their two pairs of hands. He knew now that what he saw was only himself projected against the mist and greatly magnified by the light. It was the spectre of the Brocken!

"Sometimes," says an eloquent preacher, "I think God permits us to see ourselves magnified upon the very cloud of vision. We have for a moment a glimpse of our coming estate and the magnitude of our lives, but only for a moment. The mist rolls away, the light changes its angle and bearing and the vision is gone. We come down from the mount and tell what we have seen as a matter of curiosity. Rather let us take hold of such glimpses, that we may go back to the strifes of this world with a stronger and more abiding faith in the future." *

Yes, our life is a vapor, but there are possibilities within it of which we never yet have dreamed. Browning has truly sung,

"Man is not man as yet."

A glimpse of his fuller stature, indeed, comes to him through the mists of these swiftly-passing years. Only a glimpse—and that enlarged vision of what he may be falls far below the stature of his perfect life. Yet surely there is enough of it to stimulate him into earnestness, into eagerness of preparation for the destiny which may await him. Yes, our life is a vapor! It vanishes swiftly away, but there is enough time in which to prepare for the inevitable meeting with God, and for the life of immortality. There is time enough, but there is not

* HENRY WARD BEECHER.

a moment too much! Hasten therefore to be wise, and, before this vapor life has vanished, turn in living faith and obedience to Him who waits to save you.

II. In the second place, the mist teaches us that our brief life should be a life of blessing.

In the opening pages of the book of Genesis (Genesis ii. 5–6) we have a glimpse of the ancient Paradise, the Eden home of man : "For the Lord God had not caused it to rain upon the earth, and there was not a man to till the ground, but there went up a mist from the earth and watered the whole face of the ground." In that era, therefore, as this passage reads, the mist was the great nutritive force of nature. It may be still said of mist that it serves the purpose of watering the face of the earth, for as you have already seen, if rain or dew be traced back to their origin in the atmosphere, they will be found in the form of vapor. Thus the fertilizing showers, without which earth would grow hard and chapped, and the fruits of the forest and field would be withered, may be said to be due to the same natural element that of old made Paradise for man.

What is your life? It is a vapor. Stop! is it indeed a vapor in this benevolent phase of the figure of our text? It appeareth for a little while, but does it leave behind it a blessing? Life is brief, but it may be a benediction. The one fact cannot be hindered; the other is possible to every living soul. What is the chief end of man? Man's chief end is to glorify God. But how shall one glorify God in this life? I know no other way than by purifying the fountains of one's life into holy living, and causing the issuing streams to go forth to gladden the children of men.

To my thinking, God is best glorified by an honest endeavor on the part of every man to bring and keep a blessing within the world. If indeed it be impossible thus to restore our world to the state of the primitive Eden, it is not impossible so to water the face of the earth by gracious living, by kind and noble deeds, by true and lofty aims, that this earthly home of man shall be brought as near to Paradise as may be in this mortal estate, and shall be made the high vantage ground from which man himself shall step at last into the Paradise of God. This is the purpose that ennobles, enriches, and glorifies a human life : to water the face of earth with the graces and gifts of true Christian living. Shall we not join together this hour in high consecration of the future of our lives, whether they be long or short, to such a worthy end? Live for God. Live for the human race. Live for that loftier selfhood which is within the grasp of all. Thus shall earth be better, and heaven be made sure.

Alas! how sadly in contrast with such a purpose are many of the lives that are everywhere lived around us! There is a stream in Yosemite valley that plunges from the high upland over the brink of the precipice, dashes downward beyond the front of the rocky wall, keeping for a space the form of water, but broken more and more as it falls, until at last through velocity and friction of the atmosphere, the whole descending volume of the stream is dispersed into mist that hangs for a little space around the ragged terminus of the cascade, and then slowly ascends towards the sky until it disappears within the air as invisible vapor. That waterfall is called " The Bridal Veil." It seems to me an emblem of too many lives that start upon the ventures of young manhood and young womanhood with high purposes and noble resolve, with all the force of youth's rush and vigor urging them forward, but after a brief career are dispersed into the mists of aimless living, and fade away into the life-ways surrounding them, purposeless and useless.

Is your life in this sense but a vapor? Is it to end in empty mist? Shall its effects be invisible to the hearts and lives of those who surround you? This great world is as a valley of Yosemite. Your young life rushes towards it. May God grant that instead of being frittered away and lost in aimlessness of living, you may find your place somewhere in the garden to water it, brighten it, and fructify it for those who live with you and come after you!

Let us change our figure once more. Mists when they gather above the seas are known as fogs. Produced as I have already explained, they hang above the surface of the water when the winds are calm, a perpetual element of danger to vessels passing up and down the highways of commerce. How often have you heard of collisions in the fog? How many a brave ship has gone down underneath the stroke of some sharp hull that was being pushed by careless hand or mercenary and cruel heart through the heavy mists! How many a little craft has been ruthlessly brushed from the surface of the waves to sink, unknown and uncared-for, with its humble crew to the depths of the great sea, because of criminal thoughtlessness for human life!

Friends, are there any amongst us who are thus daily running against the human lives that they meet, crushing their temporal interests, blighting their worldly hopes, ruining forever their immortal prospects? What mists are these that thus can make a mighty spirit a very pirate upon the high seas of life? Greed for gold, lust after power, the pride of wealth and station. I need not name more. These are the sins that befog many of the noblest minds, and send them forth among their fellows with all their vigor and possessions desecrated to the sad work of wreckage and destruction. Oh for a breath of God to blow these mists away from us and all ours! Oh for the clearer light that comes from the throne of the merciful Saviour, to break through these fogs of sinful selfishness and teach men that power is not meant to break, and burden, and curse, and destroy, and shatter the weak vessels of humanity, but to save and bless and fill with hope and happiness even the frailest and feeblest of our kind. Remember the words of our Lord Jesus Christ: "Inasmuch as ye did it unto one of these my brethren, even these least, ye did it unto me." And again, "Inasmuch as ye did it not unto one of these least, ye did it not unto me."*

III. Our third lesson comes to us from the obedience of the mist to the will and law of the Creator.

This fact evidently deeply impressed the minds of the ancient prophets, who were close observers of atmospheric phenomena, and drew many lessons therefrom.

---

* Matt. xxv. 40–45, R. V.

Thus the Psalmist writes: "Praise the Lord from the earth, ye dragons and all deeps, fire and hail, snow and vapor, stormy wind fulfilling his word."* Again: "He causeth the vapors to ascend from the ends of the earth."† The book of Job, the most ancient of the books of Scripture, contains the same allusion: "For he maketh small the drops of water; they pour down rain according to the vapor thereof."‡ This last is a repetition of our thought, with a fine evidence that the relation between rain and vapor was not unknown in that distant day. I will not dwell upon this point, to which I alluded in the sermon of last Sabbath upon "God as Force," but it is well to follow the spirit and letter of the ancient prophets, and hold up the obedience of the material world to the imitation of man. If there is no other way by which you may be persuaded, oh, reason-crowned men, be *shamed* into your duty by the obedience to divine law which is enstamped everywhere upon the creatures of inanimate nature. From the sun we expect sunshine, because the purpose of its being is to shine. From cloud, rain, and dew, from vapor of water, from mist we expect, always expect, expect without deviation, qualification, or delay, most implicit discharge of the functions which the Almighty Creator has imposed upon them. They never fail the hand that made them. They never go counter to the will whose force set them originally in play. They go forth upon their mission, in the impressive imagery of the Psalmist, fulfilling the word of God. That obedience is necessary. I can scarcely call it noble, for "noble" is a term that belongs to a creature of reason, of thought, of voluntary action; it belongs to man, and obedience in man is noble. There is no nobler trait.

> "Great may he be who can command
> And rule with just and tender sway;
> Yet is diviner wisdom taught
> Better by him who can obey." ⸙

IV. Our last lesson comes from the use of mist as a symbol of judgment upon the wicked.

---

* Psalms cxlviii. 7, 8. † Psalms cxxxv. 7. ‡ Job xxxvi. 27, 28.
⸙ Poems of ADELAIDE PROCTOR, "Maximus."

Elymas, the sorcerer at Paphos in Cyprus, withstood the apostles, and sought to turn away the distinguished inquirer Sergius Paulus from the faith. The apostle Paul, filled with the Holy Ghost, invoked divine judgment upon that enemy of righteousness because he perverted the right ways of the Lord, " And immediately," we read, "there fell on him a mist and a darkness, and he went about seeking some to lead him by the hand.* The wicked men whose sinful courses are set in array by St. Peter in his second epistle are described as " clouds that are carried with a tempest, to whom the mist of darkness is reserved forever." †

In the one case the judgment appears to have been a physical, in the other a spiritual one. I do not know what may have been involved in the latter. Who can say? Who would presume or wish to say? For on a subject such as this, one must feel that it is better always that the Almighty Judge should speak for Himself. This much at least we may discern, that the figurative expression "mist" is an apt symbol of that soul out of whose horizon the vision of the Sun of Righteousness with healing in his wings has been permitted to drop away. If it be but a momentary mist—"a vapor that appeareth for a little while"—even thus it is sad enough; for a life without the presence of Christ to brighten and bless it must be a hopeless one.

Too many men of high intellectual endowments, upon whom the world has laid honors, have found it in their hearts to raise before the eyes of their fellows, and becloud their spiritual future with, the mists of unbelief. In the name of science they have obscured the throne on which that Sovereign sits whose power upholds the order and laws to uncover which is the function of science. They have shut from view the ocean of eternity by the mists of doubt which they have raised before it. Such men sail no longer upon life's voyage, and outward into the illimitable future under the full sunlight of hope and joyous confidence of a happy immortality, but wander hopeless over uncertain paths,

* Acts xiii. 11.   † II. Peter ii. 17.

surrounded by fogs which make all chart and compass useless for the unhappy voyager. Who can take his latitude on this wide sea of life when for him there is no longer glimpse of sun or star of night?

In a recent magazine article the distinguished American poet, James Russel Lowell, has written a poem with such a thought as this in view. He thus represents the condition of one groping in the mists :—

> "Men feel old systems cracking under 'em ;
> Life saddens to a mere conundrum
> Which once religion solved, but she
> Has lost—has science found ?—the key."

Of those who use their scientific discoveries to promote guesses and hypotheses destructive of Christian faith, he thus writes :—

> "They make things admirably plain,
> But one hard question will remain :
> If one hypothesis you lose,
> Another in its place you choose ;
> But your faith gone, O man and brother,
> Whose shop will furnish you another—
> One that will wash, I mean, and wear,
> And wrap us warmly from despair ?"

In view of the whole field, which he is as well able to cover with his thought as any living man, he brushes away with his master pen those mists that have darkened and depressed the faith of so many, and pointing forward along the path into which the full sunlight of God pours joyfully, he thus signifies, as he sings, his purpose to hold fast to the old dear faith of childhood :—

> " I might as well
> Obey the meeting-house's bell,
> And listen while Old Hundred pours
> Forth through the summer-opened doors,
> From old and young.   I hear it yet,
> Swelled by bass-viol and clarinet,
> While the gray minister, with face
> Radiant, let loose his noble bass.
> If heaven it reached not, yet its roll
> Waked all the echoes of the soul,
> And on it many a life found wings,
> To soar away from sordid things."*

---

*James Russel Lowell—"Credidimus Jovem Regnare," *Atlantic Monthly*, February, 1887.

This, as it seems to me, is a wise decision. The rejection of Christ, the doubt of unbelief, is a mist of darkness which can only deepen the misery of man's estate. It brings to him in this life restlessness, hopelessness, and despair.

Let us devoutly hope that upon none of us shall this mist of darkness settle in the coming eternity. Is there one spirit here obscured by such a mist? Ah! brother and friend, let me invoke for you to-day the spirit of the living God. Let me beseech you to raise for yourself the prayer, Come, oh north wind, blow, oh south wind; dispel this mist of worldliness and unbelief, and show to me the blue heavens with a God of love and redemption regnant upon and beyond it, mighty and willing to save.

We often hear, perhaps too often, of men of science who have lost their faith in Christ, and forget the great number of rank and file who keep the faith and possess their souls in quietness and peace. Ten thousand ships sail the great seas safely and come and go unnoticed on their useful ways. But one goes down in the tempest or comes into port storm-bruised and broken by the waves, sails shivered, masts shattered, yards and cordage snapped, helm disabled and binnacle swept away, and lo, the whole world knows her name and her disaster! You read of one naturalist making shipwreck of the faith; do not conclude that all men of science have met a like misfortune. I doubt whether in proportion to their number such gentlemen are more liable to such disaster than those of other professions and vocations. However that may be, let me speak of one who a few years ago passed from among men—Prof. James Clerk Maxwell. He was one of the most astute minds of Great Britain. His massive intellect and great attainments in physical science and mathematics were acknowledged by the entire world of science. He was a firm and devoted follower of Jesus. Of him his biographer wrote:—

"His faith in the grand cardinal verities was firm, simple, and full; and he avowed it humbly but unhesitatingly, with the deepest gratitude for the revelation of the truth in Jesus. I do not think he had any doubts or difficulties to cloud his mind or shake his peace."*

Let such a light shine this day as a beacon, a light-house to any who are in the mists of unbelief.

"Heroic saint ! bright sufferer ! thou dost lend
  To science a new glory. Midst the press
  Of boasters, all thy meek-eyed fame confess,
And worldlings thine unworldliness commend.

Shine on, pure spirit ! though we see thee not,
  Even in thy passage thou hast purged away
The fogs of earth-born doubt and sense-bound thought
  From hearts that followed thine all-piercing ray.
And while thou soarest far from human view,
Even thy faint image shall our strength renew." †

2. It is sometimes the case in the Christian's experience that there comes a glimpse of the horror of this mist of darkness in the form of spiritual fears and doubts. These do not cover the fundamental points of faith, the being of God, the fact of immortality, the certainty of Christ's life and redemption, but simply obscure the individual's hope as to his own interest in these great facts. Am I saved? Do I truly believe in the Lord Jesus Christ?

Have you ever walked in the early morning or late at night over some familiar path covered with fogs and wondered how strange all things looked? From yon Delaware, flowing before the gates of our great city, I have often seen in the autumn the mist rolling out, hiding for a time the lovely landscapes of our suburban regions. When venturing sometimes to walk abroad through these mists, or driving from my summer lodging toward my city home, I have noted how hard it is to tell the features of the scenery. They are distorted as seen through the mist. They are obscured by the mist. The familiar landmarks are blotted out. Even the well-known pathway to home, where dearest friends await with welcome, seems strange and unknown to the eye, or is wholly hidden from sight. Yet, well did I

---

* Life of James Clerk Maxwell : McMillan & Co., London. Page 414. † From the sonnet printed on a fly-leaf of Prof. Maxwell's Biography.

know that friends and home, and blue heaven, and the light of God were all there beyond the mists, and that by and by it would thus appear to me.

Oh doubting Christian, "take it on faith a little while; soon shall you read his promise right in the full sunlight of his smile." Christ remains in spite of your doubts. Not one promise of his has been blotted out, although you may not be able to read it while that strange mist is on your eyes. Heaven and God all remain, always remain, and they all are yours.

I was driving once with a company of college friends along the valley of Chartiers creek in Western Pennsylvania. It was a foggy morning. We moved through the valley, for the road threaded the course of the stream. We wrapped our coats around us and shivered in the morning chills. Soon our path led away from the valley and stream up a sloping hillside. Higher still we mounted, up, still up, until suddenly we emerged from the mist into full sunlight. All around us and above us lay fields, hillsides, and forests beautiful in the rays of heaven's luminary that poured his morning glory on the scene. Below us, covering all the valley, lay the mist, rising here and sinking there, looking like a tossing vapor sea. We had escaped all that. We were out of the fogs. We had come out, simply by coming up.

Christian doubter, this parable is for you. Mists love the lowlands. Forsake the lowlands of that life of unbelief in which you are living. Go higher! still higher! on wings of faith mount nearer to the throne, nearer to that hill whose healing cross is the central point of human hopes. As you draw near in reverent trust, there shall fall for you the light that, if it do not disperse all mists in this weary and wicked world of ours, shall at least lift your spirit out of them, and give you that sunshine which God appoints for his own. Go upward! Live the higher life of holiness and faith! Nearer heaven—upon heights of faith men shall find brightness and joy for their souls.

> " Nearer, my God, to Thee,
> Nearer to Thee."

LECTURE III.

———

The Dew:
God's Silent Blessings.

"I will be as the dew unto Israel."—HOSEA xiv. 5.

THE DEW—GOD'S SILENT BLESSINGS.

WHEN the cover is lifted from a vegetable dish on the dinner table the inside is often found covered with dew. Whence has it come? The steam or vapor of water arising from the contents of the dish comes in contact with the cold cover, is condensed, and forms upon the inside as minute beads of moisture. An ice pitcher on a summer's day is often found covered with particles of dew which extend usually no further than the limits of the water inside. The explanation of this dew upon the pitcher is the same as that of the dew upon the inside of the dish cover, and is very simple. The layer of air in contact with the cold vessel is cooled rapidly, is condensed in the cooling, and its excess of moisture being thus squeezed out or precipitated, settles in minute drops upon the surface of the pitcher.

These familiar facts afford good illustrations of the cause of dew. It is simply the invisible vapor of the air condensed by contact with the surface of the earth, which becomes rapidly cool on clear and calm nights. During night in summer the temperature falls continually from the effects of terrestrial radiation, till the earliest dawn; when the daily rise in temperature sets in, owing to the heat reflected to the upper strata of the atmosphere which have begun to be heated and lighted up by the rays of the morning sun. As the cooling by terrestrial radiation continues, the temperature of objects on the surface is gradually lowered to the dew point, and when this point is reached the aqueous vapor begins to be condensed in dew upon their surfaces. The quantity deposited is in proportion to the degree of cold produced and the quantity of vapor in the air.*

* Encyclopædia Britannica, vol. 16, art. *Meteorology.*

But, it will be asked, what cools the earth so suddenly after the setting of the sun? This perhaps is not so evident as the cause of the coldness of our ice pitcher. The answer to this question requires us to know that the earth is moving with immense rapidity through a space whose temperature has been estimated at least two hundred and seventy (270° degrees) below zero of Fahrenheit's thermometer. Thus, like a heated cannon-ball hung in the middle of a cold room, it is continually giving out heat, or losing it by radiation. The dense atmosphere with which the earth is enveloped acts like a blanket to protect it from this intense cold of space to a certain extent. But still the constant loss of heat by radiation is so great that were the sun's rays withheld for a few days the temperature of the surface land, even in the tropics, would fall as low as it is at the poles during the long nights of Arctic winter.* When, therefore, the sun goes down radiation towards the cold regions of space takes place not only from the surface of the globe but also directly from the molecules of air and its aqueous vapor. But, as the radiation from the surface of the earth is more rapid and greater than from the stratum of atmosphere immediately surrounding it, it is obvious that the same result must follow which occurs when the ice pitcher is placed in the open room; that is to say, the moisture of the air near the surface is condensed and precipitated in the form of dew.

The natural phenomenon of dew as known to us and as above described was not unknown to the people of Palestine. In winter during fine weather dew is there deposited as in other countries by the cooling of the surface of the ground on cloudless nights. But inasmuch as winter is the one period of the year when much rain falls in tropical torrents, ordinary dew, which chiefly forms at such times, is comparatively speaking valueless.† We must therefore look for some other cause of that peculiar and inestimable blessing so often referred to by the inspired penman under the figure of dew.

---

* COOKE—" Religion and Chemistry," page 133.   † REV. JAMES NEIL—" Palestine Explored," page 133.

The nature of the difference between the dew of Holy Scripture and dew as known to us will be considered in the next discourse. At present we need only to understand that the difference is not such as to destroy the fitness of the lessons which we have to learn therefrom; for after all there is no better English word than "dew" to describe the corresponding phenomenon as it exists in Holy Land, although it has sometimes been called the "Night Mist."

This phenomenon was a matter of constant observation by the people of Bible times and lands, as we may readily see by turning to those texts which refer to the subject. For the most part Scripture writers use the dew as an emblem of divine blessing both spiritual and temporal. Isaac in bestowing his blessing upon Jacob said, "God give thee of the dew of heaven."* Moses when addressing the people of Israel in his immortal song invoked their attention on the ground that his "speech shall distill as the dew, as the small rain upon the tender herb."† Again, in the blessing which he bestowed upon the children of Israel he gave to the tribe of Joseph this benediction—"Blessed of the Lord be his land; for the precious things of heaven, for the dew."‡

The patriarch Job, among other figurative descriptions of his great blessedness in the days of his prosperity, introduces this:

> My root is spread out by the waters,
> And the dew lies all night on my branch.§

The wise proverbialist uses the same phenomenon as a figure of royal favor:

> The king's wrath is as the roaring of a lion;
> But his favor is as dew upon the grass.‖

In David's touching lament over Saul and the beloved Jonathan he utters an apostrophe describing the greatness of his grief and of the national loss by the fall of two such leaders under the striking figure, "Ye mountains of Gilboa, let there be no more dew!"¶ In all

---

* Genesis xxviii. 28. † Deut. xxxii. 2. ‡ Deut. xxxiii. 13. § Job xxix. 19. ‖ Prov. xix. 12. ¶ II. Samuel i. 21.

these references it will be observed that dew is taken as an emblem of a divine blessing either in temporal or spiritual things.

Dropping now the general symbol and entering somewhat into particulars, we shall see, first, that

I. The dew is a type of the Silent Blessings of God.

"I will be as the dew unto Israel," says Jehovah, descending with spiritual graces not only, but coming silently even as the dew falls upon the tender grass. It is not an unfamiliar thought to us that God works no less mightily because he works in silence. There hangs about the Mosaic narrative of creation a composure almost as of unconsciousness. The story of how the heavens and earth were created, reduced to orderly form and all living things brought upon the globe, is told in few words as one would tell a nursery tale, or recite the commonest incident of daily life. That spirit is a reflection of a large part of Nature's daily mood. How silently the forests grow! How silently spring up grass, herbage, and grain! We may walk on a summer day in the green fields and, except now and then a crackling of luxurious growing corn-stalks, we shall hear no sound to indicate that Nature is producing those crops which shall weight down our granaries, tax our means of railroad transportation, fill our great ships with their products, and feed the nations of the earth. Seed for the sower and bread for the eater, for all the millions of the hosts of men, are wrought out in the laboratory of Nature with scarce a sound of toil.

Go into the great forests of the Adirondacks and lie down at night by your camp fire. A silence as of death overhangs the scene. Now and then one may hear a dropping of broken twig or leaf, the hum of an insect, the restless movement of a bird upon its perch. Occasionally the forest will be startled by the sudden sweep and crash of some gigantic plant monarch as it falls seemingly without cause and awakes thunderous echoes on the silent night. The rising breeze, as it soughs and moans through limbs and leaves, will often break the stillness. But beside these external signs of life there is no voice to speak to you of that great work which Nature there is doing. And what is Nature doing? She is lifting up a forest of unnumbered trees towards the skies; she is forming timber that shall build our houses, span our rivers and streams with bridges, and frame the great ships that go down to the seas with our commence. Forest building is a silent work. Thus it is through all the realm of Creation.

Nor is it different in the kingdom of God's grace. Our Master compared the kingdom of heaven to the mustard seed and to leaven hid in a measure of meal.* The parable holds good in the matter of the silence with which the germinating seed and the fermenting germ accomplish their work. "The kingdom of God cometh not with observation." †

This lesson was never more impressively taught than to the prophet Elijah on Mount Horeb. "Go forth and stand upon the mount before the Lord!" ‡ Thus spoke the divine word. Elijah awaited the signal of God's appearance. His prophetic soul knew well to discern the awful presence. He will not go forth from his cave until God is verily there. Hark! There is a sound in the mouth of the cavern. It is the wind rising upon the mountain. Higher, fiercer, until it roars down the deep ravines that unite in front of Mount Sinai and howls through the gorges, and whips the trees into those wailing cries so familiar to mountaineers and foresters in the stormy season. The trees are uprooted and hurled down the cliff, dragging with them great quantities of soil. The landslide rushes into the plain with a crash like thunder. Thus perhaps it is that we are to understand the passage, "The wind rent the mountain and brake in pieces the rocks." It were a stout heart, indeed, that would not flinch if exposed in absolute solitude to the fury of such a mountain storm. Yet the only picture we form of the prophet is of one standing in the dim light of his cave gazing outward, straining every faculty to catch amidst the clamor of the tempest an indication of the revealing presence of his God.

---

* Luke xiii. 19, 21.   † Luke xvii. 20.   ‡ I. Kings xix. 11.

There came none to him. "The Lord was not in the wind; and after the wind an earthquake;" or, to take up the peculiar but most expressive rendering of the Chaldaic version, "After the host of the angels of the wind there was a host of the angels of commotion, but the majesty of the Lord was not in the host of the angels of commotion; and after the host of the angels of commotion, a fire, but the majesty of the Lord was not in the host of the angels of fire; and after the host of angels of fire a voice singing in silence," that is, a voice with which no other voice was mingled. It filled the air and filled Elijah's soul to the exclusion of all else. The tempest had rolled away over the mountain. The rocking cliffs were soothed into their usual stability. A calm as of death had settled upon Horeb, and through that calm more awful even than the crash of the troubled elements stole that "still small voice," "a sound of gentle stillness," * "the whisper of a voice as of a gentle breath." † The prophetic spirit discerned at once the presence of his God. "And it was so when Elijah heard it that he wrapped his face in his mantle and went out and stood in the entering in of the cave." There with his head reverently bowed within the folds of his rough sheepskin cloak he awaited the revelation. "And behold there came a voice unto him."

What is the significance of this "voice singing in silence?"—this "whisper of a voice as of a gentle breath,"—this still small voice in which Jehovah chose to commune with his prophet? It is not hard to find the answer. We have here uncovered the whole spirit of that new dispensation which Elijah was to do so much to prepare. The fire of Carmel, the storm of the Mediterranean, the earthquake revolution by which the priests of Baal and the groves were slaughtered at a blow—all that had not succeeded. Now was to begin the silent work of prayer and preaching. Conviction was to do its noiseless office. The seven thousand who had not bowed the knee to Baal were to be as a leaven silently working among the nation. Elijah was to go thence to

---

* Revised version, marginal reading.   † Septuagint version.

anoint the mild, persuasive Elisha as prophet in his own room, and then the work was to go on quietly, steadily, and hopefully as before. The still small voice should prevail. The prophet was to "learn to labor and to wait;" to be patient, and trust to the silent, steady influence of honest duty and slow growing conviction to do the work of God in men's hearts.

The truth should prevail over all. More triumphant and effective than the maledictions of Elijah, the sword of Hazael and the sword of Jehu, would be the sword of the Spirit, the Word of God. To quote the noble language of Dean Stanley, "Not in the strong east wind that parted the Red Sea, or the fire that swept the top of Sinai, or the earthquake that shook down the walls of Jericho, would God be brought so near to man, as in the still small voice of the child at Bethlehem, as in the ministrations of him whose cry was not heard in the streets, in the awful stillness of the cross, in the never-failing order of Providence, in the silent, insensible influence of good deeds and good words, of God and of man." *

This mode of divine working is profoundly effective. There is something strangely impressive in perfect silence. The silence of night overhanging the business portions of a great city; the silence of Nature in her deep solitudes; the silence that sits upon ocean and earth in the moments just before a storm; the hush of men when their souls are filled with great passions, and pause on the eve of some momentous event; the hush which marks the coming of the Holy Ghost in a revival of religion— all these mightily subdue and impress us. The animal speaks out in noise and shout; the spirit in the solemn stillness of the soul. A church fallen into silence after a congregation has retired, often seems even more like the house of God than when filled with the sounding praises of the people. I love to glide into the sanctuary when thus empty of service and worshipers, and lift my heart in voiceless prayer. At such moments one can sympathize with the ideas of worship prevailing among the Society of Friends.

---

* DEAN STANLEY—"History Jewish Church," vol. II., p. 343.

The descent of the Holy Spirit upon Jesus has been compared to the descent of a dove.* Have you ever seen a turtle-dove or wood-pigeon alight in the open fields? There is a scarcely audible flutter of wings as it falls. It drops down from the air and settles upon the ground or neighboring tree so silently that you are startled by its presence ere you had thought it near. In this respect, if in no other, it is a fitting symbol of that divine Spirit who so often speaks to the children of men in the still small voice.

These reflections should give us hope and confidence in the final success of the truth and kingdom of God. Man's heart is a tough and stubborn piece of mechanism. Nevertheless it is susceptible to the influences of gentleness, persistently and lovingly laid upon him, and by these influences God is constantly working. We may not hear the moving wings of the Holy Dove as he alights among us. We may not mark his coming, or "the hiding of his power."† His way may be in the sea, his paths in the great waters, and his footsteps not known,‡ yet nevertheless let us believe that he will accomplish his purpose, and win at last the world to himself.

The Sabbath! How easily does our theme glide into thoughts of the holy quiet of the divine day of rest! It is the time when above all others God appears as "the dew unto Israel;" when his heavenly speech "distills as the dew" upon our spirits, when our Divine King's "favor is as dew upon the grass" to our needy and seeking souls. Then indeed do our lips take up the ancient benediction of Jacob and say, "Blessed be the Lord for the precious things of heaven, for the dew!"

> With silent awe I hail the sacred morn,
>   That slowly wakes while all the fields are still!
> A soothing calm on every breeze is borne;
>   A graver murmur gurgles from the rill;
>   And echo answers softer from the hill;
> And softer sings the linnet from the thorn;
>   The skylark warbles in a tone less shrill.
> Hail! Light serene! Hail! Sacred Sabbath morn!
>   The rooks float silent by in airy drove;
>   The sun a placid yellow lustre throws;

---

* Matt. iii. 16.   † Habakkuk iii. 4.   ‡ Psalm lxxvii. 19.

The gales that lately sighed along the grove
Have hushed their downy wings in dead repose;
The hovering rack of clouds forgets to move—
So smiled the day when the first morn arose. *

II. The timeliness of the divine blessings is another lesson taught us by the dew.

There are lands that do not know the nurturing influences of the rains of heaven, but yet are fertile by reason of the dews that continually descend upon them. Even in lands favored with regular showers as was the case with Palestine, the dew had a large and helpful influence in equalizing the harvests year by year by neutralizing the results of drought. The principal seasons when a provision of the nature of dew is needed in the Holy Land, and when it is so abundantly given, are summer and autumn. Then six consecutive months of drought occur regularly, even under the most favorable circumstances. From about the first week in May to the middle of October, in the usual course, no drop of rain falls, and throughout the twelve hours of each day the sun shines with great strength, unveiled by a single cloud. In the autumn the thermometer has been known to register 118° Fahrenheit in the shade of the hot plains.† In other words, the dew comes in just where and when it is most needed, adding greatly to its benefits by the timeliness of its coming.

I am glad to believe that this is in accordance with the modes of Divine working amongst the children of men. The souls who most need the Master's tender care are those whom He most seeks to bless. The moments of our life which are most barren of ordinary joys and blessings, are those moments in which we may most securely depend upon the answering help of our Almighty Father. When the heart is parched by drought and scorched by the sun; when the rain-laden clouds refuse to gather or gather only to deceive our hopes; when the showers fall not and we lie barren of hope and joy before God, then—even then, yes, especially then will

---

* JOHN LEYDEN. † REV. JAMES NEIL—"Palestine Explored," ch. V., pp. 133-4.

He come to us if we truly seek Him. God does not seek us because we are saints, but to make us saints ; He does not visit us because our hearts are full, but in order to fill them. Human sorrow is small attraction to men, but is the lodestone that draws to us the Spirit of God. One of the sweetest sacred lyrics of an Irish bard has hymned this thought:

> O thou who driest the mourner's tear,
>   How dark this world would be,
> If, pierced by sins and sorrows here,
>   We could not fly to thee !
>
> The friends, who in our sunshine live,
>   When winter comes, are flown ;
> And he who has but tears to give,
>   Must weep those tears alone.
>
> But thou wilt heal that broken heart,
>   Which, like the plants that throw
> Their fragrance from the wounded part,
>   Breathes sweetness out of woe.
>
> Then sorrow, touched by thee, grows bright,
>   With more than rapture's ray ;
> As darkness shows us worlds of light,
>   We never saw by day.*

Yes, there is a timeliness in the help of heaven which Christian hearts have learned to count upon with the utmost confidence. "As thy days so shall thy strength be."† "My strength is made perfect in weakness."‡

It seems to me that in this respect the religion of Jesus Christ is surely like the dew in lands unwatered by the rains of heaven. For most human souls destiny lies between Religion or barrenness. There is nothing but the heavenly gift of Faith that can cause a desert heart to rejoice and a wilderness life to blossom as the rose. If Christ come not and stay not with blessings in this sinful and grief-stricken world, then indeed are we hopeless. We scan in vain the wide horizon of earthly attainments, literature, science, mechanics, law, politics, in search of fitting nurture for needy souls. Only from those sacred treasures of grace out of which distills the dew of a divine blessing can we hope for that which shall make our hearts verdant with the hopes of

---

* THOMAS MOORE.   † Deut. xxxiii. 25.   ‡ II. Cor. xii. 9.

immortality, joyful with the brightness of the Rose of Sharon, fragrant with the sweetness of the Lily of the valley, rich with the fruitage of a holy and helpful life.

Yes, yes! only the heavens, the heavens of God can drop down dew upon the heart-wastes and desolations of this world. Oh! I would despair, utterly despair of finding solace and strength for the multitude of hearts whom I know to be daily walking through this vale of tears in utmost bitterness of spirit, were not Christ in view! Every week, sometimes every day it is my duty to share the burden of others' sorrows. I stand by shattered urns which had been the repository of hopes, plans, and loves of men who bow mourning above the ruins. A merchant stands dazed amidst the wreck of his once colossal fortunes. A poor laborer stands in the market place all the day idle, sighing "no man hath hired me," although wife and weans in hunger and want await his coming home. Helpless women look upon their helpless children, and watch the meal in the barrel daily lessening like that of the widow of Sarepta, and wonder when their unwise husbands will turn from "the strike" dictated too often by selfish agitators, to give back hands of ready toil to work that will bring daily bread and fuel.

A young husband bends at the bier of his youthful wife whom he must bury to-morrow out of his sight, mourning that love's young dream has so quickly vanished away, and that all his cherished hopes are as the morning cloud. An old man sits in his arm-chair, leans upon his staff and gazes at the vacant places by his hearthstone, while memory recalls the forms of loved ones who once peopled that sacred spot. There was the wife of his youth, and merry-hearted children were there who cheered his days with prattle, laughter, and song. Alas! they all "have been scattered like roses in bloom, some at the bridal and some at the tomb." Then, there are other sorrows, "living sorrows" we call them, which we may not mention here, but are borne wearily and almost despairingly by souls that faint beneath them, or stagger on through life dumbly enduring the destiny which seems beyond reach of hopeful cure.

What is there for souls like these? Is there indeed neither comfort nor cure? There is nothing purely of earth—absolutely nothing! What then? Then, there are Faith and Hope and Heaven! Faith in God, assurance of the comfort which Heaven bestows, strength that distills like the dew into men's spirits day by day, the hope that beyond this troubled career there shall open for them the dawn of Heaven—these abide with men because their nature and needs require them.

Man's heart also belongs to Nature, and all Nature in man rises in revolt, and cries out in abhorrence against those who would blot from the heavens of God the stars of human hope that light up for us the night of tears, and point to that world beyond where night and sorrow, pain and parting are known no more, and "joy cometh in the morning." The infidel, even though he dare speak in the name of Nature, nevertheless denies Nature, tramples Nature under foot, disregards its laws and all its voices; for *Nature in the heart of man* cries out with quenchless eagerness for God and immortality!

The last utterance of the Poet Laureate of England in his "New Locksley Hall," has some striking likenesses in the general trend and tone of thought to the last song of the American bard which I quoted a Sunday ago. Tennyson's conclusion is at one with Lowell's, and they together point us to faith in God and Heaven.

Only That which made us, meant us to be mightier by and by,
Set the sphere of all the boundless heavens within the human eye,

Sent the shadow of Himself, the Boundless, thro' the human soul,
Boundless inward, in the atom, boundless outward, in the Whole.

*   *   *   *   *   *   *   *

Ere she gain her heavenly best, a God must mingle with the game:
Nay, there may be those about us which we neither see nor name,

Felt within us as ourselves, the powers of good, the powers of ill,
Strowing balm, or shedding poison in the fountains of the will.

Follow you the Star that lights a desert pathway, yours and mine
Forward, till you see the highest Human Nature is Divine.

Follow Light, and do the Right—for man can half control his
    doom—
Till you find the Deathless Angel seated in the vacant tomb.*

---

* LORD TENNYSON—"Locksley Hall Sixty Years After."

1. This is a lesson which Christians may profitably learn in their relations to their fellows. You know the old Latin proverb, "*Bis dat qui cito dat*"—He gives twice who gives quickly. There is a strong tendency among us to bestow our gifts upon those who give gifts to us. We lay our social, friendly, and material offerings upon laps that are already filled. Thus oftentimes our gifts are wasted. They go to those who do not appreciate them, who do not need them, whose hearts are filled to surfeiting, and have little added gladness therefrom. I do not mean that the opulent have no occasion for expressions of sympathy from their friends. Nay! oftentimes their hearts are empty and solitary amidst their material abundance. A timely word of sympathy, a note of condolence, a simple gift of flowers or books, an appropriate poem, tractate, or sermon sent through the mail, these or such-like things, even though of little value in themselves, will carry to such lonely hearts a blessing that silver and gold could not bestow, because rich in the tenderness and sympathy with which they are freighted.

But in those wider fields where men, women, and children are called upon to bear the burden and heat of life's struggle, there is a special need that Christian hearts should learn the lesson of timely helpfulness. It is not every one indeed who possesses the delicate spirit to discern and the gracious tact to meet the difficulties of which we are thinking, but all can at least study these, and always a warm and honest heart, a sympathy pure and sincere, will fall upon such time and manner as will best supply the barrenness of weary and embittered lives by the distilled dews of Christian aid. Happy is he who knows *how* and *when*, as well as what, to give.

III. There is yet another lesson which Holy Scripture brings to us under the form of dew, the Transient Character of much Human Goodness.

"Oh, Ephraim, what shall I do unto thee? Oh Judah, what shall I do unto thee, for your goodness is as a morning cloud, and as the early dew it goeth away!"

(Hosea vi. 4.) Of how many persons may this sad complaint be spoken? How many resolves made since this new year was born to lead a better life, to practice goodness and shun evil, have already been dispelled as dew by the morning sun? There is, perhaps, this difference to be noticed—the dew vanished and left a blessing. These broken resolves, do they leave the heart any better? Rather, it is to be feared, the heart is harder and the mind more perverted because of these failures to fulfill vows. Alas! how sad it is that the soul should once taste the sweetness of the heavenly dew and then turn from it; that God should once be seen and grasped and then permitted to vanish away from life! Are there any here to whom such sadness has come? Let me pray you turn again with prepared and receptive heart unto Him who has graciously promised to heal your backslidings. His voice still calls, " Return unto Me!" Still the Father waits to welcome the home-coming prodigal.

Will you come to Him to-day? How long, how much longer will you wait? How many times have you resolved to seek the blessedness of him whose sins are forgiven, whose iniquities are pardoned? How many half-formed resolutions lie along the pathway of your religious experience? Rose-buds! How we love them, for they speak to us of the future. They are beautiful prophecies of immortality and resurrection, and therefore we lay them around the coffins of our dead. There they speak to us through their beautiful symbolism of a life which here is all unfolden, only the budding forth of the life which shall be when unfolded into full form and blessedness in Heaven. Rose-buds! The bride bears them in her wedding bouquet as she goes to those joyful vows which unite her in love with the man of her choice. They are to her, and to all who surround her, tokens of promise; prophecy of a life of happiness, which from the budding joys of the marriage hour shall unfold from year to year into the fuller happiness of long wedded life. Rose-buds! The maiden wears them on her bosom at that interesting hour of her life when she is introduced by parents or friends to the social circles in

which her life must move.   Indeed, we call our maidens
" Rose-buds " in the season of their " coming out."   A
not unfitting word, for it bespeaks the high hopes
of friends that the sweet life of the daughter of their
love, now but in the bud, shall fulfill the prophecy of
the beautiful symbol, and open out to the full fragrance
and beauty of a noble womanly life.

Rose-buds!   Ah, but if the buds shall never bloom?
If they remain buds forever?   If there come not to
them that fullness of life which we call the seed, within
whose germs lies the fulfillment of all plant prophecy;
if the promise wrapped up within half-closed petals be
never fulfilled—what then?   What then?

Such, my friends, are lives that promise and never fulfill.   Lives that shed a momentary fragrance, that give a
passing glow of beauty, that add richness and warmth
to cheeks that blush already with pleasure and health, that
cast a momentary glow upon the face of death, but nothing more!   Lives unopened, prophecy unfulfilled, wasted
lives!   " Nothing but leaves!"   Nurtureless dew-drops
on fruitless leaves that pass away unblessing and un-
blessed!

Oh! let not the half-formed resolutions of this hour
be set towards such a destiny!   Rather, through the
grace of a divine Saviour waiting to help you and the
high purpose of your own will, may the buds of this
day's promise open from year to year more and more
until the light of heaven shall reveal their beauty, and
exhale their fragrance in the very Garden of the Lord.
There they shall bloom forever, sprinkled with the dia-
mond dew-drops of the Eternal Morning.

LECTURE IV.

—— ——— ——

The Dew of Hermon.

"Behold, how good and how pleasant it is for brethren to dwell together in unity! It is * * * *as the dew of Hermon, and as the dew that descended upon the mountains of Zion: for there the Lord commanded the blessing, even life for evermore."*— Psalm cxxxiii. 1, 3.

THE DEW OF HERMON.

During summer in Palestine vegetation becomes much parched in consequence of the continuous rainless heat, and would be altogether scorched from the face of the earth but for the following beautiful provision. At such time, and more especially towards its close in the latter part of August and during September and October, the prevalent westerly winds bring an immense quantity of moisture from the Mediterranean Sea. The watery element, with which the sea air is charged, becomes condensed when it meets the cold night air upon the land; for in Syria the nights are often as cold as the days are hot, a fact which Jacob lamented three thousand six hundred years ago. This condensation, or cloud-forming, happens more especially when the damp winds reach the hills, over the surface of which their liberated moisture rolls in masses of dense mist, which leave everywhere in their progress an immense amount of that which answers to the " dew " of the Bible.

Since the vapor becomes condensed in the air before touching the ground, in the strict scientific sense of the word it rather resembles the lightest form of Scotch mist. But then it must be remembered that this mist in Palestine never occurs in the daytime, but only forms during the night, when by radiation the earth has thrown off its heat, and the cool air above it condenses the moisture borne by the breezes from the sea. From its coming only during the hours of the night, from its not falling like other rain from the upper air, from its separation into very fine particles and not appearing to fall in drops, from the general appearance it leaves behind, and from its effect ceasing to be seen when the sun grows hot, it was rightly held to differ so much from the nature of ordinary rain as to require to be distinguished by a special technical term, " *tal*," which, fortunately for the English reader, our translators have uniformly rendered in each instance by the word " dew."

Let it be borne in mind that whenever we read of the " dew" in our Bible we must not understand such dew as we have in this country, but this copious mist shedding small, invisible rain, that comes in rich abundance every night about twelve o'clock in the hot weather when west or north-west winds blow, and which brings intense refreshment to all organized life. Mr. Neil, to whose admirable studies of Palestine I am largely indebted for these introductory facts, calls this phenomenon "night mist;" Dean Stanley speaks of it as the " dews of the mist."*

The peculiar features of this rich provision of nature, by which it differs from and greatly excels any kind of dew, and comes to be of such very great value, are threefold. First, its falling only in the hottest and driest season, when no other moisture is to be had. Secondly, its coming every night during this period when west winds blow, which they do with great regularity. Thirdly, its falling so copiously as to supply all the moisture needed for vegetation generally. The water these low clouds deposit† is perfectly sufficient to ripen the summer crops, to keep life in the pastures of the desert, to nourish the fig, fatten the berry of the olive, and give to the grape its fullness of luscious juice—in a word, to revive and sustain all hardy forms of vegetable life.‡

I. The first lesson clothed within the imagery of dew which we have to consider to-day is the Duty and Blessedness of Brotherly Unity.

All readers of the Bible are familiar with the exquisite poem on fraternal love given to the church by the inspired Psalmist. (Ps. cxxxiii.)

---

* "Sinai and Palestine," page 396.   † Thus the seemingly unnatural statement of Prov. iii. 20, that the *clouds* drop down dew," is exactly in accord with nature.   ‡ Rev. James Neil—"Palestine Explored," chapter V., pages 138–9.

> " Behold how good and how pleasant it is
> For brethren to dwell together in unity !
> Like the dew of Hermon,
> That cometh down upon the mountains of Zion:
> For there the Lord commanded the blessing,
> Even life for evermore."

Read thus from the Revised version, the thought would seem to be that just as the dews descending upon Hermon are not limited in their refreshing power to the slopes upon which they fall, so the refreshing influence of brotherly love diffuses itself through the whole community of Israel, from northern Hermon to the uttermost mountains of Zion. The Authorized version reads a little differently, and it appears to present a different shade of thought: "As the dew of Hermon and as the dew that descended upon the mountains of Zion " are words which give the idea that the refreshing mists which visit one section of the land visit all sections; a statement of which we may at least say that it is entirely in accord with Nature. The thought seems to be that just as the sacred anointing oil poured forth upon the high priest Aaron, alluded to in the preceding verse, diffuses a like fragrance whether it be on head, beard, or garment, so the dew is equally reviving and refreshing, whether it fall on the heights of Hermon or the hills of Zion. Thus, in the delighted vision of the Psalmist, was it with Israel in the day of her perfect unity. One spirit, one purpose, one faith, had fallen upon and filled all hearts, whether coming from the extreme parts of the land, far away to the north where Hermon lifts his snowy head fast by the foot of Lebanon, or from those sacred and more famous heights where the city of Zion sits among her hills. Where such a spirit as this prevails, there the Lord commands his blessing.

1. The imagery is true of the family. The happiness of household life depends upon the unity of its members, and it is equally true that its prosperity is closely related to the same. There is no more attractive sight than a family united in the bonds of a holy affection. They are strong because they are happy, happy because

they are united. In such a household the angel of love is continually playing upon the heartstrings soft melodies that float through the soul like voices of birds in the morning. Their echoes roll out upon the waters of strife like the Lord's commanded " Peace, be still !" on stormy Galilee. These are indeed songs in the night. We may well pray God that the angel of domestic love may thus sing to us all and make us all such singers. The children's hymn is very sweet and true :—

"There is beauty all around
    When there's love at home ;
There is joy in every sound
    When there's love at home."

2. In national relations we know how certain it is that in unity there is strength. All the blessings of national life are scattered before the winds of discord; but upon a united people prosperity and peace are sure to descend even as dew upon the mountains from Hermon unto Zion. Our own nation is known as the " United States," or as it is more briefly expressed, the " Union." In the very terms there is a teaching of the fact that our national vigor and prosperity, our good name among nations, nay, our very life depend upon the preservation of those bonds by which the widely-separated sections of the country are united into one nation—"Distinct like the billows, yet one like the sea."

3. It is in the matter of religious and church life, however, that we need here most to consider the lesson which the dew brings us. The prosperity of the Church of Jesus Christ, its glory and beauty in the eyes of the nations, must ever depend upon the spirit of brotherly love which it maintains. It has often been a reproach to the Church Universal or Catholic that it is divided into many sections or "sects." In so far as this has any just cause, it is our duty, and it ought to be our pleasure, to labor to remove it. First, however, we require to know what is the true ground of reproach in the premises. The adversaries of the Church may have exaggerated facts, and those who have not thought deeply enough

upon the subject of church catholicity, may have misunderstood it. If we look beneath the surface of external differences, we may often find substantial unity. May it not be so with the Church?

He who will run his thoughts backward along the entire history of the Church shall find a substantial concensus of faith in the central truths of Christianity. It would be possible to select from every branch of the Church, to-day, a college of learned theologians who would express unity of faith upon the fundamental doctrines of religion. The being of God; the existence of God in the tri-personality of the Father, Son, and Holy Ghost; the doctrine of Providence; the immortality of the soul; the inspiration and Divine authority of Holy Scripture; the life and ministry of Christ; his passion upon the cross; his resurrection from the grave; his ascension into heaven; his intercession for his people forever—these are truths upon which the Church has always been, as it is to-day, substantially one. The Apostles' Creed, so called, is accepted and uttered with little change of form, and certainly with no essential change of meaning, by all who to-day confess and call themselves Christians. Here is unity, if there be not uniformity. One type of doctrine fundamental to Christianity marks the Church catholic.

Undoubtedly there is a difference in the external forms in which these fundamental truths are presented to the world. But why should not the Church be permitted a liberty which is everywhere manifest in nature? Variety is as certainly a character of the natural world as unity. The dew is one, but I venture the doubt whether any two kindred drops are moulded into exactly the same shape and size. The tree is one, but there are no two leaves upon the tree that are shaped precisely alike. The fruit of the tree is one, but there are no two apples hanging from the boughs that are modeled alike. You cast your eye over a landscape, and your heart rejoices in the harmony unfolded from the scene before you, yet there is everywhere a difference in manifestation. In the beauty and grace of the forms which you see, in the spirit which insensibly reveals itself to you from wood and stream, lake, meadow, and mountain side, you feel the sense of oneness. One Mind has evidently planned all this. One Hand, through whatever channels of physical force, has manifestly moulded all this. Yet, when group by group and item by item, you turn your eye and thought upon the objects of this landscape, you note how wide the difference is between the one and the other.

May it not be thus also with the Church of the living God? May not the blessing of Divine grace rest, and the sweetness of brotherly unity abide equally upon the hills of God's universal Zion, whether they tower from the north in the peaks of Hermon, or roll away south-ward to the mountains round about Jerusalem? I am not justifying those differences in the external manifesta-tions of Christ's Church which are set so sharp-edged, and reared so mountainous high that they divide be-tween followers of Christ, and keep hearts separate that, like kindred drops of dew, would fain melt into one and fall together into the sacred heart of the Divine Rose of Sharon. I am simply pleading for justice and truth in the face of assaults made upon the Church from the standpoint of its divided ranks. I ask that the spirit of agreement in fundamental truth should be regarded in all such cases, as well as the differences in external form and manifestation.

Not only is there unity in the fundamental theology of the Church, but there is unity in its fundamental Christian life. There is one type of Christian character which would be accepted to-day in its substantial fea-tures as the type which lies nearest the thought of Christ.

Photography within a few years has presented to us some strange results gathered from what is known as the Galton process. This consists briefly in taking a group of faces, many or few, and causing them one after another to be presented before a sensitized plate. The time necessary to produce a perfect picture is divided between the members of the whole group so that to each one but a fraction of a minute may be allowed. The result is curious and instructive. I have here before me a series of such composite photographs. One pre-

sents the picture of sixteen naturalists.* The resulting
face is one which has caught the harmonious features of
each individual and rejected those which are not common. It is what may be called the typical face of all
these men of science. It is a strong, manly, thoughtful,
and well-seeming face. As one looks upon it he observes that it is not a close likeness of any one, yet carries something of every one of the group, and thus he is
compelled to acknowledge that it is a well-defined and
typical countenance.

When I gazed upon that face for the first time, my
thoughts insensibly turned into the channel which they
are here pursuing. Is not this a parable of the Christian
life? Is there not amidst all the varieties of Christian
men and women a common type? Would it not be
possible to take from this Church and that, from Latin,
Greek, Armenian, Protestant, and from all the representative denominations of Protestantism, individuals whose
common characteristics would present to us the typical
character of the man of God as he is in Christ Jesus? I
believe that it is possible. I am sure that it is possible.
The "Imitation of Christ" by Thomas A'Kempis is a
book wrought out by a disciple of the Church of Rome,
but it has found its way into the hearts of the Universal
Church, and no man asks or thinks as he reads the devout meditations of this godly character, to what branch
of the Christian Church did he belong? He belongs in
the widest sense to " the Holy Catholic Church." There,
indeed, in spite of whatever barriers, he always belonged
and always will be classed. His is a typical character,
one which is recognized without question in all ages by
all believers.

Again, look at the subject in the light of the Hymnology of the Church. There are indeed hymns through
whose refrains one may hear the discords of denomina-
tional shibboleths; but for the most part the hymns that
have fastened themselves upon the hearts of the devout
in any one branch of the Church are those hymns which
are loved and used by all who honor and love the name

---

* "Science," vol. V., No. 118, May 8th, 1885.

of Christ. This is true because all genuine devotion bears the common type of Christian character. In all ages the truly devout are one in sympathy, and therefore the forms of praise which utter the devotions of one heart bear alike to God the aspirations of another. The Calvinistic Toplady, Watts and Bonar, the Arminian Wesleys, the Anglican Heber and Ken, the Tractarian Keble, the Romanist Faber, and all the goodly company of the sons and daughters of Asaph when uttering the devotions of their hearts speak in one tongue. There is something divine in the flame of sacred poesy that burns out therefrom the dross of sect. Pious tongues loathe the flavor of *isms* in their holy songs. The hymns of the most rigid denominations are rarely sectarian. There is not a presbyter or priest in this whole land, with due tact and good faith, who could not conduct a mission or service of song as chaplain of a company of soldiers made up of Protestants and Roman Catholics of all phases of ecclesiastical opinions, without one discordant note and with perfect approval and enjoyment of all ! Thus it has come that as we open our own Hymnal, and it is true of every other Church, we find their sacred songs jostling one another upon the same page. Jostling, did I say ? Nay, I recall the phrase and rather say, lovingly facing and embracing one another; their thoughts equally borne up to God upon the wings of Christian devotion as the expression of that type of Christian character which represents now as in all ages the brotherly unity of believers.

Yes! the dew is one, whether it descend upon the mountains of Hermon or the hills of Zion, and through it God commandeth his blessing, even life for ever more. This truth is never more surely recognized than when we stand together upon the brink of the eternal world or set our faces outward and upward to the great eternity.

It is a fact with which we are familiar from infancy, that all the heavenly bodies, sun, moon, and stars, seem to be set in an azure vault which, rising high over our heads, curves down to the horizon on every side. This celestial vault above us, with a corresponding one below us, forms a complete sphere, which has been known in all ages as the celestial sphere.* True, it is imaginary, but that does not diminish its value as enabling us to form definite ideas of the directions of heavenly bodies from us. Think of it! Those bodies, well nigh innumerable, are scattered everywhere throughout the stellar space, and yet as the eye looks heavenward they seem smoothed out upon the plane of the celestial arch, and move in groups and constellations of individual stars and suns *as one host*, the mighty host of the heavens of God. Their lines are never broken, their order is never disturbed, but they march on forever in harmonious line, and unity so perfect that the expression " The music of the spheres" is rather a fact of science than a figure of poetry.

Thus it is, as it seems to me, not only with individual Christians, but with those groups and constellations known as congregations and Churches, when they are looked at with the eye toward the infinite and eternal world. They are all projected upon the celestial sphere as one harmonious host. When we lift our eyes from earth's narrow fields; when our vision rises above man's passions, prejudices, and ambitions; when we take the wider range and clearer view which come from those who have eternity in sight, one after another the differences that had seemed to us great are overbridged, and men and churches " dwell together in unity."

Surely, my friends, we must believe that this is the spirit and teaching of Christ. In his great high-priestly prayer in the seventeenth chapter of John, He utters in behalf of his people the supplication that they may be one. We have seen that in a certain sense, perhaps in the deepest and most important sense, that prayer has not been refused. In spirit the Church is one. Yet may we, and ought we to stand in our places day by day, and so work that the differences between us may be minimized, our common resemblances magnified, and the spirit of love by which we are to be bound in one be cultivated more and more.

Even those who do not walk as disciples of Christ discern this truth. The men of France in the barricades of

* NEWCOMB—"Popular Astronomy," page 7.

Paris once looked, it is said, upon an image of Christ and bowed to Him in reverence—not in religious reverence or recognition of his place as divine Author of the faith, but because, as they declared, " He first taught fraternity to men." Aye! the Brotherhood of man lies close within the central doctrine of our theology, the Fatherhood of God. We are one in Christ Jesus. Let no petty spirit of jealousy consume us, but whether the dews of heaven descend upon this mountain or on that, on the hills of Zion or on the slopes of Hermon, let our hearts equally rejoice. In the camp of Israel of old, before the tent of the congregation the Spirit of the Lord rested upon the elders of Israel and they prophesied. Meanwhile beyond those sacred precincts were two men, Eldad and Medad, on whom the Spirit also rested, and they prophesied in the camp. Then there ran a young man and told Moses, and said " Eldad and Medad do prophesy in the camp!" Joshua spoke up, (and one sees how possible it is for the grandest characters to err), and said—" My lord Moses, forbid them!" and Moses said unto him, " Art thou jealous for my sake? would God that all the Lord's people were prophets, and that the Lord would put his Spirit upon them!"*

Moses was a prophet like unto Christ, and never was this likeness more manifest than on the day when he uttered so broad and catholic a desire as this. Let us take up the request. Let us hope for all denominations and branches of the Church of God, the outpoured spirit of prophecy, the blessing of the Lord to descend as the dew on Hermon and on the hills of Zion.

Brethren, we *must* do it! Enemies of the faith are multiplying on every hand. It is most unwise to show our divisions in the presence of the foe. " *Divide et impera*"—divide and conquer—has long been a maxim of the great adversary of the Church. Shall we divide or shall we close up our divisions? The ancient Romans, armed with shield and spear, when they moved forward to the charge placed their shields in front and over their heads inclined backward, so that shield lapped on shield

---

* Numbers xi. 26–30.

like the scales upon a fish. Thus was formed one solid
shell of opposing shields, which from this peculiar form
was known in military parlance as the "testudo" or tor-
toise. In solid phalanx, and with this solid covering,
they marched against their foes, whose arrows and spears
fell upon the common defense and found no victim in
the united ranks.

Our Faith the Holy Spirit has likened to a shield,
"the shield of faith." Let churches and individual
Christians join shield to shield, and thus in united rank
and solid host move against the foes of Christ and his
holy faith. Be assured that such union will give us
strength and victory; that the blessing of God shall be
commanded upon us, even life forever more.

II. The next lesson is one of encouragement to ourselves in the Discharge of daily Duty, and the Exercise
of Ordinary Influence among our Fellows.

The dew-drop, we are told, has within it a latent
thunderbolt, yet it melts away into the corol of the wild
flower and does its gentle work of nurture so silently
that no ear can mark it. There are many men, and yet
more women, who sink mildly into the earth-currents of
life like a dew-drop, who have latent thunder enough
within them to shake society if it should once go forth
in that wise. But would their power for good be thereby any greater? Is not that a false estimate of moral
forces which measures them by the noise and stir, the
flash and thunderous echoes which result from their
exercise? Are not gentleness and repose after all the
mightiest powers? Let those who love and choose to
have their words distill as the dew remember that in the
silent, unobtrusive acts of daily life they may be treas-
uring up in other hearts forces which in their final outcome will give countless blessings to the world.

A dew-drop is a very little thing, yet every drop of
dew is itself an accumulation of many minute particles
of vapor. These have been distilled from the atmosphere, atom by atom, during the night long, and have
gradually gathered together in little beads of moisture.
They catch the morning sunbeams, and glitter from

every leaf and flower; they shine like strings of beaded pearls from the round webs of Orbweaving spiders; they twinkle upon the flossy threads of Lineweavers that everywhere mesh the bearded grasses and leafy shrubs; they sparkle like diamonds from the whole face of nature.

It needs some such revelation as that which the sun gives to nature to disclose the daily accumulations and whole life gatherings of " little deeds of kindness," little words of care, silent acts rendered almost unconsciously to our fellows, that distill from loving hearts and lips like the dew of evening. That revealing sunlight may not come to us here, but in the Future, when all the issues of life, when all forces latent and manifest, when all actions silent or audible shall be uncovered by the all-searching light of the eternal day in the presence of the Sun of righteousness, then shall come the revelation! Then forgotten or unknown deeds of love, which have distilled like vapor of evening, shall shine like dew-drops of the morning, and be as precious diamonds in the coronal of your eternal rejoicing and reward.

III. Our third lesson teaches the Blessedness of Charity.

You have observed when walking in the country, or through the pretty grounds that surround so many of our West Philadelphia homes, that early in the evening the grass will already be wet while the gravel walk over which you tread, or some outcropping rock in the midst of the field, is perfectly dry. You perhaps know that the reason is that radiation from plant surfaces is far more rapid than from sand, stones, and gravel. The leaves give out their heat rapidly and abundantly; therefore the invisible moisture of the air seeks them, clings to them, and gathers upon them in beaded dew-drops, thus quenching their thirst and bringing nurture to their life. Fields, orchards, and forests are enriched with grain and covered with fruits because they freely yield to the air daily and nightly the warmth that is in them. On the other hand, the barren rock and sandy desert give out nothing of the heat which the sun has poured into their laps the whole day long, and lie arid and sterile.

Hermon's grassy slopes invited and compelled the dewy mists to settle upon them, while Hermon's rocky cliffs lay hard and dry.

Is there not here also for us a lesson from the parable of the dew? He who gives shall get; he who gets should give. "Unto every one that hath shall be given."* He who pours forth freely into this world the warmth which so freely came into his own hand through the helpful influences of heaven, home, society, church, and state, shall find the answer in richer gifts of heaven, which shall nurture and beautify his spiritual life. But he whose soul is as a rocky cliff on Hermon, a stone in the field of this world, who yields up nothing of that warmth which heaven has poured upon him, may remain eternally solitary in his own fruitlessness, unblest of heaven because bringing no blessing to others. "There is that scattereth and increaseth yet more; and there is that witholdeth more than is meet, but it tendeth only to poverty. The liberal soul shall be made fat, and he that watereth shall be watered also himself."† The dew-drops love a heat-yielding surface, but shun the selfish rocks that treasure their own warmth and yield nothing to the air. Let us learn from this a lesson also.

IV. Our next lesson from the dew is one of Consecration of Early Life and of Life's Freshest Powers to God.

This duty is beautifully conveyed to us in the 110th Psalm (verse 3): "Thy people shall be willing in the day of thy power, in the beauties of holiness from the womb of the morning, thou hast the dew of thy youth." There is a melodious rhythm about this text which has fixed it in the memories of many, but are you right sure you understand it? We shall understand it better, at least, if we learn that the expression "youth" is not equivalent to early years or childhood, but is used in the sense of young people, young men. The text is therefore equivalent to this—Thy youth are to thee as the dew out of the womb of the morning. Hengstenburg reads it, "Thy youth-like soldiers are as dew for beauty."

---

* Matt. xxv. 29. † Prov. xi. 24, 25.

Now if we turn to the Psalm we shall see that it is a promise of Jehovah to the Divine Messiah, and that it looks forward to the time when men throughout the Church and world shall yield themselves as willing offerings to the Saviour. " Thy people offer themselves willingly in the day of thy power." Among those who thus offer themselves, a most grateful gift indeed, are the strong young men and maidens fair of the land. These are given to God in their morning freshness like the dew for beauty. We might thus render somewhat freely the second and third verses.*

> 2. The sceptre of Thy righteousness
>   From Zion shall the Lord send forth :
>   Be Ruler, Thou, among Thy foes !

> 3. Thy people to Thy muster troop
>   In sacred festal dress arrayed,
>   More than the drops of morning's womb ;
>   Like morning dew spring forth thy youth.

Yes, and we may carry our figure further. Like the dew the holy youth shall come in perpetual succession, for children are the hope of the Church; like the drops of dew they come in number, too. Like the dew also they suddenly appear, seen all at once under the new-risen Sun of righteousness. And may we not adopt another thought from Hengstenburg and say that they come, " Altogether begotten from above."† The metre version of Tate and Brady has thus expressed the coming to Christ of those who

> "Shall all, redeemed from error's night—
> Appear as nnmberless and bright
> As crystal drops of morning dew."

This is indeed a sweet prophecy. What hopes it stirs within our hearts concerning the youth of this and every land ! Would that these hopes to-day might be fulfilled in the rendering up to God, as a sweet and acceptable sacrifice, all the youth to whom this message comes!

---

* See DELITSCH, *in loc.*   † BONAR — "Commentary on the Psalms," *in loc.*

While the fragrance and the beauty of our morning round us lies,
We would of the heart's libation pour to Thee a sacrifice ;
Trustful that the Hand which scatters blessings every morning new,
Would refill the urn of offering, as a floweret with the dew :
Pure and sweet the exhalations from a grateful heart to Heaven ;
Unto Thee then be the incense of our Cardiphonia given,
Ere the noontide sun shall wither, or the gathering twilight hour
Closes the outpouring chalice of the morn's expanded flower.*

V. We have yet another lesson to learn from the dew, a lesson of Preparation to Receive the Gifts of God.

However full the air may be of invisible vapor or moisture in the form of mist, there will be no deposit of dew until the temperature of the earth has reached a certain degree, which is called " the dew point." That represents the point at which vapor will condense upon earth surfaces in tiny drops of water. Now, Heaven's gifts, like the invisible moisture of the atmosphere, everywhere overhang the souls of men. They are present in the greatest abundance, and they come very near to us. We walk in the midst of them. They push themselves against us, and solicit us to appropriate them to ourselves. Why then are not our hearts enriched thereby ? Simply because we fail in preparation. We have not reached the spiritual Dew Point ! There are always two sides to this matter of spiritual blessings. One side is that of Heaven which gives, gives freely, gives always. The other side is that of earth. It is of you, my friend! The mercies of God will not be, and cannot be forced upon an unwilling soul. There must be on your part that condition of faith and willingness which will cause the mercies of Heaven at once to distill upon your heart like the dew of heaven upon the thirsty grass. " Behold," says the Divine Master, " I stand at the door and knock. If any man hear my voice and open the door, I will come in."† " Open to me, * * * for my head is filled with dew, and my locks with the drops of the night."‡ You hear that voice to-day. Will you open the door ? Will you seek that preparation of heart to which Heaven's blessings may respond ? If so, be assured that you shall this hour be blessed by the benedictions of a bountiful God.

---

* HANNAH LLOYD NEAL. † Rev. iii. 20. ‡ Canticles v. 2.

LECTURE V.

Hail: God's Reserves of War.

"Hast thou seen the treasures of the hail, which I have reserved against the time of trouble, against the day of battle and war?"—JOB xxxviii. 22, 23.

HAIL—GOD'S RESERVES OF WAR.

WE are already familiar with the fact that the atmosphere surrounding us is an immense ocean of vapor. Lieutenant Maury made an estimate based upon the average annual rain-fall, which is sufficient to cover the earth to the depth of five feet, that this atmospheric ocean contains an amount of water equal to a lake sixteen feet deep, three thousand miles broad, and twenty-four thousand miles long.* From this reservoir of moisture we have already learned that mist and dew are continually precipitated upon the earth.† From this same storehouse issue forth those other phenomena which we have yet to consider—hail, snow, and rain. The challenge made to Job, " Hast thou seen the treasures of the hail ?" was perhaps unanswerable in the days of the patriarch. In a measure it is still unanswered; but modern investigations in meteorology have enabled us to draw aside the cloud-curtain, peep into Nature's laboratory, and obtain a reasonably clear mental insight of the formation of hail.

Hail is formed only in summer, and is almost invariably an accompaniment of tornadoes. It is found in one or sometimes two belts outside of the tornado track and parallel to it.‡

If a large hailstone is cut in two the centre or nucleus is found to be a minute snow-ball; then comes a ring of clear ice, then a ring of snow-ball-like conglomerate, and so on. This indicates that two different influences following each other in repeated succession have caused the formation. What are those influences?

A tornado or whirlwind may be described as a hollow cone of air in violent spiral motion around its own

---

* MAURY—"Sailing Directions," vol. I., page 28. 1858. † Lectures II., III., IV. ‡ BLASIUS—"Storms : their Nature, Classification, and Laws," page 140.

axis, which is continually moving forward. The walls of moist warm air are in the highest state of saturation and compression, as well as motion ; the centre or vortex is comparatively calm. The humid air continually drops into the vortex and passes under conditions of much diminished pressure. Rapid expansion follows ; the temperature is greatly reduced, the moisture condenses and freezes. Thus are formed the little snow-ball nuclei of the hailstones. Up they go, borne along their spiral road by the gyrations of the tornado. As they mount aloft they are tossed to and fro in all directions by the surging air, aided perhaps by electrical attraction. The impinging pellets are kneaded and balled together by regelation. This process continues until the weight of the accumulated masses enables them to overcome the vortex motion of the air currents and the attraction of electricity which is commonly formed under such circumstances, when they break away from the warring elements in which they had their formation and fall to the earth as hailstones.

But it is possible that in the wild commotion of those upper regions these icy drops may not be permitted to fall directly to the ground. They may be caught in their descent upon the edges of some eddy and whirled in again towards the vortex by the inflowing currents, and once more be borne swiftly aloft into the freezing regions. This process may occur again and again, and several revolutions of ascent and descent be made before the hailstones are able to fall to the earth. While crossing the region lower down, where they meet the yet unfrozen rain, they receive a coat of solid ice on precisely the same principle that a cold stone pavement will often have an icy surface on a warm winter morning. Thus alternate coatings of snow and ice are received, and the number of such icy jackets carried by each hailstone indicates the number of revolutions described before they began their headlong descent to the ground.

It has already been intimated that during the process of hail formation electricity is usually generated. In fact hail generally precedes, and sometimes accompanies thunder and lightning. The sharp rattling noise of hailstones against each other during a hail-storm is in part probably electrical, and the electricity doubtless has something to do in attracting the minute ice masses to each other. Electricity, however, is not the origin of hail as has sometimes been supposed, but rather electricity and hail are results of the same combination of causes. At all events the association of thunder and lightning with the hail-storm was observed by the ancient writers, as may readily be seen in the Psalmist's noble description of the tempest.

9. He bowed the heavens also, and came down;
   And darkness thick was underneath his feet.
10. And he rode upon a cherub, and did fly :
    Yea, swiftly flew upon the wings of the wind.
11. Darkness he made his hiding place, his pavilion round about him;
    Darkness of waters, and thick clouds of the skies.
12. Out of the brightness before him there broke through his clouds,
    Hailstones and coals of fire !
13. The Lord also thundered in the heavens,
    And the Most High uttered his voice ;
    Hailstones and coals of fire !
14. And he sent out his arrows, and scattered them ;
    Yea, lightnings manifold, and discomfited them.*

I. The hail teaches the Providential Interposition of God in Human Affairs.

God rules. That is a lesson which men have learned in all ages, and which God himself will see to it that they never shall forget. "Hast thou seen the treasures of the hail," He asked Job, "which I have reserved against the day of battle and war?" What does He mean by this? In what sense are hail-storms God's Reserves of War? "Reserves," in military usage, are troops kept back from the battle line and held ready for any exigency. Is any point of attack weakened? They are ordered to strengthen it. Does the foe assault from some unexpected quarter? The "reserves" are ordered to meet him. Does he waver so that a little more pressure will break his ranks? Forth rush the "reserves" to strike and rout the wavering line. Has God such "reserves" held back by Him to turn the tide of battle, and support his struggling

* Psalm xviii. 9-14.

hosts of truth in an hour of emergency? Yes. The allusion of the text is plainly to a class of facts in the Divine Providence which have abundant illustration in the history of Israel. Let us notice two of these.

The battle of Beth Horon is not often alluded to in military histories, yet it is one of the most important ever waged. It decided the destiny of Palestine, settled the land firmly in the possession of the Hebrew nation, and thus laid the foundations of that sacred history whose opening chapters are recorded in the Old Testament Scriptures; whose grand development appears in the Christianity of the New Testament; whose magnificent continuance we may read in the records of the last eighteen centuries, and whose glorious unfolding lies before us in that future upon which the nations of Christendom are entering. What was the battle of Beth Horon?

The venerable general, Joshua, who led the Hebrew hosts across the Jordan, first destroyed Jericho, which was the eastern key to the country commanding the approach from the plains of the Jordan valley. He then found himself at the foot of the mountain regions of which the heart of Palestine consists, and which had to be won before the country could be possessed. He began by seizing the pass of Ai. He entered into a treaty of offense and defense with the citizens of Gibeon, a town at the head of the pass, and then marched back to his camp at Gilgal. The Canaanitish tribes, enraged at the conduct of their countrymen, gathered from far and near and marched against Gibeon to destroy it. The Gibeonites sent swift messengers to their new ally. Joshua, with the true instincts of a great commander, saw that the pivotal conflict of the war was upon him. Gibeon was the key of the interior country. To advance and strike terror at once into the Canaanites was a first necessity. A forced march was made up the mountain, and in the course of a little more than a night he accomplished a three days' journey. Falling suddenly upon the Canaanitish troops who were beleaguering the city of Gibeon, he drove them before him up the mountain roads until they reached the head of the pass where they could look westward upon the Mediterranean Sea. Over the summits of the mountains the Hebrew soldiers poured. Now there came to their aid those reserves of war of which the Almighty speaks in our text. A cloud gathered in the eastern sky. It darkened over the horizon. The wind rose; flashes of lightning illumined the scene, and the noise of elemental war mingled with the sound of mortal battle. Suddenly there fell from the heavens a storm of hail. It beat upon the backs of the Hebrew soldiers, but as it swept toward the east it came full in the faces of the army of the Canaanites as they slowly retired towards the western horizon. "And it came to pass as they fled from before the Lord, while they were in the going down of Beth Horon, that the Lord cast down great stones from heaven upon them, and they died. There were more which died with the hailstones than they whom the children of Israel slew with the sword."* In other words, the influence of the storm upon the already disheartened troops of Canaan was more disastrous than the swords of the victorious Hebrews.

Now, the devout warriors and people of that olden time believed that no event came without the permissive will or active purpose of God. There was no doubt in the mind of Joshua and his soldiers that this storm which had prevented the enemy from rallying in the familiar passes of Beth Horon, and which had enabled them to push the battle forward to the very extermination of the army, was a direct interposition of Jehovah their God. In that hail-storm they saw those reserves of war which God had held back against this day for them, and at the very crucial moment of the fight had let loose upon the enemy, and thus obtained for Israel the victory.

Take another illustration from Hebrew history. We go forward a little in point of time to the age of Deborah, the warrior prophetess, judge, and poetess of ancient Israel. The Hebrew people, by one of those reverses which are continually occurring in history, had lost their

---

*Joshua x. 11.

grip upon the people of the land and were "mightily oppressed" by King Jabin and his general Sisera.* The spirit of Deborah revolted against this degradation. She sought to inspire Barak to active opposition, and when his laggard spirit refused the whole responsibility, she herself summoned the tribes of Israel to rendezvous, and, accompanied by Barak, marched forth against the Canaanites. The scene of the battle was the beautiful plain of Esdraelon. It lies between the foot hills of Lebanon on the north where the town of Nazareth looks down upon it, and the hills of Gilboa and the mountains of Ephraim on the south. On the west the high shoulder of Mount Carmel pushes into it, and eastward are the hills that border the river Jordan. Directly through this plain flows the river Kishon with its branches, which are known as the "waters of Megiddo." In the northeastern corner of this plain Mount Tabor rises upwards to the height of eighteen hundred feet, a solitary elevation. Along the wooded slopes of this mountain was encamped the army of Deborah and Barak, numbering ten thousand foot soldiers. Directly south-westward, thirteen miles away, across the beautiful valley and branching streams that flowed amongst green fields and flowery meadows, the Canaanitish tribes were encamped at an ancient fortress called Taanach. They were under the command of Sisera.

That stretch of land lying between the two armies is a famous battle-field of the old world. In and adjacent to the plain Gideon achieved his triumph over the Amalekites, and here too the glory of Israel was darkened for a time by the fall of Saul and Jonathan upon Gilboa. It was adjacent to Aphek, in the plain, that Ahab and the Israelites obtained a miraculous victory over the Syrians under Benhadad, while at Megiddo the pious Joshua fell in battle against the Egyptian monarch. Then came the times of the Romans with battles under Gabinius and Vespasian. The period of the Crusades furnishes its account of the contests in and around the plain. At Hattin the renown of the Crusaders sank be-

---

* Judges iv. 2.

fore the crescent of Saladin. Almost in our own day the battle of Mount Tabor was one of the triumphs of Napoleon, while at Akka, near Carmel, he was baffled and driven back from Syria.*

These historic associations were all in the future as that little band of ill-armed and undisciplined Israelites faced their powerful, well-armed, well-organized, and victorious enemies advancing from the heights across the plain. They needed all the inspiration that Deborah could give them to urge them to the attack. With unhesitating confidence she raised her battle cry, "Awake, Deborah! † Arise, Barak! Up! for this is the day in which the Lord hath delivered Sisera into thy hand."‡

Down from the wooded heights descended Barak and his ten thousand men. They moved westward along the plain which here forms a large bay to the south. The great caravan route from Damascus to Egypt passes, and probably at that time already passed across it.§

When the little army of Israelites saw the dense array of the enemy and their nine hundred chariots of war, a terrible enginery for infantry to face, they and their commander Barak, says Josephus, " were so frightened that they were resolved to march off had not Deborah retained them, and commanded them to fight the enemy that very day, for that they should conquer them, and God would be their assistance. So the battle began."‖ Thus centuries before the Maid of Orleans this Hebrew Joan of Arc led armed men into battle.

What the issue of the contest might have been had it been left to the unaided valor of the Hebrews we cannot say. Fortunately that Divine Ruler whom they believed superior to all kings and potentates, held in his Hand the Reserves of War which were to decide the battle. As the armies closed, the skies darkened above them. A storm swiftly swept from the north-east out of the hills of Hermon and Lebanon, a fruitful breeder of storms in Palestine, as Pike's Peak is in Colorado. The tempest rushed across the plain and burst with fury in the midst

---

* "Robinson's Researches," vol. II., page 366. †Judges v. 12.
‡ *Id.*, iv. 14. §STANLEY—"History Jewish Church," vol. I., Lecture XIV. ‖JOSEPHUS—"Antiquities," book 5, chapter 5, section 3.

of the combatants. Remember, now, that the army of the Canaanites was marching eastward while the Israelites were marching westward. The storm, therefore, coming from the east, broke upon the backs of the Hebrews, but beat full in the faces of their enemies. It was accompanied with a vast downfall of rain and hail. It darkened the eyes of the Canaanitish soldiers so that their arrows and slings were of no advantage to them. It chilled their hands, so that the soldiers could not make use of their swords.* The Hebrew warriors saw in this hail-storm a direct interposition of Providence in their behalf. It seemed to them the fulfillment of Deborah's prophecy. Their hearts were strengthened, their fears dispelled, and with fresh courage and vigor they threw themselves upon their foes. They knew the value as well as the source of these Reserves of War, which from the forces of nature had come to their aid.

The waters of the storm fell so copiously, that the plain was soon beaten into mud beneath the hoofs of the horses and wheels of the chariots.

The numerous rivulets began to overflow their banks, and added to the inconvenience of managing the cavalry. The dreaded and terrible engineery upon which Sisera had so strongly relied, became an element of danger.

The horses, made frantic by the hail, pranced and plunged as we have seen these animals do in our city streets,† and turned back upon their own lines. The footmen were thrown into disorder, and, rendered helpless by the blinding storm, broke their ranks. In the degree that their enemies' hearts sank, the courage and hope of the Hebrews rose, so that they fought with increasing bravery and success. Panic seized the Canaanites, and then the end soon came. The army dissolved, and a vast number perished. Their general Sisera dismounted from his chariot and fled, only to find an ignominious death at the hand of Jael the Kenite. The battle was decisive; Israel was delivered from subjection, and began anew her noble career as an independent nation. The victory was celebrated by the prophetess in

---

* JOSEPHUS. † During the hailstorm of May 3d, 1870.

those triumphal odes known as Deborah's Song, whose artistic forms and elevated nature with all its antique simplicity show to what refined art lyric poetry aspired, and what a delicate perception of beauty already breathed through it.*   The portion of Deborah's Song descriptive of the battle, together with the conclusion, I venture to present in the following version :—

*   *   *   *   *   *   *

VII. The Battle and Flight.

19. There came kings and fought,
       Then fought the kings of Canaan
   At Taanach, on Megiddo's waters ;
       Spoils of silver they took not !

20. From Heaven they fought ; the stars
   From their orbits fought with Sisera.

21. The torrents of Kishon swept them away,
   That ancient river, the river Kishon.
   Trample down, O my soul, their strength !
   Then stamped the hoofs of the horses,
   From the plungings of mighty ones,
   The plungings in morass and flood !

*   *   *   *   *   *   *

X. The Mother's Watch.

28. The mother of Sisera leaned through the window,
   And thus she lamented through the lattice :
   " Why is his chariot long in coming ?
   Why do the wheels of his chariot tarry ? "

29. The wise ones among her princesses answer
   Yea, she repeats to herself their answer .

30. " They are surely finding, dividing the prey,
   One damsel,—two, for the head of each hero !
   Prey of divers colors for Sisera,
   Prey of divers colors of broidery,
   One of mixed colors, two of embroidery,
   For the necks of damsels token as prey."

XI. The Conclusion.

31. So let all thine enemies perish,
       O Lord Jehovah !
   But them that love Him be as the sun
       When he goeth forth in his might !

---

* Ewald—" History of Israel," II., page 354.

Does it seem to you that God does not deal in this way with nations at the present time? Then you have read modern history neither wisely nor devoutly. Was not England saved by the storms that scattered the Spanish Armada? Go back to the War of the Rebellion, and you will find as striking evidences of God's interposition as any that are recorded in the history of Israel. Time and again were those Reserves of War which God keeps within the forces of nature, sent out to strike in behalf of our Republic. Take one example. On the eighth of March, A. D. 1862, there occurred an extraordinary event in Hampton Roads near Norfolk, Virginia. The Confederates had converted the United States' frigate Merrimac into an iron-clad ram. Our fleet of wooden frigates lay in Hampton Roads besieging Norfolk. You may remember still the tremor that every now and then shook the hearts of Philadelphians, as their well-grounded fears were awakened by the rumor that some formidable sea monster was being prepared, which would crush through our wooden hulls like egg-shells, and make its way to the cities of the North, carrying destruction and levying tribute. That day seemed to have dawned at last. The mail-clad Merrimac steamed out from Norfolk to attack our blockading fleet. She dashed her iron prow into their wooden sides, while their cannon-balls rolled from her own armored walls as if they had been paper pellets. When evening had fallen, the Cumberland had gone down with all on board; the Congress had been forced to surrender; the Minnesota was run aground, and apparently destined to fall an easy prey on the morrow to this monster of the sea. It was a black night in the history of our Republic.

What would the morrow bring? How *could* the morrow bring deliverance? What power would come to our assistance to fray from us the awful disaster that seemed impending? Humanly speaking, the fate of the nation was in the balance, with scarce a hope that the scales would swing to our favor. But during that night a strange-looking object, resembling more a cheese box upon a raft than a vessel of war, appeared upon the scene. It was the "Monitor" of Ericsson, a small steam floating battery, with a revolving turret within which two 11-inch guns were placed. Morning dawned; the Merrimac, confident of her irresistible power, and certain of complete success, steamed out to renew her ravages only to be brought to bay by this new-come adversary. The two vessels fought for hours when the Merrimac was compelled to fall back into Norfolk, leaving the little Monitor in possession of the field.* The honor of the navy was restored. The nation was saved. The ports of New York and Philadelphia and all our northern seaboard were delivered from devastation. Those of you whose memories can go back to that period will recollect that this sudden and most timely appearance of the Monitor was regarded universally as an Act of Providence. We saw in it the Hand of a good God interposing in our behalf. We were filled with the sentiment which during that troubled period stamped upon our coin the national motto " In God we trust," and gave us the " Battle Hymn of the Republic." True, men had shown wisdom and skill in devising and constructing this vessel, but what wisdom or skill could have so timed the appearance of the vessel? At least all devout hearts must believe and feel that He who guards the destinies of nations and of men, who holds in His hands those unseen reserves of war by whose sudden coming upon scenes of human conflict destinies are so often settled; that He had held the winds and the waves in the hollow of His Hand, and had so timed all the exigencies and incidents surrounding the Monitor that it was permitted to steam silently, in the very nick of time, to the duty and service which saved the Republic.

No wonder the soldiers of that great conflict could sing: " Mine eyes have seen the glory of the coming of the Lord!"

I have seen Him in the watch-fires of a hundred circling camps ;
They have builded Him an altar in the evening dews and damps
I can read His righteous sentence by the dim and flaring lamps :
   His day is marching on ! †

2. As it is with nations so it is with individuals. The Bible everywhere teaches that God carries the same

---

* See "The Century," March, 1885. † JULIA WARD HOWE.

methods into the spheres of individual life that are displayed in the broader fields of national destiny. Indeed it could not be otherwise. Society is made up of individuals, and the aggregate can only be regulated by regulating the units. To say, therefore, that God overrules the destinies of nations is but to say in another form that he overrules the destinies of men. "The greatest rivers," says a Chinese proverb, "are cradled in the leaves of the pine." In a measure that is true. The vast forests of coniferous trees which cover the sides of mountains and send up their myriads of delicate, needle-like leaves toward the sky, present so many attracting points to the over-passing clouds, and help to draw down to themselves and the earth that moisture which feeds the sources of rivers. So the mighty streams of national destiny have their rise in individual life and action. He who thinks of great events must not separate his thoughts from the little things that encompass and control their origin. You know how beautifully our Divine Lord taught this truth: "Behold the fowls of the air, for they sow not, neither do they reap, nor gather into barns; yet your Heavenly Father feedeth them. Are ye not much better than they?"*

Every man is permitted to think of himself as the direct object of Divine care. I spoke in my last lecture of that celestial sphere, as astronomers have called it, which appears to surround the earth. The directions or apparent positions of the heavenly bodies, as well as their apparent motions, have always been defined by their situation and motion on this sphere. "It matters not," says an American astronomer, "how large we suppose this sphere, so long as we always suppose the observer to be in the centre of it, so that it shall surround him on all sides at an equal distance. But in' the language and reasoning of exact astronomy, it is always supposed to be infinite, as then an observer may conceive of himself as transported to another point, even one of the heavenly bodies themselves, and still be for all practical purposes in the centre of this sphere."†

---

* Matthew vi. 26.　† NEWCOMB—"Popular Astronomy," chapter I.

Now it seems to me that this conception of an all-en-compassing celestial sphere which every individual must make for the practical uses of astronomy, is one which is just as necessary to make for the practical uses of our spiritual life. Every living soul may dare to conceive himself as a central point of celestial thought and care, towards whom, in all the exigencies of life, shall centre and focus whatever agencies of help God may think needful. God is not unmindful of the struggles which human hearts have to endure in this life. "He knoweth our frame; he remembereth that we are dust."* He knows the enemies against whom we contend, so nu-merous, so insatiable, so much more powerful than our-selves. He knows the secret foes who too often hold possession of the fortress of the heart, and stand ready to betray us to God's enemies and our own. Be sure, then, that in the crisis of spiritual conflicts, in the hour of greatest temporal need, our heavenly Commander, from his high vantage point of observation viewing all the field, will send forth his Reserves of grace to strengthen us and preserve us. We must not let go faith in this great truth. God rules. He rules for *us*. We may trust Him implicitly. We may venture into the conflict, not rashly, not self-confidently, not presumptuously, but as-sured that if our strength should fail there are reserves in heaven, hosts of God, agencies at his command that shall be bidden forth to our rescue.

This is a very comforting truth. The soldier who goes into battle has always more confidence because he remembers that behind him wait the reserves, often the very flower of the army. If there shall be need, they will dash forward at the commander's order to strike here and there, to strengthen a wavering line, or charge with fresh energy when the enemy's line has been broken, and thus make assurance doubly sure. Should not the Christian soldier in like manner be confident as he goes forth to the conflict; more cheerful, more coura-geous, more hopeful of success, because he knows well that God's Reserves of War are waiting to serve him in any hour of need?

* Psalm ciii. 14.

II. Our next lesson from the hail is one of Divine Judgment upon the Ungodly.

God not only rules, but he rules in righteousness. The prophet Isaiah* expresses the judgment of the Lord upon the Assyrians under the figures of the lighting down of his arm, with indignation of his anger and tempest and hailstones. In the book of Revelation † the opening of the seals and the pouring forth of the vials upon the nations is associated with hail: "And there fell upon men a great hail out of heaven, every stone about the weight of a talent." As the weight of a talent is a hundred and twenty-five pounds troy, the figure becomes a very strong expression of the judgment of destruction which it conveyed. It is not necessary perhaps to explain it literally, and yet we have records ‡ of hailstones ranging in size from a half-brick to that of a sheep and even of an elephant. The simple point with us, however, is to grasp the lesson which God would teach through this imagery.

Justice is one of the attributes of the Divine nature. It is impossible for us to conceive of that nature as a perfect one without enthroning justice within it. There is no quality of the human heart that is more admirable than justice. "A just man" is a tribute of highest praise. No higher encomium can be passed upon an executive and judicial officer than "He is a just ruler;" "he is a just judge." There is no virtue whose practice would be more likely to bring harmony out of the discords of society than justice. Long ago the inspired writer gave the best solution of the actual or imaginary "conflict" between Labor and Capital. "Masters, render unto your servants that which is just and equality." "Servants, obey not with eye service, but with singleness of heart, fearing God." § For "masters" read "employers," and for "servants" read "employees," and you have at once a principle that will cause these elements to combine. Unjust words hastily spoken, unjust thoughts entertained within the heart, unjust actions

---

* Chapter xxx. 30.   † Chapter viii. 7, and xvi. 21.   ‡ Chambers' Encyclopædia, art. *Hail*.   § Coloss. iii. 22, and iv. 1.

towards individuals or parties—these are the seeds whose sowing surely will result in a harvest of discord and regrets. Justice is expediency. Justice is harmony. Nay, justice is benevolence.

It would be impossible on earth to administer government without the quality of justice. It is equally impossible for Heaven to rule without the same quality. But justice implies judgment upon the offender; and as long as there are men who dishonor every noble quality of manhood—who offend God, trample virtue under foot, disregard law, mercy, righteousness, and truth—just so long must Heaven be armed with the sword to administer fitting penalty and preserve in the midst of the world the sovereignty of Divine Law.

A duty devolves upon all public teachers, indeed on every man and woman in society, to keep alive in human hearts a sense of indignation against moral evil. Selfishness, impurity, falsehood are very strongly intrenched within human nature, and may easily get the mastery of men unless they be kept under subjection by the force of a well-disciplined conscience and right public sentiment. Justice is often represented as blind. Certainly, at least, she often has her eyes closed, and he who keeps his eyes long closed will surely fall asleep. When justice sleeps the community is in peril. She needs to be awakened, even by the loud cries of a righteous indignation. Those cries are often heard. Alas! too frequently there occur outbreakings of human depravity of such especial heinousness that the whole community—the whole world, at times—is shocked, and instinctively men cry out for justice upon the offenders. I believe that that voice, which never is wholly silenced from the human breast, is an utterance from that Divine Image and Likeness enstamped upon man in his origin. Justice is Divine! and the execution of judgment upon the sinner must surely be regarded as in the line of righteous and necessary action. Shall we suppose an example?

There is a young woman whose fair, sweet face bears in every feature the stamp of virtue. That maiden's guileless heart has never cherished a thought of sin or

suspicion of impurity for herself or for any fellow-
creature. But see! she is met face to face by a man
—by one who bears at least the form of man. In
his impure heart he has marked that maiden as his victim. He is the master of all the arts by which unsuspicious women are persuaded to trust with unwavering
confidence those in whom their hearts become enlisted.
Day by day, week by week with stealthy approach, with
unrelenting purpose he plies his awful art until at last his
purpose is on the verge of its dreadful accomplishment.
I have seen a large beautiful cat creeping through a mass
of bright green grass bedecked with lovely flowers,
moving with the noiseless gliding stride characteristic of
the feline species, its great green eyes fixed yonder upon
some object that I could not quite discern among the
low-hanging boughs of a tree. On, across the beds of
flowers; on, across the lovely lawn, until at last the
creature pauses. It raises its head, curves its back, sinks
upon its haunches, crouching to spring upon what I
now see is a fledgling bird innocently twittering and disporting upon that, hanging branch. The cat is doing
nothing foreign to its nature, only indeed that which
nature taught it. Yet every impulse of your being, were
you a witness of such a scene, would prompt you to rush
forward as I do with a cry of alarm to fray away the
skulking beast, and save the little birdling from its
threatened doom. Yes, you are angry at poor Puss.
You strike her with indignant outthrust of your foot.

Ah! but this creature who bears the form of man, this
beast in manhood's fleshly livery, who has deliberately
plotted and waits upon the execution of his lustful purpose—what vial of wrath so full, so fierce that your
hand would not pour out upon *him?* But let us suppose, further, that this stealthy beast of prey meets no
interposing hand to drive him from his victim; that this
unsuspicious maiden hears no voice raised to warn her of
her danger, and bid her flee. The deed is done. That
fair life is blasted. That soul is sullied with an impurity
that never here, and mayhap never hereafter, shall be
washed away. Human justice is foiled in the pursuit and
punishment of her seducer. Nay, on the contrary, he en-

joys wealth, honor, and public station. What then? Is justice indeed blind? Is justice asleep? Is justice dead? Is there *no* justice that can overtake a wretch like that and visit him with the penalty which such crime demands?

Yes, my friends, God has his reserves of war! Let wicked men tremble as they remember that God is Just, and turn from the purposes of evil upon which their hearts are fixed. I know that on earth justice seems to tarry long, and hearts grow weary in their cry to the Almighty to make bare his Arm and interpose for the protection and defense of truth and innocence. But if not here, then hereafter Justice shall be vindicated. There is nothing that seems to me to present a stronger argument for a future being, for an immortal life in which the inequalities of this world shall be rendered even by the All-just Rector of the world, than the fact that so much injustice does prevail in this life, so many wrongs go unrighted, and so many sins unpunished. Surely, since justice is an attribute infinite, eternal, and unchangeable of the Almighty God, somewhere—SOMEWHERE He has appointed a Judgment Seat at whose bar the unpunished criminal shall be judged.

Anne of Austria, the Queen of France, had in the great Prime Minister Richelieu a relentless enemy. On one occasion, it is said, the queen thus addressed the minister: " My Lord Cardinal, there is one fact which you seem to have entirely forgotten. God is a sure paymaster. He may not pay at the end of every week, or month, or year, but I charge you remember that he pays in the end." Yes, though long delayed, justice shall fall at last.

A sentiment not unlike this was uttered by the editor of a weekly newspaper in a section of Illinois near which I began my ministry. An infidel farmer in the neighborhood sent to the editor a letter of this substance : " SIR :—I have been trying an experiment. I have a field of Indian corn, which I plowed on Sunday. I planted it on Sunday. I did all the cultivating which it received on Sunday. I gathered the crop on Sunday, and on Sunday hauled it to my barn; and I find that I have more corn to the acre than has been gathered by any of my neighbors during this October." The editor was not a religious man ; was rather a rough sort of personage, such as one often meets with in new countries. His general character, indeed, had given the infidel farmer the impression that he might perhaps be in sympathy with his scepticism. In fact, the editor did publish the letter, word for word as it had been written, but underneath it he placed two index marks, one at the beginning and one at the end of a short line. That line was printed in bold-faced capital types, and read thus: "GOD DOES NOT ALWAYS SETTLE HIS ACCOUNTS IN OCTOBER."

Though the mills of God grind slowly, yet they grind exceeding
    small ;
Though with patience He stands waiting, with exactness grinds
    He all.*

III. A third lesson from the Scriptural use of hail is that there is no Safety for human souls except beneath the Saving Rule of God.

One great purpose of Divine judgments is undoubtedly to awaken the human conscience and turn man from sin unto God. " I smote you with hail," said the Lord unto his people, "and ye turned not to me."† Evidently the purpose of God in this judgment of hail was to turn his people to him, although they refused to learn from the discipline of his hand. The Plague of Hail was one of those sent upon Pharoah and his kingdom to compel the Egyptians to listen to the voice of God and let his oppressed people go forth into freedom. Moses fully warned the Egyptian monarch of the coming judgment and bade him and his people provide against it. Some of the subjects of Pharaoh, we are told, were wise enough to make their servants and cattle flee into houses, and thus escaped. But " He that regarded not the word of the Lord left his servants and his cattle in the fields,"‡ and the hail smote them both man and beast. The safety of these people lay in their obedience of the will of God. "Only in the land of Goshen where the children of Israel were was there no hail."§

How thoroughly this illustrates that blessed Refuge

* LONGFELLOW.   †Haggai ii. 17.   ‡Exodus ix. 20-21.   § *Id.* verse 26.

to Whom we all may flee, and in Whom, we are assured by God's own word, we shall be safe from Divine judgment. Christ Jesus is the Refuge of souls. He who by faith commits himself to the sovereign care of the Redeemer, he who lives in humble following of this Saviour a life of loving obedience and holiness, whatever storms shall beat upon the wicked in the day of judgment—he shall be safe.

> "Safe in the arms of Jesus,
> Safe on his gentle breast."

Is there no other refuge? I know of none. Can the soul be safe from Divine judgment outside of Jesus Christ? I know no other way of safety. "I am the way," said Jesus. "Neither is there salvation in any other."* All other refuges are compared by the prophet Ezekiel† to a wall daubed with untempered mortar against which "there shall be an overflowing shower, and ye, oh great hailstones shall fall, and the stormy winds shall rend it. And it shall fall and ye shall be consumed in the midst thereof." The prophets who invite weary and sinful souls to take refuge behind such an untempered wall as this are denounced by the Almighty as those who "have seduced my people, saying, peace, peace, and there is no peace." Our blessed Saviour himself compared trust in all other hopes and faiths to the action of one who laid a foundation to build a house upon the sands, against which the waves and winds and rains beat, and it fell, and great was the fall thereof.‡ Once more, Jehovah, through the lips of Isaiah, declares that those who put their trust in other than Himself "have made lies their refuge and have hid themselves under falsehood." "Therefore, thus saith the Lord God, behold I have laid in Zion for a foundation stone, a tried stone, a precious corner-stone of sure foundation. He that believeth shall not make haste. And I will make judgment the line, and righteousness the plummet, and the hail shall sweep away the refuge of lies."§ Thus God sets before the souls of men the

---

* Acts iv. 12. † Ch. xiii. 10–12. ‡ Matt. vii. 27. § Isaiah xxviii. 16–17.

folly of seeking refuge from the storms of judgment in fragile hopes, vain delusions, and presumptuous self-confidence, and in the same breath sets before them the one sure Foundation of human trust. To that Foundation I invite you to-day. Flee! Flee, O sinner, from the impending wrath of God, and build all your hopes for eternity upon Him who is the Chief Stone of the Corner. Who is He? He is the Christ! The Messiah of God, who shall help you in the fight against sin, will bruise for you the Dragon's head, and swallow up Death in Victory.

I have read a fiery gospel writ in burnish'd rows of steel :
"As ye deal with my contemners, so with you my grace shall deal ;"
Let the Hero, born of woman, crush the serpent with his heel,
    Since God is marching on.

He has sounded forth the trumpet that shall never call retreat ;
He is sifting out the hearts of men before his judgment-seat :
Oh, be swift, my soul, to answer him ! be jubilant, my feet !
    Our God is marching on.*

---

  * Mrs. Howe's "Battle Hymn of the Republic."

LECTURE VI.

Snow Crystals:
God as Geometer.

"Hast thou entered into the treasuries of the snow?"
—JOB xxxviii. 22.

SNOW CRYSTALS: GOD AS GEOMETER.

THE molecules and atoms of all substances when allowed free play have a tendency to definite forms called crystals, which for the most part are very beautiful. The familiar confection known as rock candy is simply a mass of crystals of sugar which have been produced by dissolving the sugar in water and permitting the water to evaporate. Crystals of alum may be produced in the same way, and are familiar objects in druggists' windows. Water, indeed, is almost a universal solvent, and there are but few substances that are not to a greater or less degree dissolved by it. The magnificent crystals which we frequently find in the rocks are formed in almost every case by a deposition of mineral substance from a state of solution in water. Many of the large crystals in cabinets of minerals have been unquestionably thousands of years in formation.* Thus the solvent power of water studs the cavities of rocks with crystal gems. Flints, dissolved as they sometimes are in nature and permitted to crystallize, yield prisms and pyramids of rock crystal. Chalk dissolved and crystallized yields Iceland spar, and diamonds are crystallized carbon. All our precious stones, ruby, sapphire, beryl, topaz, and emerald are examples of this crystallizing power.

Snow is simply the vapor of water in a crystallized form. Indeed, the term "crystal" found in most of the European languages is derived from the Greek χρύσταλλος (*krustallos*), meaning ice or frozen water, and was subsequently transferred to pure transparent stones cut into seals, which, as was thought, were produced only in the extreme cold of lofty passes of the Alps. The atmosphere is charged with watery vapor to an immense extent, and when the temperature is sufficiently low to

---

*COOKE—"Religion and Chemistry," page 156.

freeze this moisture, snow is formed. When produced in calm air the icy particles build themselves into beautiful stellar shapes, each star possessing six rays. More fully described, snow crystals are six-pointed stars or hexagonal plates, which exhibit the greatest variety of beautiful forms, one thousand different kinds having been observed. These numerous forms Scoresby reduced to five principal varieties: (1.) Thin plates, comprising several hundred forms of the most exquisite beauty; (2.) A nucleus of plane figure, studded with needle-shaped crystals; (3.) Six-sided, more rarely three-sided, crystals; (4.) Pyramids of six sides; (5.) Prismatic crystals, having at the ends and middle thin plates perpendicular to their length. The flakes vary from seven-hundredths of an inch to an inch in diameter, the smallest occurring with low temperatures and the largest when the temperature approaches thirty-two degrees. If the temperature is a little higher, the snow-flakes are partially thawed in passing through it, and fall as sleet.

One who chooses to experiment for himself may catch the falling flakes upon a cold hand mirror, slate, or a bit of window glass. With an ordinary magnifying lens he can then observe the crystal forms of the flakes, which will commonly have a similar structure in any one snow-fall. Thus examined the water crystals of snow will awaken the utmost admiration for their beauty. How beautiful they are may be seen by examining the figures of them made by Messrs. Scoresby and Glaisher, for the most part, as they are reproduced in various cyclopædias, commentaries, and works on meteorology.* These forms have been frequently used for decorative purposes, being wrought into the figures on wall paper, prints, laces, and other objects of domestic use.

It is not, however, from the beauty of snow-crystals that we are to derive the lesson of this lecture, but from the geometrical form of their structure, which I shall take as a type of that order which is everywhere manifest in the material world. To this typical character of

---

* See Barnes' "Commentary on Job;" Tyndall's "Forms of Water;" and Chambers' Encyclopædia, art. *Snow;* also, the drawings in No. 1, of "The Swiss Cross."

snow-flakes Whittier alludes in the description of a snow-storm with which he begins his poem, " Snow-Bound."

> " In tiny spherule traced with lines
> Of Nature's geometric signs,
> In starry flake, and pellicle,
> All day the hoary meteor fell."

I. The first and chief lesson which we are to draw out of the Treasury or Storehouse of the snow is the Active Presence in nature of a Divine Orderly Mind.

The text is a part of that remarkable poetic passage in the book of Job* in which Jehovah responds to the patriarch's plea, " May the Almighty answer me !" † He surprises him with questions which are intended to bring him indirectly to consciousness of the wrong and absurdity of his challenge. In language, not of wrath, but of loving condescension, and yet earnest reproof, he makes the Titan puny in his own eyes, in order to exalt him who is outwardly and inwardly humbled.‡ Over against the Infinite Power and Wisdom of the Divine working in nature God sets the insignificance of Job's human weakness. Thus, as the vision of the Almightiness rounds out larger before the defiant patriarch's soul, he gets new glimpses and true views of his own littleness. Let us read in the connection of our text a few of these questions which Jehovah put to Job out of the storm :—

*   *   *   *   *   *   *   *   *   *

VI.

22 Hast thou reached to the storehouse of the snow?
Or hast thou seen the treasures of the hail,

23 Which for the time of trouble I reserve,
Against the day of battle and of war?

24 Along what track is light distributed?
How spreads the east wind o'er the face of earth?

25 Who cleaves a channel for the flood of rain,
And marks a pathway for the thunder-flash,

26 So that upon the land where no man dwells,
The desert tenantless, the rain descends,

27 To satisfy the waste and wilderness,
And cause the tender shoot of grass to spring?

---

*Job xxxviii. 22, *sqq.*   † *Id.*, chap. xxxi. 35.   ‡ DELITZSCH— " Commentary," *in loc.*

VII.

28 Is there a father to the rain? And who
   Begetteth to the morn the drops of dew?

29 Out of whose womb hath issued forth the ice?
   And who hath borne the hoar-frost of heaven,

30 So that the waters harden like the stone,
   The surface of the deep together cleaves?

It is still true, as in the days of Humboldt, that among these questions "there are many which the natural philosophy of the present day can frame more scientifically but cannot satisfactorily solve."* The question concerning the storehouse of the snow, and the formation of crystal within it, is one of these. Crystals may be seen, as in the time of Leeuwenhoek, springing out of solutions under the microscope and continuing to increase in size, but the powers that are active escape our notice, and we are still left almost in the same region of speculation as our predecessors. We can at this moment form no adequate idea of the complex and beautiful organization of these apparently simple bodies.†

The physical properties of crystals indicate a close dependence on their geometric character. The same systems shown by their mathematical forms and optic properties reappear in reference to their relations to heat, magnetism, electricity, and other properties.‡ Let us pursue this fact a little further. We must not weary of the details; the conclusion I trust will repay us for any tediousness in the process by which it is reached. We have seen that when water containing saline matter in solution is allowed to evaporate slowly, the salt it contains is thrown down in bodies of peculiar forms, bounded by smooth, even surfaces meeting in straight lines. We have learned that fused metals consolidating in certain favorable conditions appear as similar bodies; and that in nature, also, in cracks or fissures of the rocks, or imbedded in their mass, minerals resembling these in form are frequently found. These regular polyhedric or many-sided bodies, whether natural or artificial, we know,

---

*Von Humboldt—"Cosmos," II., page 48. † *Crystallography*, Ency. Brit., vol. VI., page 675. ‡ *Id.*, page 677.

are called crystals, and the science naming and describing the forms they assume, and pointing out the relations that exist among them, is termed crystallography. Now, let us emphasize the fact that in a theoretical point of view this science may be regarded *as a branch of mathematics*, and might be studied independent altogether of the fact of any material bodies existing in the forms described.

It is easy for the least scientific observer to determine for himself that the entire structure of crystals is based upon mathematical laws and relations. Visit the extensive collection of minerals in the museum of the Academy of Natural Sciences, or in the Vaux Collection under the same roof, or any one of the valuable private collections possessed by gentlemen in our city. The visit, besides affording you a day of exquisite enjoyment in the contemplation of some of nature's most lovely forms, will give you new ideas of the vast variety and infinite wealth of taste manifest in the works of the Creator. You will see at a glance that all these crystal forms are geometric. . Angles, edges, and faces will remind you of those forms which, if you have ever studied geometry at all, continually figured upon the pages of your Euclid, and which to-day are familiar in the Kindergartens of our young children.

Converse for a little while with the mineralogists who own or have studied these specimens ; or, open such a well-known book as Professor Dana's " Mineralogy," and you will find yourself at once overwhelmed with geometric terms, which, even should you not happen to comprehend them, will at least give you the undoubted impression that you are greeted with the terms and facts of a mathematical science. You will hear, perhaps, of the nucleus of a crystal, and learn that in fluor spar the nucleus is an octahedron ; in heavy spar, a right prism with rhombic base ; in galena or sulphate of lead, a cube, and so of other substances. You will hear, perhaps, of Haüy's theory of the structure of crystals ; of six primitive forms—the parallelopiped, the octahedron, the tetrahedron, the regular hexahedron prism, the duodecahedron with equal and similar rhombic faces, and the duodecahedron with triangular faces consisting of two regular six-sided pyramids joined base to base. Proceeding a little further in your study of the growth of the science, you will learn of the theory of Weiss which allows the ascertained knowledge of mathematical laws and relations of crystalline structure to come out purely. You will hear of the law that the indices marking the relative dimensions of the pirameters are always rational numbers. In short, you are in a realm of geometry! By whatever energy the objects before you have been formed, it has been operated under mathematical laws, has been subservient to mathematical principles. Whence these laws and principles? How shall we describe that ultimate Power to which they must be traced? How shall we name It? It is mathematical; is It a Mathematician? It is geometrical; is It a Geometer?

The laws and relations which we observe in crystals are not peculiar to them. In fact, mathematical laws form the basis of nearly all operations of nature. They constitute, as it were, the very framework of the material world.* Galileo's discussion of the cycloid proved, long afterward, to be a key to problems concerning the pendulum, falling bodies, and resistance to transverse pressure. Four centuries before Christ, Plato and his scholars were occupied upon the ellipse as a purely geometric speculation, and Socrates seemed inclined to reprove them for their waste of time. But in the seventeenth century after Christ, Kepler discovered that the Architect of the heavens had given us magnificent diagrams of the ellipse in the starry sky; and, since that time, all the navigation, architecture, and engineering of the nineteenth century have been built on these speculations of Plato.†

The physical universe has perhaps no more general characteristic than this, its laws are mathematical relations. The law of gravitation which rules all masses of matter, great or small, heavy or light, at all distances, is a definite numerical law. The curves which the heavenly bodies describe under the influence of that law are

---

* HITCHCOCK—"Religion and Geology," page 387. † PROFESSOR FLINT—"Theism," page 368.

the ellipse, circle, parabola, and hyperbola. Or in other words, they all belong to the class of curves called conic sections, the properties of which mathematicians had begun to investigate twenty centuries before Newton. Sir Isaac Newton showed that whatever was true of these curves might be directly transferred to the heavens, since the planets revolve in ellipses, the satellites of Jupiter in circles, and the comets in elliptic, parabolic, and hyperbolic orbits.* The relative intensity of magnetic attraction is expressed in mathematical terms.†

The law of chemical combination through which the whole world of matter has been built up out of a few elements always admits of precise numerical expression. Each color in the rainbow is due to a certain number of vibrations in a given time. So is each note in the scale of harmony. Numerical order marks the vegetable kingdom.‡

The "tens of thousands of kinds of plants all harmonize with each other, like the parts of concerted music;"§ the movements of plants and climbing vines are expressed in mathematical terms, such as ellipses, ovals, curves, spirals, circular spirals.|| The feathers in the wings and tails of birds are numbered.¶ A study of the spiral configuration of the wing of a bird and its spiral, tail-like, lashing movement involves some of the most profound questions in mathematics.** These references might be carried into every department of physics and natural history and multiplied indefinitely.

Now, if nature had not thus been ruled by numerical laws, the mathematical sciences could not have become, as they are, great instruments of physical investigation. They could not have been applied to the universe at all unless its order had been of the exact numerical and geometrical kind which has been indicated.†† The pro-

---

* PROFESSOR NEWCOMB — "Popular Astronomy," page 377.
† QUACKENBOSS—"Natural Philosophy," page 338. ‡ McCOSH—"Typical Forms in Creation," page 18. § PROFESSOR ASA GRAY —"How Plants Grow," page 17. || DARWIN—"Power of Movement in Plants," pages 1, 2; "Climbing Plants," pages 124, 125. ¶ DUKE OF ARGYLE—"Reign of Law," page 56. ** PETTIGREW—"Animal Locomotion," page 154. †† PROFESSOR FLINT—"Theism," page 135.

phet Isaiah does not exceed the exact statements of modern science when he declares that the waters had been measured in the hollow of the Divine Hand, the heavens meted out as with a span, the dust of the earth comprehended in a measure, the mountains weighed in scales, and the hills in a balance.*

The science of chemistry, which has appeared upon the scene at a late period as compared with astronomy, mathematics, and geometry, has recently carried its triumphs beyond this world. We know something now of the chemistry of other worlds. The constituents of the sun and stars have been revealed to us through the spectroscope. In those far-away worlds we find the same elements existing that enter into the make-up of our globe. We find those elements operated according to the same general laws. We find, in short, throughout the whole stellar realms, and we may infer also throughout universal space, that order of the strictest kind, the most definite proportions are wrought into the very structure of every world and of every compound in the world, air and water, earth and mineral, plant and animal. Thus, wherever human mind directs its thought, it is brought face to face with the fact that order, mathematical order, geometric order, pervades all the arrangements of the universe.

Can we forbear to start the question, How came this so? The question forces itself upon us. Reason demands an answer, an answer that will satisfy the very conditions of our being as reasoning creatures. Could anything else than intelligence thus weigh, calculate, measure, or number? Could mere matter know the most abstruse properties of space and time and number so as to obey them in the way it does? It requires the finest mathematical knowledge to apprehend the relations which exist between the stellar worlds, and the nature of their movements. How much profounder the skill and learning needed to discover and verify by mathematical science these motions and relations! Could all these have originated with what is ignorant

---

* Isai. xl. 12.

of quantitative relations? Shall we stand in the light of these facts and perceive no Mind behind them all? Is it not one of the plainest conclusions to human reason that these objects have all the characteristics of machines, constructed, directed, and maintained in motion by exact mathematical forces, and have been under the influence, at some period, of the Mind of a Geometrician, a Mathematician, a Numberer, and a Calculator?

Wherever we see order we infer the presence of mind. If you enter a house, though it be in the loneliest desert, and see around you the many items of domestic comfort and taste which go into the make-up of a modern home, arranged in that exquisite order and delicacy of placement and grouping which mark woman's taste within our own homes, what inference would you make? Surely you would say, "These things did not *happen* so!" You would not attribute these harmonious relations of one object to another object, of a room to the furniture and appointments of that room, simply to some inherent tendency of the matter within those articles themselves to thus assume relations? You would say, "There has been here present a mind, an intelligent personality!" And the attributes of that personality you would probably to some extent rightly infer from the conditions and qualities of the objects upon which you look. Why should you not reason in like manner when you survey through your hand-lens the beautiful forms, the harmonious adjustments, the orderly relations of the snow-crystals, and their various parts? Whose Mind suggested and enforces that order?

Suppose, further, that you throw your eye upon a corner of the stairway in our imagined solitary house, and behold standing there a great Dutch clock, its pendulum ticking through its arc, its second hand swinging around its circuit, its hour and minute hands in proper place and movement, the mimic moon above the dial showing the exact phase of that satellite, while in another corner the day and month are properly indicated. You would hardly say that there was within that clock some inherent quality by which all these delicate adjustments and skillful arrangements had been executed.

Would the thought ever enter your mind, "This clock simply happened here and so"? No! The presence of order, the mechanical obedience to some unseen power which you know to lie within the machinery of the clock, would tell you that there had been present a mind with the sense of proportion and mathematical relations, that that mind had directed the construction of the machine producing before you such accurate and useful reports of time and seasons.

Why should you reason otherwise when you observe through the help of science the movements of the stellar worlds that whirl in space,—" great clocks of Eternity, which beat ages as ours beat seconds?" They move on across the dial of the heavens in beautiful harmony, in perfect regularity, throughout orbits and at times which, as we have seen, are adjusted with perfect geometrical accuracy; they are appointed for day and night, for seasons and years, and they roll on unchanged so that seed time and harvest, summer and winter do not fail. Science at such and such a date says they shall be there or here, and at that date they report tnemselves in the places assigned to them. Is it not inevitable that reasoning man must declare that behind this intricate machinery, regulated in such strict mathematical order and by such geometric law, there must have been and there must be a Mind conversant with the laws of mathematics? If the universe were created by an Intelligence conversant with quantitative truth, it is easy to understand, says Professor Flint, why it should be ruled by definitely quantitative laws, but that there should be such laws in a universe that did not originate in Intelligence is not only inexplicable but an inconceivable improbability. Apart from the supposition of the Supreme Intelligence, the chances of disorder against order, of chaos against cosmos, of the numerically indefinite and inconstant against the definite and constant, must be pronounced all but nothing. The belief in a Divine Reason is alone capable of rendering rational the fact that mathematical truths are realized in the material world.*

---

* "Theism," page 137.

This is the impartial conclusion of the profoundest thinking upon the latest facts of science by the most vigorous philosophical minds of the present day. It is only an echo of the utterance of one of the earliest meditations upon a like theme, that of Canon Derham, who a century and a quarter ago made this observation:—
"That every Planet should have as many, and various Motions, and those as regularly, and well-contrived and ordered, as the World and its Inhabitants have Occasion for, what could all this be but the Work of a wise and kind, as well as omnipotent CREATOR, and ORDERER of the World's Affairs? A Work which is as plain a Signal of GOD, as that of a Clock, or other Machine is of Man."*

"It is impossible," says the great philosopher, Immanuel Kant,† "to contemplate the fabric of the world without recognizing the admirable order of its arrangement, and the certain manifestation of the Hand of God in the perfection of its correlations. Reason, when once it has considered and admired so much beauty and so much perfection, feels a just indignation at the dauntless folly which dares ascribe all this to chance and a happy accident. It must be that the Highest Wisdom conceived the plan, and Infinite Power carried it into execution." Kant has not always been credited with entertaining views so sound as these upon this fundamental principle of Theology. Perhaps, therefore, all the more readily I may obtain through the great philosopher a hearing for the truth, which many men might deny to a humble minister of the Gospel. Hear him further:—

"All things which set forth reciprocal harmonies in nature must be bound together in a single Existence on which they collectively depend. Thus there exists a Being of all beings, an Infinite Understanding and a Self-existent Wisdom, from which nature, in the whole aggregate of her correlations, derives existence. Further, it is not allowable to maintain that the activity

---

*CANON DERHAM—"Astro-Theology," page 73. London, A. D. 1758. † "General History of Nature," quoted in Professor Winchell's "World-Life; or, Comparative Geology," where an admirable abstract of this valuable essay will be found.

of nature is prejudicial to the existence of a Highest Being; the more perfect it is in its developments, the better its general laws contribute to order and harmony, the more conclusive is the demonstration of the Godhead from whom these relations are borrowed. His productiveness is no longer the operation of chance, or the consequence of accident; from Him flows everything according to unalterable laws, which, therefore, must produce only what is fit, because they are only the reflection of a scheme infinitely wise, from which all disorder is banished. It is not the fortuitous concourse of the atoms of Lucretius which has builded the world, implanted forces and laws whose source is the wisest Understanding, and have been the unvarying cause of that order which can only flow from them, not by chance but by Ordination."*

II. Our second lesson from the snow-crystals is a practical one. Let us imitate the Great Creator in Faithful Doing of all Life's Work and Duty.

The simplest creatures of the Divine Hand and the minutest details of their structure are not deemed unworthy of Infinite Power. Who could have thought these crystals of the snow-storm worthy of such care? Only a snow-flake! Is it not a waste of beauty? What unnumbered myriads of them are floating there through the skies! How they blanket the fields; drift in great banks along the fences and railway tracks; fill the ravines in the hills; pack the gorges of the mountain; and lie heaps on heaps upon the highest summits! Surely, as we think of the seeming wastage of beauty, we may sing over these flowers of the snow, these crystal gems of the winter storm, as Gray sang in his " Elegy:"—

> Full many a gem of purest ray serene
>   The dark unfathom'd caves of ocean bear;
> Full many a flower is born to blush unseen,
>   And waste its sweetness on the desert air.

Yes! These flowers of the snow, these gems of the winter storm, God has wrought out with as careful touch

---

* KANT—'' Allgemeine Naturgeschichte und Theorie des Himmels," page 315, *sqq.*

as the Victoria Regia of the Nile or the twinkling lustre of Venus, the Evening Star.

Our wonder is still more awakened when we remember what force is pnt into the creation of every one of these snow-flakes. A learned naturalist has declared that to produce from the vapor of water a quantity of snow-flakes which a child could carry, would demand energy competent to gather up the shattered blocks of the largest stone avalanche of the Alps, and pitch them twice the height from which they fell. If a single baby handful require such force for its creation, what power must have been put forth to produce the thick blanketing of snow that lies upon the Northland, from mountain top to valley, during the winter season? Indeed, this is a very wonderful reflection. Yet, it is not the thought of reckless waste that comes to me; not the suggestion that this is but the play of blind Titans, giants of force, throwing away their might in these careless disportings, as little thoughtful of the results of work or play as a sporting group of children. Rather I see in this that infinite exactness in the smallest details of nature's work which marks the structure of everything whether organic or inorganic. Here I learn that what is worth doing at all is worth doing well. And it is worth well doing for the sake of well doing, because perfection is a quality of the noblest mind, and above all is the quality of the Infinite Mind; and therefore the works of the Divine Hand must in themselves be perfect.

Is it your lot in life to labor in wood, or stone, or iron, or paper, or cloth, or other material or fabric? See to it that in imitation of the infinite Architect and all-wise Artisan, you carry with you to your toil a sense of joy and pride in your labor. Cherish the desire and purpose to do your best for the sake of doing your best, to produce the most perfect work, not simply because it pays, not simply because you are under pecuniary obligations so to do, but because in the exercise of your noblest manhood and womanhood you esteem it a part of your life to make your life's products as near perfection as your conditions and abilities will allow. I never knew a good mechanic who was not proud of what he is pleased to call his "job," and who did not work upon it conscientiously, lovingly, framing it to the best of his lofty ideal even though he should receive for it no extra pay and no extra praise.

To such a man or woman the satisfaction of doing good work is a part of his reward. The careless worker is never happy in his toil. His slipshod structures and slighted jobs can carry no lofty pleasure to his mind. His ideal is lost. He labors simply with "eye service" as a man pleaser. He does not strike with hammer, or shove plane and saw, or hold the plow, or drive the shuttle, or draw thread and needle, or swing mallet to chisel, or wield yardstick and scissors, or push the pen, or do whatever work as unto God, knowing that He, the Master Worker Divine, before whom all men and their work must stand in judgment, in making the smallest product of nature leaves upon it the stamp of minutest care.

III. Our last lesson is one of Faith and Comfort in the Assurance of our Heavenly Father's Care.

Recently I looked into the Last Journals of David Livingstone, that hero and martyr of modern missions, to fortify a reference to a simple point of natural history. I found the allusion which I sought—an observation upon the habits of African sunbirds, who use the spinning work of spiders to make their little nests. Upon the same page immediately following this reference to the spider, a creature so commonly despised and deemed unworthy of the slightest human sympathy, I read these words, written in the heart of the dark continent, which in a short time received to itself its noblest sacrifice, the life of the venerable man.

"What is the atonement of Christ? It is Himself: It is the inherent and everlasting mercy of God made apparent to human eyes and ears. The everlasting Love was disclosed by our Lord's life and death. It showed that God forgives, because he loves to forgive. He works by smiles if possible, if not by frowns; pain is only a means of enforcing love.

"If we speak of strength, lo! He is strong. The

Almighty; the Over-power; the Mind of the universe. The heart thrills at the idea of his greatness. All the great among men have been remarkable at once for the grasp and minuteness of their knowledge. Great astronomers seem to know every iota of the knowable. The great Duke, when at the head of armies, could give all the particulars to be observed in a cavalry charge, and took care to have food ready for all his troops. Men think that greatness consists in lofty indifference to all trivial things. The Grand Llama, sitting in immovable contemplation of nothing, is a good example of what a human mind would regard as majesty; but the Gospels reveal Jesus, the manifestation of the blessed God over all, as minute in his care of all. He exercises a vigilance more constant, complete, and comprehensive, every hour and every minute, over each of his people than their utmost self-love could ever attain. His tender love is more exquisite than a mother's heart can feel."*

Is not this also a most inspiring truth: He so clothes the lilies of the field that they outvie in beauty Solomon's imperial robes. Not a sparrow shall fall without our Father. He builds the crystal structure of the snow-flake as carefully as he rounds out the proportions of the mightiest sun. He colors the insect, whose painted wing is expanded within the solitudes of a Brazilian forest, as carefully as he tints the glory of the Moon, that shines in the face of all mankind. Is not man, the crown of Creation's work, equally a subject of the Creator's care? Surely, surely! Yes, *how much more*, is the conclusion of the blessed Lord, shall he care for you, oh, ye of little faith! No man is so insignificant among his fellows; no life is so obscure in the multitude of pushing life forces of this great world; no child is so small, so weak, so poor; no plan for honest work is so limited in its sphere,—as to lie outside of the benevolent thought and helping force of the Almighty Father. Who need despair with a truth like this written on his heart? Who need hesitate to engage in labor for the advancement of mankind, with encouraging

---

* LIVINGSTONE—"Last Journals," page 453.

facts like these shining before him on the Inspired Page, set in the heavens everywhere around him, and showering upon him in the winter storm, out of the Crystal Treasures of the snow? "Consider the lilies of the field," said Jesus. The fields are lying white to-day with their lilies locked up in their bosoms. But consider the lilies of the sky, the beautiful crystals of snow, and they will teach you the same lesson of the All-Father's love and tenderest care.

LECTURE VII.

Snow Beds:
The Uses of Adversity.

For He saith to the snow, Fall thou on the earth.
Whether it be for correction, or for his land,
Or for mercy, that He cause it to come."
                                        —JOB xxxvii. 6, 13.

SNOW–BEDS : THE USES OF ADVERSITY.

By the term snow-beds as used in this lecture I express the covering of snow which during the winter remains in greater or less thickness upon the ground. There is at least one Scriptural reference to the formation of these beds, although the passage is regarded by commentators as somewhat obscure. In the war song and victory hymn given in the sixty-eighth Psalm there is this striking and somewhat puzzling allusion to snow.

> 13 When ye bivouac among the sheep folds
> It is as the dove's wings covered with silver,
> And her feathers with glistening gold.
> 14 When the Almighty scattered kings therein
> It is as when it snoweth in Zalmon.

The first figure is one of peace. The Israelites are viewed in their night bivouac among the folds of sheep, and the joy of their prosperity and ease is compared to the varied hues of a dove disporting in the sun. In contrast with this peaceful rural scene is drawn an image of war. Israel's enemies are routed. The vast army is seen scattered over the heights of Zalmon; the shining armor of the fleeing soldiers, compared, as in the Homeric figure, to the snow,* is likened to the tumultuous rushing of snow-flakes through the air; and the glistening helmets, shields, and spears cast away upon the ground are likened to the snow-beds after a storm whitening the face of the mountain.

The formation of these snow-beds has been well described by one of our own poets :—

> The snow had begun in the gloaming,
> And busily all the night
> Had been heaping field and highway
> With a silence deep and white.
>
> Every pine, and fir, and hemlock
> Wore ermine too dear for an earl,
> And the poorest twig on the elm-tree
> Was ringed inch-deep with pearl.

---

* Iliad, xix. 357–361.

From sheds new-roofed with Carrara
Came chanticleer's muffled crow,
The stiff rails were soften'd to swan's-down,
And still fluttered down the snow.*

The advantage of these beds or blanketings of snow is in a measure apprehended, but there are few persons who really estimate in full their value to the soil and to mankind at large. A few facts briefly stated must suffice to uncover this truth. Most of you are familiar with what is known as snow-crust. In our own latitude of Philadelphia it may be occasionally seen in open fields. But in more northern sections, as New England, northern New York, and Canada, a crust forms upon the surface of the snow and remains during the greater portion of the year. What has formed that crust? " It is frozen water, to be sure, thawed out from the snow on a bright day." Such is the common thought. Some portion of the crust may be attributed to this cause, but for the most part it is probably produced by the moisture of the air which is precipitated upon it, precisely as dew is formed upon the cold earth in summer. In other words, whenever the humidity of the atmosphere in contact with snow is above the point of saturation at the temperature to which the air is cooled by such contact, the superfluous moisture is absorbed by the snow or condensed and frozen upon its surface.† This of course adds to the winter supply of water received from the snow by the ground, and no doubt far exceeds the amount which is lost by evaporation from the surface of the snows.

A second fact is to be noted. Snow is of a color unfavorable for the radiation of heat. It follows that when heavy beds are laid upon the earth they act precisely as do bed-coverings or clothes to the human body. The warmth of the covered soil is kept within itself. Moreover, to some extent the rays of the sun penetrate the snow even when it is of considerable thickness. From these two facts results a third fact; viz., that the upper or surface stratum of the ground, even though it be frozen at

---

* JAMES RUSSELL LOWELL—" The First Snow-Fall."   † MARSH —"The Earth as Modified by Human Action," page 209.

the first fall of the snow, is soon thawed out and does not again fall below the freezing point during the winter, at least while the snow lasts. In Vermont, for four successive days of one winter, the temperature immediately above the snow was thirteen degrees below zero. Beneath the snow, which was four inches deep, the temperature was nineteen degrees above zero, a difference of thirty-two degrees within four or five inches of space. Under a drift of snow two feet deep the temperature was twenty-seven degrees above zero, thus making a difference of forty degrees, showing that the soil beneath the snow-beds was from thirty-two to forty degrees warmer than the temperature of the air.* The value of this fact in preserving the life and vigor of plants is at once apparent. It is for this reason that in the borders and glades of our American woods and forests violets and other small plants begin to vegetate as soon as the snow has thawed the soil around their roots, and they are not unfrequently found in full flower under two or three feet of snow.†

A third fact is now to be considered. The layer of snow lying nearest to the soil, having a heavy bed above it with its enclosing crust, soon begins to melt. This process continues more or less abundantly according to the temperature during the winter. What becomes of the water thus formed? It is slowly imbibed by the vegetable mould, sinks into the under surface of the earth, and finds its way into the springs and streams which are the sources of our creeks and rivers. Very little water runs off in the winter by superficial watercourses, except in rare cases of sudden thaw, and there can be no question that much the greater part of the snow deposited, in the forests at least, is slowly melted and absorbed by the earth. It is questionable whether the snow in certain latitudes has not as much to do with the fertility of the land and fullness of the springs and water-courses as the rain. The rains of summer coming with sudden dash run away from the soil faster than the ground can imbibe them; but it is not so with the snow.

---

* Reports Department Agriculture, 1872, May and June. † American Naturalist, May, 1869, page 155–6.

It lies in beds upon the top of the ground, and, as we have seen, the process of infiltration continues the winter through.   Thus the moisture precipitated throughout winter months in the form of snow is imbibed by the earth in far greater proportion than are the rains of summer.   This fact was not unknown to the writers of Holy Scripture.   The prophet Isaiah alludes to it in the familiar verse: "For as the rain cometh down and the snow from heaven and returneth not thither till it has moistened the earth and fertilized it and made it green, and offered seed to the sower and bread to the eater, so will my word be which goeth forth out of my mouth."* It is a striking evidence of the closeness and accuracy of the prophet's observation of nature that he should thus have given snow a place side by side with rain in watering and fertilizing the earth, a position upon which few of us, perhaps, would have ventured.

I. The first and chief lesson which we are to learn from Beds of Snow is conveyed in the old adage— Sweet are the Uses of Adversity.

From its loose texture and from the fact that it contains several times its bulk of air, snow is a very bad conductor of heat.   It is ranked with wool among the poorest of conductors, and thus it forms an admirable covering for the ground from the effects of radiation. It is relatively as warm to the earth in its thick enswathement of white packed crystals as is the softest wool to the human body.   It has happened not unfrequently in times of great cold that the soil is forty degrees warmer than the surface of the overlying snow. These facts will suffice to show the value of the snowy mantle which God sends to the earth during the severe frosts of winter.   Yet, as a rule, those who live in cities can hardly be said to welcome with much enthusiasm the coming of a heavy snow-storm.

It is indeed a beautiful sight when the white flakes tumble through the air, and fall softly, eddying, sporting, rising, and sinking ere they drop upon their final

---

* Isaiah lv. 10, 11.

resting-place. It is not an unpleasant sight presented by streets and houses when whitened over with the first clean flakes. They hide away for the moment the foulness of our streets, and all the uncouth, ungraceful, and repulsive objects that so frequently greet our city-environed eyes. The snow will stir a momentary joy in the city maiden's heart as visions of sleigh ride and toboggan slide dance through her brain. The schoolboy is filled with enthusiasm as the circling crystals greet his vision through school-room windows.

> "It snows!" cries the schoolboy, "Hurrah!" and his shout
>   Is ringing through parlor and hall,
> While swift as the wing of a swallow he's out,
>   And his playmates have answered his call;
> It makes the heart leap but to witness their joy;
>   Proud wealth has no pleasure, I trow,
> Like the rapture that throbs in the pulse of the boy
>   As he gathers his treasures of snow.

Nevertheless, to the great mass of dwellers within city walls, snow is an unmitigated nuisance. It blocks up the tramways, the cable tracks, the lines of transportation and business. It becomes trampled and soiled in a little while, and lies along the edges of the pavements in great winrows that day by day grow more unlovely to the eyes as the sweeping machines pile upon them the accumulated filth of the streets. We could easily spare the snow from our city limits. But beyond city walls the farmer and gardener look upon the falling flakes with different feelings. As they come flying through the air and slowly gather upon fields of grain and meadows of grass, and pack around the roots of growing trees in nursery and orchard, the agriculturist is glad. His farm is not as beautiful to your eyes as in the freshness of the early spring, or the maturity of summer's beauty, but the farmer will tell you that his grain and grass lie snugly beneath the snow through the whole winter, quite protected from the sharp frosts. When the sun gains strength in the spring time, and the warm currents flow once more through the earth, and the snow is melted and gone, up spring the tender blades. Then, when harvest is over, well-packed hay-mows and granaries heaped with yellow grain tell that the cheer-less-looking snow was after all a kindly friend to the farmer.

It has served the florist quite as well, for underneath its fleecy beds the flower plants have snugly slept and prepared them for their early spring awakening. Our Quaker poet voiced this fact in his beautiful apostrophe to the snow.

> Fill soft and deep, O winter snow,
>   The sweet azalea's oaken dells,
> And hide the bank where roses blow,
>   And swung the azure bells!
>
> O'erlay the amber violet's leaves,
>   The purple aster's brook-side home,
> Guard all the flowers her pencil gives
>   A life beyond their bloom.
>
> And she, when spring comes round again,
>   By greening slope and singing flood
> Shall wander, seeking, not in vain,
>   Her darlings of the wood.*

It is often thus with the soul, upon whom fall the trials and sorrows of this earthly career. "Now no affliction for the present seemeth to be joyous, but grievous; nevertheless, afterwards it yieldeth peaceable fruits." The experience of men asserts it to be true that burdens on the human heart, like snow-beds on the breast of meadow, field, and orchard, prevent radiation of the soul's warmth; retain within the heart the graces and blessings of the spiritual life; save the soul from chilling amidst the cold currents of worldliness and self-ishness, and make the nature rich and fertile with the blessings of a holy life.

A distinguished naturalist has been recently reported as declaiming against the character of God, as it is wit-nessed in the life of living creatures. Suffering so pre-dominates from the lowest organization to the highest; there are so many scenes that stir one's pity as he be-holds, that the question will start up, how can these things be beneath the dominion of an all-merciful Crea-tor? Passing into the sphere of human life one sees not

* JOHN GREENLEAF WHITTIER—"Flowers in Winter."

only those physical sufferings by which man is allied to the lower animals, but also those mental and spiritual conflicts and griefs which seem to be reserved for him alone by reason of those endowments which make him more sensitive to both pleasure and pain. Surely the Christian philosopher needs to ponder but a moment a difficulty like this, as far, at least, as it relates to men. The answer springs readily to his heart and tongue, " Whom the Lord loveth he chasteneth."* " Consider in thine heart, that, as a man chasteneth his son, so the Lord chasteneth thee."† " Furthermore, we had the fathers of our flesh to chasten us, and we gave them reverence; shall we not much rather be in subjection unto the Father of spirits, and live ? For they verily for a few days chastened us as seemed good to them; but he for our profit, that we may be partakers of his holiness. All chastening seemeth for the present to be not joyous, but grievous ; yet afterwards it yieldeth peaceable fruit unto them that have been exercised thereby, even the fruit of righteousness. Wherefore lift up the hands that hang down, and the palsied knees; and make straight paths for your feet, that that which is lame be not turned out of the way, but rather be healed."‡

To the Christian, development of a holy character after the likeness of the eternal God is the chief end of all things. Nature's noblest efforts look toward man himself. Man stands at the apex of the zoological pyramid. All life centres towards him; types and shadows of the past; typical forms of being; the physical outcome of all the convulsions and changes of the geologic ages; the processes by which the surface of the earth was diversified and made a fitting home for man ; the excess of vegetation in the carboniferous era by which the treasures of coal were locked up within the earth's surface to await man's use and forward the highest development of his character and abilities,§ all these, and all other things seem to have been wrought out with a view to the introduction upon the scene of that which is nature's sublimest product—man himself. These and

* Heb. xii. 6. † Deut. viii. 5. ‡ Heb. xii. 9-13. § McCosh and Dickie—" Typical Forms," page 350.

multitudes of other arrangements, collocations, structures, and products of a useful and beneficent character, are so many indications that during the long process of the world's fitting up, while yet the human era was contemplated as we contemplate the millennium, Man, the nature of Man, and the wants of Man, constituted at least one of the objective points of cycles of geological preparation.*   Even the evolutionary philosophers recognize this fact, and are ready to assert that the noblest outcome of the claimed processes of evolution is the human species; that Man is the consummate fruition of creative energy, and the chief object of Divine care.† Now, as in nature the greatest of all things is man, so in man the greatest of all things is the immortal soul. Shall we accept the thought that nature has labored so long toward the development of his physical being and refuse the reflection that the spiritual nature of man is worthy of the richest endowments and highest development at whatever cost?   In point of fact it is true that the highest spiritual as well as the highest physical is procured at the heaviest cost, is the outcome of convulsions, struggles, pains.

There are few who will question the statement that discipline is good for nations and the race at large.

The lands familiar with snow rear the hardiest children. The discipline that comes through a conflict with winter and storm develops the manly and womanly virtues into vigorous action. A nature too rich, too prodigal of her gifts, does not compel man to snatch from her his daily bread by his daily toil. A regular climate, the absence of a dormant season, render forethought of little use to him; nothing invites him to that struggle of intelligence against nature, which raises the forces of man to so high a pitch. Thus he never dreams of resisting this all powerful physical nature; he is conquered by her; he submits to the yoke, and becomes again the animal man, in proportion as he abandons himseif to these influences, forgetful of his high moral destination. In the temperate climates all is activity, movement. The

---

* PROFESSOR WINCHELL—"Sketches of Creation," page 336.
† PROFESSOR FISKE—"The Destiny of Man," page 111.

alternations of heat and cold, the changes of the seasons, a fresher and more bracing air, incite man to a constant struggle, to forethought, to the vigorous employment of all his faculties.*

Narrowing, now, the sphere of our application, we observe that it is good for man to bear the yoke in his youth.† There are many persons prominent to-day in the circles of human activity who can trace back their productive power in society, their usefulness among their fellows, the growth and nurture of their intellects and abilities into those proportions which have given them fame and made them a blessing, to the hard apprenticeship of trial, buffeting, and struggle which in earlier life disciplined their powers.

> Plants reared with tenderness are seldom strong;
> Man's coltish disposition needs a thong;
> And without discipline the foolish child,
> Like a neglected forester, runs wild.‡

Is not this also true in the development of a moral character, or a spiritual life? Has not the history of the Church borne testimony time and again to the truth that persecution has been a purifier? That the tempests which have beaten upon the growing plants of faith have only caused them to root themselves more firmly and lay faster hold upon the eternal Rock? That the winds of trial which have swept the face of Christendom have only borne aloft the seeds of truth as a summer zephyr scatters the downy seeds of the dandelion, and have scattered them over the face of the earth to find lodging and become the centres of a new and better life? The blood of the martyrs has ever been the seed of the Church!

The influence of trial in developing the spiritual character of the sufferer is not the only benefit which we may discern. Its reflex influence upon society is very great. How often has the influence of an invalid in the home circle caused the development of the noblest form of manhood and the sweetest virtues of womanhood in those members of the household whose thoughts have

---

* GUYOT—"Earth and Man," page 269. † Lamentations iii. 27.
‡ COWPER.

been centred upon the suffering one! What has done so much to develop the true Christian character of men and women in Christian lands, as those noble institutions of charity provided for all forms of suffering humanity? Our hospitals, asylums, homes, institutions, refuges, retreats, orphanages, and societies well-nigh without number, are among the most beautiful evidences of the loving hearts and noble instincts of our people, but they all have their growth and development around the fact of human misery. Self-denial, compassion, philanthropy, generosity, charity—these are graces most lovely to behold, which enfold with their sweetest charm the sons and daughters of our generation and our faith. But how could they be—*would* they be?—were it not for those trials on the part of their fellow-creatures which have opened up the fountains of sympathy and caused those streams to gush forth, which have watered the garden of the heart, and made it bloom with heavenly charity? So far then as man himself is concerned, it seems to me that it is a sufficient answer to all objections to the Divine administration of this world raised from the standpoint of human misery, to say that suffering is a discipline of good; that sorrows and trials are but the snows of winter storms, that pack the fields of human life, preserving them from spiritual sterility and the binding frosts of selfishness and unbelief.

II. Our second lesson from the Snow-Beds is simply an outgrowth of our first thought, namely, the Strength and Beauty of Home Life.

In the book of Proverbs we have a remarkable poetical description of a thrifty and virtuous housewife, which is attributed to the mother of Lemuel. In the course of the poem occurs the stanza:—

> She is not afraid of the snow for her household,
> For all her household are clothed with scarlet.*

In other words, this wise, loving, and industrious woman had foreseen the time of the snow, and provided against its rigors the warm clothing necessary for her

---

* Prov. xxxi. 21.

family. The necessity that compelled such action was largely instrumental in calling into play and in strengthening the home virtues here celebrated. Such characters as this woman are most common in lands where snow falls. Winter is the creator of home, and the sweetest home-life is fostered by the frosts of the Northland. Home-life grows and thrives best in the light and warmth of the fireside.

"Announced by all the trumpets of the sky,
Arrives the snow ; and, driving o'er the fields,
Seems nowhere to alight ; the whited air
Hides hills and woods, the river and the heaven,
And veils the farm-house at the garden's end.
The sled of the traveler stopped, the courier's feet
Delayed, all friends shut out, the housemates meet
Around the radiant fireplace, enclosed
In a tumultuous privacy of storm."*

This " tumultuous privacy of storm," winter's rigor, thus brings with it the advantage that it draws men and women in-doors, fosters home life, develops home virtues, throws man upon his inward resources, strengthening his intellectual and spiritual life, and thus develops nobler characters both in women and men. I believe it may be asserted that the strongest and loveliest characters, and I might add the strongest and best governments, are found amongst those nations who have the profoundest insight of the benefits of Home. It is a matter for sincere congratulation that American men are in such large proportion men of domestic habits. While this fact remains I shall not despair of the Republic. The brightest spot left to man, since Paradise was lost through sin, is his own fireside. At the hearthstone which glows with the light of earthly affection, sanctified by a Heavenly Love, there, if ever, Paradise is regained on earth.

Let us count it then as one of the most valuable incidental results of the rigors of winter, when the world is made inhospitable by the beds of snow lying on forest and field, that men are driven to build themselves altars at the Fireside of Home.

---

* RALPH WALDO EMERSON.

III. We are to carry our lesson still further, and learn that these Life-Rigors and Trials, of which the Snow-Beds are emblems, prepare us for and open the way for us to the Heavenly Home.

Life itself will bring healing to many wounds of death, and there are griefs which Time, dropping moments after moments into the scar, will cover over, as the snow-beds cover the fields. Lowell has very sweetly uttered this thought:—

> I stood and watched by the window
>   The noiseless work of the sky,
> And the sudden flurries of snow-birds,
>   Like brown leaves whirling by.
>
> I thought of a mound in sweet Auburn,
>   Where a little headstone stood ;
> How the flakes were folding it gently,
>   As did robins the babes in the wood.
>
> Up spoke our own little Mabel,
>   Saying, "Father, who makes it snow?"
> And I told of the good all-Father,
>   Who cares for us here below.
>
> Again I looked at the snow-fall,
>   And thought of the leaden sky
> That arched o'er our first great sorrow,
>   When that mound was heaped so high.
>
> I remembered the gradual patience
>   That fell from that cloud like snow,
> Flake by flake, healing and hiding
>   The scar of our deep-plunged woe.
>
> And again to the child I whispered,
>   "The snow that husheth all,
> Darling, the merciful Father
>   Alone can make it fall!"*

But there are wounds which life and time cannot heal; aches that will not be hushed; scars that cannot be covered save as Heaven casts the mantle of Divine consolation thereon.

One striking form which snow-beds take is that of the glacier. This is the name given to an immense mass of moving snow and ice. The glacier is in fact a river of ice, whose sources are the snows that, summer and win-

---

* JAMES RUSSELL LOWELL—"The First Snow-Fall."

ter alike, fall upon lofty mountain summits. In process of time the snow becomes hard-packed, and by reason of great pressure and alternate thawing and freezing is solidified, so that as it passes gradually into the valley, it goes down as a rugged river of frozen snow and ice held within the walls of mountain gorges, as a stream of water runs between its banks.

The melting of the ice on the surface of the glacier produces streams whose course is often broken by crevasses, or deep cliffs, down which the water descends, and after being increased by like rivulets, it issues at last as a stream, or creek, or river, through the cavernous mouth of the vault at the termination of the glacier. Thus these strange phenomena of nature have their origin in the region of perpetual snow, and reach far down into the valley. That of Bossons, which comes from the highest part of Mont Blanc, reaches a point five thousand five hundred feet below the snow-line, where it is embosomed among luxuriant woods, and is almost in contact with the wheat-fields of the vale of Chamouni.

A curious and interesting career is that of the melted snow-flakes. Born high up amid eternal winter, trickling down through the crevasse along secret springs and channels of the glacier, issuing at last immediately from its dark, icy vault into sunlight, amid the fragrance of flowers and sweet-smelling hay-fields, it flows forth among human habitations, to bless and beautify the gardens, meadows, and fields of men. The river Arveiron is born of the Glacier des Bois. Flower-decked Chamouni —sweet Chamouni, whose beauty dwells as a pleasing memory in the mind of every tourist to Switzerland—is a creature of streams of snow-water flowing from the ice-bound channels of glaciers of the Alps.

As it is here, so shall it be Hereafter. To the Christian thought the uses of adversity extend beyond the margin of this life and enrich for us, indeed I may say, often procure for us the life of the eternal world. I have read a story of a chamois hunter of the Alps, for the truth of which I do not vouch, and whose probability, indeed, I cannot affirm. I only know that it points the lesson which I am bringing you to-day. The hunter in pursuit of his wild mountain game followed to the upper regions of the glacier. In the intense eagerness of chase he was careless of his footing, stepped upon false ground and slid rapidly down the mountain over the edge of a deep crevasse. He was not killed, scarcely more than bruised. But as he slowly recovered and looked around him, he felt that he had fallen upon a doom worse than outright death. Between the icy walls of the crevasse, rising two hundred feet or more, he saw far, far above him the blue sky. "This must be my icy sepulchre!" he cried. In despair he threw himself upon his knees and prayed. Now he noticed the little crevasse stream flowing just at his feet. "I will follow this," he said. As he went on and on, the stream was broadened by in-flowing rivulets, until at last it emptied into a wide pool. Beyond that was a solid wall of ice. There the crevasse ended! All avenue of escape was cut off. He was still entombed within that icy gorge.

Is it a hopeless case? Not quite; a thought had come to him, that there was one possible—the only possible path of deliverance. It lay through the swirling waters of that pool! "It is but death," he said, "whether I stay or go. I will make the venture!" He lifted his heart to Heaven in silent prayer. Then he laid aside his knapsack and coat. He poised himself a moment upon the brink of the pool, whose waters as they whirled around and sank out of sight, showed that the stream must issue somewhere beyond. Then he plunged head foremost into the vortex. There was a moment of darkness; a moment of chill; a chill that struck to his very heart as he was sucked down into the icy pool. There followed a moment of unconsciousness as he was borne swiftly along by some unseen power, and then—he was thrown out into the clear vault of the glacier stream, and borne upon the bosom of its waters into the fields of Chamouni! The green fields and bright woods of his own beautiful valley were around him. He was safe! Safe and at home!

O my friends, the time shall come, may soon come to some of us, when we shall stand on the brink of that dread water which men call Death. Let us believe, for it is the voice of the Master who assures us, that beyond its vortex, beyond that unknown pathway to an Unseen World, there shall open to us a view of Heaven. The dread plunge; the icy chill that strikes through heart and flesh; a moment of unconsciousness, and then, then in a brighter vale than Chamouni, where fragrant flowers immortal bloom; where the Tree of Life grows evergreen on the banks of the River of Life; where the voice of friends shall greet us, and never again fade from our hearing; where the Summer of our Soul shall shine in beauty sempervirent; there, in Heaven, our soul's Eternal Rest, we shall dwell forever more!

Haply in that day one may ask, as it was asked of St. John of old, "These which are arrayed in white robes, who are they, and whence came they?" Then shall the answer come as it came to the inspired Apostle, "These are they which came out of the great tribulation, and they washed their robes and made them white in the blood of the Lamb. *Therefore* are they before the throne of God, and they serve him day and night in his temple."*

---

* Rev. vii., 14–15.

LECTURE VIII.

Snow-Whiteness:
The Glory of Christ.

*"And in the midst of the candlesticks one like unto the Son of Man.   *   *   *   *   *   And his head and his hair were white as white wool, white as snow."*—REVELATION i. 13, 14.

SNOW–WHITENESS: THE GLORY OF CHRIST.

"As white as snow" is a proverb as old as the days of David and Isaiah. What produces snow-whiteness? To answer the question you may be reminded that there are certain colors of the solar spectrum which, when combined in due proportion, will produce white. These are red and green, yellow and violet, orange and blue; they are known as complementary colors, and are distant from each other half the length of the spectrum. Now, the minute snow-crystals have the quality possessed by other crystals of reflecting light, and the combination of the different prismatic rays issuing from them produces the white color so familiar to us. In other words, the complementary colors reflected in due proportion from the facets of the crystals appear to the eye as white. In the more technical language of physical science, the phenomenon of snow-whiteness may be explained thus: the optical severance of the particles giving rise to the multitude of reflections of the white solar light at their surfaces produces the whiteness of the snow-crystals.*

There is yet another element that enters into the color of snow; viz., the air. If they be examined carefully the individual particles of snow may be seen as transparent. In the case of transparent bodies whiteness results from the mixture of the particles with small spaces of air. The particles of glass or crystal when crushed for this reason become a white powder. The whiteness of paper is produced by the composition of innumerable fibres which are individually transparent. The whiteness of ice when it is chopped or broken, and which you have often ob-

---

* TYNDALL—"Forms of Water, page 176."

(137)

served in contrast with the clear bluish color of the entire block, is caused in the same way. Ice formed in the freezing machines, which are so common in many of our Southern States, is usually white, a fact due to the air-bubbles with which it is filled, they being entangled by the rapid process of congelation. When the freezing of water is extremely slow and the crystallizing force pushes the air effectually aside, the resulting ice is transparent.

This is the explanation presented by physicists of the beautiful white color of snow, which as we have seen is produced separately or jointly by two causes; either, first, the reflection of white solar light from the faces of the crystals, or second, by the admixture of minute bubbles of air with the particles of snow. Why the snow crystals possess this quality we cannot say further than that so they were constituted by the Creator, who saith to the snow—"Be thou on the earth!" and whose sovereign power bestowed upon them, as upon all things else, their natural characteristics. We pass now from this explanation of the phenomenon of Snow-Whiteness to consider the lessons which Holy Scripture teaches us under the figure of that phenomenon.

I. The Snow-Whiteness teaches us the Divine Nature and Authority of our Lord Jesus Christ.

In the symbolism of the Scriptures, which is largely in sympathy with the ideas of all ancient races, and indeed I may say of all mankind, white is used to express various ideas, as innocence, purity, victory, and joy. Of these we shall have something to say in our next lecture. To-day we are to consider whiteness as the symbol of Glory and Majesty. It is the color that expresses above all others the idea of Deity, and no doubt this is so because it is the color of light. There can be no more fitting natural emblem of the Divine glory than the sun; hence, by a perversion of judgment and feeling which marks the religious history of the race, the sun itself has been a favorite object of worship. In the Old Testament the most majestic pictures of the Almighty are associated with the color of light. God is represented as covering himself with light as with a garment.* In the glowing imagery of Habbakuk Jehovah is compared to the rising sun within whose rays His omnipotence is environed.

> 3 His splendor covered the heavens,
>   And the earth was full of His glory;
> 4 And brightness arose like sunlight,
>   He had rays coming forth from His sides,
>   And there was the hiding of His power.†

For the origin of the imagery used by St. John in our text, we must doubtless go back to the book of Daniel.‡ The prophet Daniel beholds seated in the midst of the prostrate thrones of world powers, "One that was Ancient of days. His raiment was white as snow, and the hair of his head like pure wool. His throne was fiery flames, and the wheels thereof burning fire."

The entire imagery of this visional Figure is intended to impress the mind with the sense of Divine Majesty. The patriarchal age, the wool-white hairs, the snow-white raiment, the environment of light, all these in the well-understood figures of oriental thought and speech depict One who without doubt must be recognized as the Eternal God.

We take another step in developing the meaning of snow-whiteness as applied to the Christ. A year before his death, our Lord Jesus retired with three of his disciples to one of the spurs of Mount Hermon and was there "transfigured" before them. On this occasion, Matthew records that our Saviour's "face did shine as the sun, and his raiment was white as light.§ St. Mark, that " His garment became glistening, exceeding white, so as no fuller on earth can whiten them."‖ The record of St. Luke is that the "fashion of his countenance was altered, and his raiment became white and dazzling."¶ This peculiar appearance of our Saviour's person is associated with a corresponding appearance of the heavenly visitors

---

* Psalm civ. 2. † Hab. iii. 3, 4, R. V., and KEIL and DELITZSCH, *in loc.* ‡ Daniel vii. 9. § Matthew xvii. 2. ‖ Mark ix. 3. ¶ Luke ix. 29.

Moses and Elias, who, we are told by St. Luke, "appeared in glory;" and also of the overshadowing cloud out of which the Eternal Father spoke, which is described by Matthew as "a bright cloud." St. Peter speaks of it as "the excellent glory."

These are the external or symbolic associations of the event. The spiritual significance of it we may readily learn from the impression which was made upon the minds of at least two of its witnesses. Says John, "We beheld his Glory as of the only begotten of the Father."* Says Peter, "We were eye witnesses of his Majesty when we were with him in the holy mount."† It is doubtless chiefly from this standpoint that we must review the whole event, remembering also its relations to the preceding announcement of the crucifixion. We may think of the dazzling whiteness of our Lord's outward appearance as the result and manifestation of the glory of his Divine Nature, which was commonly restrained within usual human semblance, but then burst forth and illuminated not only his body, but his clothing and all surrounding objects. There is no ground to think that this bodily illumination was a reflection of the glory surrounding Moses and Elias, for it was Christ's "own glory" which chiefly attracted the apostles' eyes,‡ and the bright cloud did not appear until after the transfiguration.

It was needful that the disciples should have this manifestation of the glorious Majesty of the Lord Jesus Christ, so that amid the humiliations of his human life and approaching death they should not forget that He was indeed the Son of the Highest. The theme of conversation between those exalted delegates from the spirit world, Moses the giver of the Law and Elijah the restorer of Prophecy, and Jesus Christ himself in whom Law and Prophecy were fulfilled, was, we are told, the decease of Jesus, or as the Greek expresses it, "The exodus" or departure of him which he was about to accomplish at Jerusalem.§ Thus the apostles were led to associate the Heavenly Glory with the earthly hu-

---

*John i. 14.   † II. Peter i. 16–18.   ‡ Luke ix. 32.   § Luke ix. 32.

miliation, the Conquering with the suffering Messiah. Henceforth the glory of the cross would quench its shame, and the doubting disciples learn the exaltation of the one great theme of their future ministry. Thus we are led through the significance of the snow-whiteness of our Saviour's person on the Transfiguration Mount to the lesson of his Divine Majesty, his heavenly and earthly Glory.

We come now to that emblem from which we have our text, namely, the vision of the Son of Man in the midst of the seven golden candlesticks. He is represented as clothed with the long "talar" or garment of the High Priest which reached down to the feet. After the manner of high priests and kings he was girt about the breast with the golden girdle. "His head and his hair were white as white wool, white as snow; his eyes were as a flame of fire; his feet like unto a stream of molten metal as it had been glowing in a furnace;* and his countenance was as the sun shineth in his strength."†

This visional image with his venerable head and snow-white hairs, presents to us an object of reverent honor. The white hairs as the symbol of old age would alone have taught this lesson. Veneration of age was a part of the Jewish religion, and one of the most binding duties of ancient social life. "Thou shalt rise up before the hoary head, and honor the face of the old man, and fear thy God: I am the Lord," said the law of Leviticus.‡ Again, the proverb says:§ "The hoary head is a crown of glory, if it be found in the way of righteousness." It is in the spirit·of this law and custom that St. John must have seen among the candlesticks One before whom he should rise up in worship as in the presence of the most venerated Patriarch and Ruler.

I might venture to plead the spirit of our modern customs also as pointing the same lesson. I know that it is often said, "Ah! our young people do not honor the aged as they used to do." Perhaps there is ground in some quarters for the charge, but I cannot think it true of the majority of the young men and women of this

---

* LANGE. † Rev. i. 14, 15. ‡ Lev. xix. 32. § Prov. xvi. 31.

generation. There were not wanting in ancient time those who violated law and custom in this regard. Such were the young men who publicly jeered Elisha, following him with the cry, "Go up, thou bald-head!"* Such was Rehoboam, who despised the counsel of the old men and allied himself with the young men of his court.† This irreverent generation has its succession still on earth; but of most of our youth I believe it may be said that reverence for the aged is a strong sentiment within their hearts.

Perhaps the aged are not careful enough to strengthen and compel this following; perhaps they are too ready, in our land at least, to retire from the scene of duty and activity; perhaps they have not enough confidence in the willingness of young men to follow them. If so, they surely err. Age does not disqualify for leadership any more than youth. The leaders of the great movements of Scripture were many of them aged men, as Abraham, Moses, and Joshua. We may even include Jacob, the old wanderer, "the Hebrew Ulysses," as Dean Stanley has called him,‡ who led his people into Egypt at his new call to a new migration, with new trials and a new glory before him.

> "Something ere the end.
> Some work of noble note may yet be done,
> 'Tis not too late to seek a newer world,
> Made weak by time and fate, but strong in will—
> To strive, to seek, to find, and not to yield."

Were our aged Christians and citizens to take the place, duty, and leadership which their years allow, and summon the young men of this land, like those of Europe who so ardently have followed the aged Premiers Disraeli, Gladstone, and Bismarck, I believe that they also would be found following the white hairs of age into the thickest conflict against all evil, even as the Huguenots at Ivry rallied to the white-plumed helmet of Henry of Navarre. Be that as it may, it is manifest that there is much in every civilized society which responds to the

---

* II. Kings ii. 23. † I. Kings xi. 14. ‡ Jewish Church, vol. I., page 80.

Scripture laws and customs upon which is based the symbolic teaching now before us, namely, the Lord Jesus Christ is an object of reverence. He is to be honored as the Ancient of days, the Venerable, the Patriarch, the Ruler, the Lord.

But it is something more than the aspect of antiquity that we must consider in the drapery of this image among the candlesticks. The majestic Being of John's vision is clothed with all the symbolic drapery with which the prophets associated Jehovah. One who will read the description of the Almighty as presented in Daniel's vision side by side with this image of John's Revelation will be led inevitably to the conclusion that the same attributes of Divine Majesty and Glory attributed by the prophet to the One Being, are by the apostle attributed to the Other. It is not within the bounds of sober thought that John, himself a Jew, educated in the strictest sect of Israel and associated intimately with the most zealous adherents and loftiest representatives of his faith, would have clothed Jesus Christ with the accepted Scriptural symbols of the Divine Nature were he not entirely convinced that Jesus Christ is indeed Divine. So that, resting upon Scriptural symbolism alone, we are led to the conclusion which is held by the well-nigh Universal Church of Christ, that Jesus is the Second Person of the adorable Trinity, is possessed of Divine glory, and is to receive worship and service as such.

In the well-known admirable answer of the Westminster Shorter Catechism to the question "What is God?" He is declared to be infinite, eternal, and unchangeable in seven attributes. Those attributes are the Divine Being, Wisdom, Power, Holiness, Justice, Goodness, and Truth. Light is composed of seven primary colors, red, orange, yellow, green, blue, indigo, and violet. Let us imagine every one of the seven branches of the great candlestick of St. John's vision to shed forth one of these seven colors; and further, think of each color as typical of one of the seven Divine attributes.* What, then, shall we see? The seven colors combine and in due propor-

---

* McCook—"Object and Outline Teaching," page 262.

tion form the white solar ray. The Visional Image in their midst is bathed in white light. Light? Yes! It is the color of the Deity. The divine attributes are blended upon One Being. That Being is the Christ; those blended rays give forth Love, the sum of all the attributes of God! Behold the man! Behold the God! "Herein is Love!" This is "the true Light which lighteth every man that cometh into the world."*

2. We turn now from the testimony of Scriptural symbolism to examine for a few moments other lines of evidence which assert the Divine Majesty of Christ. Let us consider the Personal Testimony of Christ's Disciples.

Said Jesus to the woman of Samaria, "Salvation is of the Jews."† The saying covers more than at first thought appears. Ewald has reminded us that the student of history has observed in the various nations of antiquity, strong, special tendencies toward which the national efforts constantly pointed. A grand ambition towered over all common aims and necessities. Amid prosperity and adversity it was pursued with a constancy fixed enough to leave its mark upon the national remains. With the Egyptians this aim was the grandeur of architecture and the perfection of civilization. With the Phœnicians it was commerce and navigation. With the Roman it was the perfect code of law. With the Greek the perfect art and literature. With the Jew it was the perfect religion.‡

Much as the Hebrew attained in other, indeed in all branches of human improvement, upon this the noblest of all aims his highest endeavors were fixed. Through many centuries of varied national fortunes he wavered not from his lofty purpose. The promise of his God to "send to him a Saviour and a Great One"§ shone before him like the north star to the ancient mariner. His course across the ages was lighted and guided thereby. And God was with him. Heaven bent down to meet

*John i. 9.. †John iv. 22. ‡EWALD—"History of Israel," I., page 4. §Isaiah xix. 20.

the aspirations of his heart, and fill with the coveted prize the hands that had reached out unweariedly for it through years that had grown into millenniums.

In Jesus Christ the high hopes and aims of Israel culminated. The rose of Sharon was the perfect bloom upon the stem of Jesse. With Jesus the great salvation came. With Jesus it was complete. Israel had wrought out her national destiny and so passed away. Though as a people she rejected the true Christ, yet multitudes of her best sons and daughters embraced the perfect faith. Thenceforth as the eagle stirreth up her nest and casts her young upon the wind that they may learn the eagle's flight,* these Christian Israelites were sent forth of God to carry upon all the surface of the earth their holy possession. They invariably bore witness to the glory of Jesus, a glory as of the only begotten from the Father,† the true Messiah of Israel.

Most of them had known him from childhood. They were companions and friends of his entire public ministry; his private life, his secret thoughts, his character, aims, motives, were uncovered before them. What a record is that which they left us! Let us seek to condense it within a few sentences. To his disciples Jesus was the incarnation of knowledge, loveliness, and truth. He knew all things, even the thoughts of men,‡ for he had learned the secret of eternity as he lay in the Father's bosom, his only begotten Son.§ He was full of grace and truth, the true vine,‖ the pearl of great price, the Alpha and Omega, the bright and morning Star.¶ The apostles looked upon the heavens above, the earth and seas beneath, and they saw in these creative wonders the work of their Master's hand. All things were made by him; without him was not anything made which was made;** by him they were and for him they were created.††

In those disciples' thoughts all history hinged upon the glory of Jesus. His will was the spring of Providence.‡‡ The stormy flood grew calm at his word.§§ The food of multitudes multiplied in his hand.‖‖ Devils

---

* Deut. xxxii. 11. † John i. 14. ‡ Matt. xii. 25. § John i. 18. ‖ John xv. 1. ¶ Rev. xx. 13, 16. ** John i. 3. †† Col. i. 16. ‡‡ John xiv. 14. §§ Mark iv 39. ‖‖ Luke ix. 13.

trembled in his presence.* Legions of angels awaited
his pleasure.† Disease in her hundred-fold horrors resigned her hold upon poor humanity at his touch.‡ His
voice shattered the sceptre of death,§ shot back bolts of
the grave, and summoned forth the dead into the world
of life.‖

In gentleness, sympathy, and meekness he passed the
tenderness of woman. Yet in courage he shamed the bold-
est of his disciples, and stood calm, undaunted, a king of
men alone in the face and power of cruelest foes.¶

His words were savory in the ears of the common
people, who heard him gladly ; ** yet the keenest
intellects, the most learned and cultured minds of the
profoundest nation of antiquity, quailed and failed before
the might of his genius.†† Rulers of Israel sought his
counsel, and acknowledged him a teacher come from
God ; ‡‡ yet he loved the prattle and simplicity of little
children, whom he blessed and held in his arms.§§

Great as he was in life, in death he was greater still.
He died for the truth that he gave; he died for the
world that he loved. He paused in the awful agony of
the cross to give hope to other breaking hearts, triumph-
ing thus over self—most worthy of victories!—amid the
torments of pain. On the one hand he turned to win an
unknown dying thief to God ;‖‖ on the other to commend
his mother to the care of a faithful friend.¶¶ Yes, more
than that, amid the jeers of his persecutors and execu-
tioners, he raised his voice to Heaven, and spent his dying
strength in prayer for them: " Father, forgive them, they
know not what they do."*** Well might the sceptic
Rousseau exclaim in view of this: "If the life and
death of Socrates were those of a sage, the life and
death of Jesus were those of, a God."

There were no terms of too exalted use for these disciples to apply to Christ. The high priest of Israel was
the sacred head of her religious, and often of her secular affairs. He was revered above all other men. Yet

---

* Matt. viii. 31. † Matt. xxvi. 53. ‡ Mark i. 34. § Luke vii. 12.
‖ John xi. 43. ¶ John xviii. 37. ** Mark xii. 37. †† Matt. xxii. 46.
‡‡ John iii. 2. §§ Mark x. 16. ‖‖ Luke xxiv. 43. ¶¶ John xix. 26.
*** Luke xxiii. 34.

Jesus is to his inspired biographers the Great High Priest of men, greater even than he of the Aaronic priesthood, a high priest forever after the order of Melchisedec.* He has power to forgive sins, as God; he is Prophet,† he is exalted to be a Prince, he is King; he is Master, he is Lord even of the Sabbath;‡ he is the anointed of God, the Messiah of his people, he is Redeemer, Saviour, the Foundation of the church;§ with him is the Power of God;‖ he is the Word of God, yea, culmination of all titles of greatness, " In the beginning was the Word, and the Word was with God, and the Word was GOD!"¶ Angels worship him. Through the doors of heaven the prophet of the Revelation sees Jesus of Nazareth on the Throne of God and the Lamb, the centre of all praise that rises from the holy intelligences of Heaven and the Universe of the Almighty.** Words can go no further in laying the mantle of greatness upon any being than the apostle's words have gone in crowning Christ Jesus Lord of All!††

3. Shall we appeal the question of Christ's greatness to the judgment of great minds? What a library of testimonies might one compile, all drawn from the greatest or the best of men! Let me recite but two, perhaps among the most impartial. The first is the noble eulogy of Napoleon Bonaparte. " Everything in Christ astonishes me. His Spirit overcomes me, and his will confounds me. His ideas and his sentiments, the truths which he announces, his manner of convincing, are not explained, either by human observation or the nature of things. His birth and the history of his life; the profundity of his doctrine, which grapples the mightiest difficulties, and which is of those difficulties the most admirable solution; his gospel; his apparition; his empire; his march across the ages and the realms; everything is to me a prodigy, a mystery insoluble, which plunges me into a revery from which I cannot escape—a mystery which is there before my eyes, a mystery which I can

---

* Heb. v. 10.   † Matt. ix. 6.   ‡ Luke vi. 5.   § I. Cor. iii. 11.
‖ I. Cor. i. 24.   ¶ John i. 1.   ** Rev. v. 12.   †† Acts x. 36.

neither deny nor explain. Here I see nothing human. Everything is above me. Everything remains grand— of the Grandeur which overpowers. His religion is a revelation from an Intelligence which certainly is not that of man."

The other testimony which I present is that of the French Rationalist Renan, who seeks to account for the phenomena of Christ and Christianity on simple historic and natural principles, and who views Jesus Christ as a human force alone. He says: "Jesus is that individual who has caused his species to make the greatest advance toward the Divine. Humanity as a whole presents an assemblage of beings low, selfish, superior to the animal only in this that their selfishness is more premeditated. But in the midst of this uniform vulgarity, pillars rise towards heaven and attest a more noble destiny. Jesus is the highest of these pillars which show to man whence he came and whither he should tend. In him is condensed all that is good and lofty in our nature. * * Whatever may be the surprises of the future, Jesus will never be surpassed. His worship will grow young without ceasing; his legend will call forth tears without end; his sufferings will melt the noblest heart; all ages will proclaim that among the sons of men there is none born greater than Jesus."*

Nor has this testimony waxed weak or narrowed the circle of witnesses as the ages have receded from Golgotha. The greatest men and women of the world in the past have called, and the greatest men of to-day do call Jesus of Nazareth Lord. The prophecy is fulfilled. God hath given him the nations for an inheritance. Over millions of the earth's noblest sons and daughters, Jesus *does* reign

> " Where'er the sun
> Doth his successive journeys run !"

4. Shall we try the greatness of Jesus by the results of his life ? To the mind of most men success is the standard of greatness. What has one done ? What are the fruits of his life ? We need not fear this test in

* RENAN—" Life of Christ," pages 375–6.

the case of Jesus; He himself challenged it when he said: " By their fruits ye shall know them.* Do men gather grapes of thorns, or figs of thistles?" Once it was a prophetic metaphor, but now it is a historic fact that the Christ of God is the Dayspring from on high!† The cross and sepulchre have been the rising points of an influence that has been to the world a veritable Sun of Righteousness with healing in its wings.‡ From these as from a focal point, rays, beams, floods, seas of light have swept over all ages in an ever-expanding way, bright with comfort and eternal hope. Education has arisen along this path. Star-eyed Science has lifted up her head to scan and note the works of heaven, earth and sea. Faith, Hope, and Love have spread their pinions above the sorrowing, bringing shelter, nurture, and cheer. Christ gave to man a new word—Charity, and that one word has transformed society. He emancipated and exalted woman; he redeemed childhood, theretofore undervalued and oppressed, and set upon it a price beyond the gold of Ophir. In short, he created the highest civilization that humanity has attained— the civilization of Christianity. He imposed a code of morals that is faultless. He established principles of honor, justice, kindliness, peace, industry, self-denial that have become the bulwarks of nations, the vital elements of the very race.

II. We must not forget that the Glory of the Christ is associated with His human life and office. Our last thought, therefore, will present as an element in that Glory His Faithfulness as the Messenger of Divine Love and the Friend of sinners.

One of the Scriptural lessons taught under the imagery of snow is faithfulness in message-bearing. Says the Proverbialist,§

> "As the cold of snow in the time of harvest,
> So is the faithful messenger to them that sent him ;
> For he refresheth the soul of his masters."

---

* Matthew vii. 16. † Luke i. 79. ‡ Mal. iv. 2. § Proverbs xxv. 13.

One who reads this passage without knowing the customs of the people of Holy Land would be greatly puzzled to understand how snow could fall in summer time or harvest; or if such should occur, as possibly it might,* how it could be regarded as in any sense refreshing. However, we have only to carry our thoughts to the heated days of our own summertide, and the refreshing draughts of ice water or iced lemonade, to have a natural and sufficient explanation of the proverb. In point of fact the ancient Israelites appear to have understood quite as well as ourselves the mode of tempering the heats of summer by the preserved frosts of a winter region. Even to-day we are told that at Damascus snow procured from Anti-Lebanon is kept for sale in the bazaars in the hot months, and being mixed with the juice of pomegranates forms a favorite beverage. In the heat of the day, says a modern traveler, the Jews in northern Galilee offered us water cooled with snow from Jebel esh Sheik, the modern Mount Hermon.† This mountain is ten thousand feet above the Mediterranean Sea, and the top is partially covered with snow, or rather ice, during the whole year, which, however, lies only in the ravines, and thus presents at a distance the appearance of radiant stripes around and below the summit.‡ Nature has thus made a large provision of material to be used in the manner suggested by the Proverbialist. Countless loads of snow, says another traveler, are brought down to Beirut from the sides of Sannin, one of the highest peaks of Lebanon, to freshen the water, otherwise hardly fit to drink. The practical use of snow in this manner existed also among the Greeks and Romans.§

We shall not be misunderstood nor, we are certain, shall we belittle the Glorious Majesty of Him whom we seek to serve, if we apply the central lesson of this proverb to our blessed Lord himself. It is indeed a part of his glory that he has placed himself in our stead, that he has humbled himself to our position, and become a

---

* See Proverbs xxvi. 1. † WILSON—"Lands of the Bible," II., 186. ‡ ROBINSON's Researches, Vol. II., 437. § SMITH's Bible Dictionary.

veritable Messenger to us. "The Son of Man is come not to be ministered to, but to minister.*

In the first chapter of the Revelation in close connection with the image amidst the candlesticks we read the assertion of St. John that his message is "From Jesus Christ, who is the faithful Witness."† In the messages to the churches of Asia, subsequently delivered, this glorious Being from the midst of the candlesticks thus speaks, "These things saith the Amen, the faithful and true Witness."‡ When in the hour of his great humiliation Jesus stood captive in the presence of Pontius Pilate, he declared to the Roman knight that the purpose of his coming and birth into the world was that he might bear witness to the truth, and therein, he added, consisted his true kingship.§ This character as messenger and witness, the bearer of the gospel, the good tidings, is that which was predicted by the prophets concerning the Messiah. In the last of the canonical books of the Old Testament the predicted Christ is called the "Messenger of the Covenant."‖ Indeed this title of Messenger or Angel, for the words are the same, belongs to the Second Person of the Godhead, who appears in the ancient Scriptures as the Angel of the Covenant, the Angel of the Lord.

We need only read the Gospels in order to see how faithful Jesus was to this his character as a Messenger. He declared the truth, the whole truth, and nothing but the truth. His joy was to do the will of Him that sent him, to hold up before the children of men the message which he had come to bring them, to tell them of their loss, and point them the way of salvation; to show them their sins, and provide for them a way of escape; to remind them of the fleeting nature of this life, and fix their thoughts upon that immortal home where the wicked cease from troubling and where the weary are at rest. In order to bear this message to men he shunned no labor, he begrudged no cost, he withheld no pain, but freely bore and yielded all things, even life itself amid the terrors and contumely of the shameful cross.

---

*Matthew xx. 28. † Revelation i. 5. ‡ Revelation iii. 14. § John xviii. 37. ‖ Malachi iii. 1.

In bringing this message into the world how truly has he refreshed the souls of those to whom, for the time, he became a servant! As the ice-cold water to the fever-consumed patient, so is this message to the souls who are parched and consumed by the sins and miseries, the vanities and falseness of the world of guilt and misery in which they live. Oh! you whose hearts are burning with life's fitful fever, whose souls are bitterly athirst, behold, this message comes to you to-day! Drink and live! Refresh yourselves with the waters that flow from the perennial fountains opened by the hand of the Christ upon the Mountains of Holiness in the Paradise of God.

2. Again, the Christ is not only faithful as the Divine Messenger, but as the sinner's Friend. One interesting and curious Scripture lesson derived from snow is that taught by the patriarch Job. He uses the snows that melt before the influence of the summer heat as an emblem of Faithless Friendship.

I have stood in my tent door in the Garden of the gods of Colorado, and watched the snow-storm drifting around the summit of Pike's Peak until it had been covered with a white mantle. The flakes accumulated in thick drifts in the deep ravines. On the sudden slopes they lightly bordered the fissures like a delicate lace veil. On the abrupt declivities they showed themselves here and there in brilliant spots. Every deep in the mountain was marked out from afar by the brilliant mould of snow which filled it. This transient snow enveloping the mountain like a veil, which so far from concealing its form reveals it in its smallest details, has well been called the coquetry of nature.* The next day when the summer sun arose, the grand old beacon of the American desert, whose lofty poll had thus been whitened the night before, gradually dropped off his snowy mantle and stood out in naked massive proportions against the sky. Such a phenomenon as this might well have been taken as a fitting emblem of the transient

---

* RECLUS—"The History of a Mountain," page 77

nature of human affection or of any other human beauty, grace, or service; but Job appears to have had something else in his mind, the breaking up of the winter snow.

When the soft south wind blows in the spring, and the heat of the sun acquires fresh fervor, the snows piled upon the mountain slopes, packed within ravines, and spread upon the surface of the streams, begin slowly to dwindle and melt and glide away, until at last they and the mountain torrents into which they have been merged are alike extinct. Such is the patriarch's figure of a friendship which, like the snows and snow-fed torrents of a mountain, yields and disappears before the fierce beating of affliction and poverty. You will permit me to present his words in a form of English verse which perhaps may convey to you more thoroughly the sense of its poetic figure and beauty.

14 To one who is consumed by burning grief
   Consideration from a friend is due.
15 My brothers as the torrent have been false,
   As winter torrents when they fade away.
16 The streams were dark by reason of the ice;
   The snows within their bosom hid themselves.
17 When spring time comes to breathe upon them warmth,
   They melt, they dwindle :—summer comes with heat,
   And from their channels are the streams extinct.

18 Their branching brooklets wind along the sands.
   They mount up in the waste, in vapor die!
19 The traveling bands of Tema looked for them;
   The caravans of Seba hoped for them;
20 They were confounded, for their trust was great,
   They burned with grief upon the empty banks.

   Thus ye too are become a dried-up brook :
   Ye saw my troubles and ye stood amazed.*

There are parables of contrast as well as of comparison, and here all is contrast. Whatever charge of fickleness and faithlessness may be laid against human friendships, none such can be urged against Him who is the Friend of the sinner. His love passeth that of woman. He is the Friend that sticketh closer than a brother. His friendship has not been wearied by your faults; has

---

* Job vi.

not been alienated by your follies; has not been broken by wrongs that you have inflicted thereon; has not been exhausted by the heavy and frequent drafts which you have made upon it by your unworthiness and contempt of his love. Poverty has laid no strain upon the friendship of Jesus. The enmity of man has not broken the cord that binds the heart of Christ to the helpless. Those who have least of human friendship, to whom has come. least of earth's treasures and joys, are those who may most surely count upon the abiding friendship of Jesus. His love antedated the life of the world: "Yea, I have loved thee with an everlasting love." It will outlive the life of worlds, for having loved his own he will love them to the end. He is the same yesterday, to-day, and forever; the same loving Friend of the friendless, Helper of the needy, Comforter of the sorrowing; pouring the wealth of his infinite Friendship upon the waifs of life, wooing the unfortunate and the sinful back through Himself to the paths of virtue and peace. Oh, friendless hearts! Oh, sin-bruised spirits, come to this Friend and be made happy and holy forever by partaking of his heavenly love! This Glory bends down to-day to encompass and enfold you. Will you lift up your life to be received therein, to be glorified thereby? If you would be crowned with his Glory in the presence of the great White Throne, you must share with him on earth both glory and shame. All human glories are as the flowers of the field; they will perish in your hand, and their faded beauty drop from your lifeless fingers at the touch of Death. But the Glory which Jesus offers to divide with you is Fadeless and Eternal.

While walking up the street one evening during an election canvass I saw rockets flaring aloft leaving behind them trails of glittering sparks. There was a rush along a graceful curve, a momentary twinkling, a brief explosion, a beautiful display of colors, and then all was quenched in darkness. Over against these flaring rockets, its light momentarily hidden by them, shone the Evening Star; shone on steadily, shining out brightly when the rocket's brief glamour had faded into the night. It had been shining since the morning stars sang together the hymnal of creation's dawn, and it shall shine on until the heavens be rolled together as a scroll, and the elements melt with fervent heat. Here, I thought, is the type of the human and the Divine. The glory of man is as the rocket whose beauty and lustre arrest for a moment the admiration of beholders and fade away forever. But the glory and beauty of Christ, Heaven's "Bright and Morning Star," shall shine on eternally. O soul, turn thou from following the fading lustre of earthly honors, and fix thy faith and love upon Him whose Glory is quenchless, whose Infinite Splendor shall illumine Heaven and all its innumerable Host, world without end!

———

Snow-Purity:
Human Perfection.

"*Her nobles were purer than snow, they were whiter than milk.*"—LAMENTATIONS iv. 7.

"*Wash me and I shall be whiter than snow.*"—PSALM li. 7.

SNOW-PURITY: HUMAN PERFECTION.

In works of art our Lord Jesus Christ is usually represented in white garments. This symbolism expresses, as we have seen in the last lecture, his Divine Glory. But the white garments of the Christ express also the idea of purity, for always, as it is to-day, whiteness has been the emblem of innocence. The angels of God as ministers of the Most High are clad with power which they exercise among men and over nature; but that quality which appears to have been taken as especially characteristic of them is holiness. Hence they are known as " the holy angels," " the holy ones," and therefore they are always represented in the Scriptures as clothed in white. The angel of the Lord who rolled away the stone from the grave of Jesus on the morning of the Resurrection was clad in raiment white as snow.* The angels who visited the disciples as they stood looking steadfastly into heaven after the ascended Lord were clad in white apparel.†

A like symbolism is used to express the holiness of men. Jeremiah expresses the righteousness of Zion in her days of faithfulness to Jehovah by declaring that " her nobles (or Nazarites) were purer than snow." The saints in glory shall walk with Christ in white, because they are worthy, not having defiled their garments.‡ The four-and-twenty elders upon the thrones are arrayed in white.§ In the judgment day the saints shall receive " the white stone,"|| the token of acquittal and recognition of the righteousness of their new life, as the white ballot or ball in certain American societies is the sign of the elector's approval of an applicant for membership. This symbol is transferred to the Church considered in its Catholic unity, for we are told that the Bride, which is the Lamb's wife, at the marriage of the Lamb, shall

* Matt. xxviii. 3. † Acts i. 10. ‡ Rev. iii. 4. § Rev. iv. 4. || Rev. ii. 17.

array herself in fine linen, bright and pure, for the fine linen is the righteous acts of the saints.*

Under the Jewish ritual on the great day of Atonement the High Priest was required to put on his linen coat, even the holy garments, and thus he was to make atonement for the holy sanctuary, for the priests and for all the people.† The official garments of the priests and Levites in the Jewish temple service were undoubtedly white. A similar dress prevailed in the Christian Church as early at least as the fourth century, and is retained among the ministers of the Anglican, Episcopal and Roman Churches, although it may be considered very doubtful whether it was a return to the priestly habit of the Hebrew ritual, or a simple development from the ordinary garments of the laity of early times as maintained by Dean Stanley.‡ Even choristers and choir boys are clad in white linen garments, in token of that purity of life which ought to be the mark of those who officiate in the song service of God's holy house.

We are thus led to that subject which is naturally associated with Snow-Purity, viz., personal purity, holiness or perfection. The term perfection may be used in current theological language in a three-fold sense. First, it expresses the perfection of man at his origin as regarded from the view point of the Bible narrative of creation. Second, it expresses that legal perfection which is bestowed in the act of justification and pardon through the soul's faith in Jesus Christ. Third, it expresses the actual possession by man of the germ of a holy life and his progress therein, known as sanctification, and which is consummated at the general resurrection, when God's saints are " made perfect in holiness." The present discourse will be concerned chiefly with the first two of these meanings.

I. We turn, in the first place, to consider man's Primitive Holiness. The Bible pictures the original man in a condition far from savagery. It is also widely separate from an estate of civilization as known among us. Of the

---

* Rev. xix. 8. † Lev. xvi. 33. ‡ STANLEY—"Christian Institutions," chapter VIII., page 178.

arts and sciences, and ordinary comforts and luxuries of
society, the primitive pair knew nothing. These rapidly
arose, however, for we find music, the invention of the
pipe and organ, the keeping of flocks and herds, the
forging of copper and iron, the making of cutting instruments, and such-like arts, already appearing in the
family of Cain, showing that the inherent tendencies of
man in that direction were strong at the very outset.*
What Holy Scriptures present, and what our faith affirms,
concerning man's original nature is that he was made in
the image of God. St. Paul, writing to the church of
Colosse,† said: "And have put on the new man which
is renewed in Knowledge after the image of Him that
created him." Writing to the Ephesians,‡ he says: "Put
on the new man which after God is created in Righteousness and true Holiness." It is plain from these passages that knowledge, righteousness, and holiness are
elements of the image of God in which man was originally created. Adam, as soon as he began to be, had
self-knowledge. He was conscious of his own being,
faculties, and states. He had also the knowledge of
what was outside of himself, or he had what modern
philosophy calls world-consciousness.§

It is, of course, unnecessary for us to affirm, in declaring that original man was a creature of knowledge, that
he knew everything. His knowledge of material things
was undoubtedly imperfect. It was certainly sufficient
to maintain life and health, to defend himself against
such inconveniences and obstacles as his primitive condition might have presented, although we know from
Scripture that it was,|| and infer from science that it must
have been, extremely favorable in all its surroundings.¶
The Bible record of what Adam knew of the external
world is limited chiefly to the statement that his mind
was deeply interested in the living things near his abode;
and that he was able to distinguish one from the other,

---

* Genesis iv. 20–23. † Col. iii. 10. ‡ Eph. iv. 24. § Dr. Chas.
Hodge—"Systematic Theology," vol. II., page 101. || Gen. ii. 8.
¶ Sir William Dawson—"Story of the Earth and Man," page
367. Wallace—"On Natural Selection," page 320. Winchell
—"Preadamites," page 356.

to name them, and perhaps in a rude way to classify them.* The first Academy of Natural Sciences was established in the groves of Eden.

The chief thing for us to believe is that Adam knew God, whom to know is life eternal; that he had knowledge of himself and of his relations to God; that his moral nature was in full exercise, and that in all essential particulars his soul was pure. Such an estate does not require us to suppose the learning of the schools, the skill of the mechanic arts, and the culture and polish of manners which obtain among the most highly civilized modern nations. With respect to these attainments, we may perhaps agree that man at his origin was neither savage nor civilized, but simply undeveloped.† It is an experience with which we are continually meeting, and which may be observed in all parts of Christendom today, that the greatest vigor of intellect and strongest moral sense may be associated with the humblest surroundings and simplest forms of life and manners.

There is a pride of civilization which is fed or rather inflated by very superficial material. There are many whose ideas of "high society," of "nobility," of lofty development, and "enlightenment" are inseparable from palatial dwellings—I do not say "homes"—splendid furniture, costly works of art, luxurious entertainment, abundant and disciplined service. Even here in Republican America multitudes genuflect and cringe covetously before wealth and its accessories, as though they were the standard of all worth and manhood. You shall see the ideas of such folks whirl and somersault through whole arcs and circles of admiration at a sudden announcement that such and such a man is a millionaire; that this or that lady is an heiress! There are men in high regard in this and all other cities simply for their money who, independent of that, would not be thought worthy of a passing recognition. Yes, we may see men who are moral lepers, polluted to the core of their lives, not only tolerated but fawned over, fêted, served, because they have seized power and wealth. Shame! Let us clear our

---

* Gen. ii. 19, 20.   † Professor Harris—"The Self-Revelation of God," page 346.

thinking of such fogs; let us purify our moral atmosphere of such miasmatic ideas, and exalt pure, true
manhood and womanhood, irrespective of the tinsel of
outward estate. Let us remember that the most heroic
ages of our Republic were times of simplicity of manners and life. Let us away forever with the notion that
the veneer of modern luxury and riches is necessary to
high and pure character!

For one moment draw in your mind a contrast between
two states of society in our Mother country, and which
may easily be reproduced here. One is limned to us by
the pen of daily journalism, whose often too prurient hand
plucks aside the veil that barely hides from public view
the social life of some degraded examples of England's
proud nobility or America's inflated plutocracy. One
glance—I dare not bid you take more—and lo! a group
more loathsome than lepers, putrescent at the very seat
of life, reveling amidst the fairest creations of modern
civilization. Drop the veil! Shut out the infected spot,
and let us look now at a picture drawn from the " other
extreme of the social scale," to use the swelling phrase of
caste. It is the matchless picture of the Scotch peasant's
home, written by Robert Burns. The Saturday night
gathering of children from their weekly toil, the simple
tale of love, the humble surroundings, the patriarchal act
of evening worship, are depicted in matchless phrasing.

> Then homeward all take off their sev'ral way ;
>   The youngling cottagers retire to rest ;
> The parent pair their secret homage pay,
>   And proffer up to Heaven the warm request
> That He who stills the raven's clam'rous nest,
>   And decks the lily fair in flow'ry pride,
> Would, in the way his Wisdom sees the best,
>   For them and for their little ones provide ;
>   But chiefly, in their hearts with Grace Divine preside.
>
> From scenes like these old Scotia's grandeur springs,
>   That makes her loved at home, revered abroad ;
> Princes and lords are but the breath of kings,
>   "An honest man's the noblest work of God ;"
> And certes, in fair Virtue's heavenly road,
>   The cottage leaves the palace far behind.
> What is a lordling's pomp? A cumbrous load
>   Disguising oft the wretch of human kind
>   Studied in arts of hell, in wickedness refined !*

---

* BURNS—"The Cotter's Saturday Night "

Do not misunderstand; there are women and men of rank and wealth who adorn ·the highest circles of the true nobility of nature and grace. They live to honor God and bless their fellows; they are foremost in every work of self-denial and bounty that can add force to the leverage whose uplift shall raise mankind to a loftier plane of character and life. On the other hand, there are poor dwellers in lowly and ill-furnished homes who are as far removed from the high moral altitude of Burns' cotter as is the stainless snow of a country field from the winrows of frozen filth that fringe our city streets. They live in rural hut and cottage; in New York tenement houses, like ant-hills in their swarming life, but unlike them *toto cœlo* in every element of physical and moral purity; yes, they live also in Philadelphia's pretty little brick homes with their white marble trimmings. God pity and keep them all! But the point which I seek here to emphasize is that mere social condition, whether high or low, does not now and never did determine man's rank in personal purity and nobility of character. These are mere secondary elements which we may readily separate from the question of the real standing of Adam as a perfect man.

2. There is nothing contrary to the fullest actual attainments of modern science in the belief that man at his origin was in this sense a perfect being. If we think of his physical nature simply, there is not a scintilla of testimony, entitled to consideration as scientific evidence, that fossil man, so called, was any different in his physical characteristics from man as he is to-day.* Whatever the future may uncover, this is the present condition of our knowledge.†

This is certainly according to the analogy of nature. I think I may affirm without fear of contradiction that no fossil animal has ever been uncovered from any geological horizon which, so far as could be determined, did not possess in all plenitude and amplitude of its faunal characteristics everything necessary to insure its

---

* WALLACE—"Natural Selection," page 327. † HUXLEY—"Man's Place in Nature," page 159.

perfect life amidst the conditions of its being. Numbers of species have been preserved to us from very early periods which have their close representatives in living creatures. In so far as a comparison between the two classes can determine, the oldest are as perfect after their kind as the latest. The earliest fossil spiders of which I have any knowledge appear to be as perfectly adapted to the conditions of their life as those which spin and weave and capture their prey every summer in our gardens and fields. A series of figures of fossil spiders collected in Colorado,* might well be taken for drawings of a number of badly-damaged species of our current fauna. Moreover, the only example of the industry of these remarkable creatures which has been preserved to us from early periods, a little fossil cocoon or egg-sac,† appears to be as perfect as are the egg-nests of the genus‡ to which it probably belongs, as they may be found every summer in the shady ravines of Delaware county, or hanging underneath the rocky ledges in Fairmount Park. The beautifully preserved fossil araneads of the amber§ of Europe are in every essential respect identical with recent genera.

The point which I am here seeking to emphasize is that the habit of nature appears to be to present its new forms of life as perfect forms. Their first apparition above the geologic horizon in which they are discovered, presents them to the vision of science full-orbed species, well furnished, and completely outfitted for their place in nature.

There is indeed a tendency of low types to appear first, but appear in their highest perfection and variety;|| sometimes, like the fishes of the Upper Silurian, they appear at once as "kings of their class." Why, therefore, should we suppose any exception in the case of man? Why, at least, should we be surprised at the statement that man, when he appeared, made his apparition with all his physical characteristics, a perfect man?

* S. H. SCUDDER — "Tertiary Insects of North America." † *Aranea Columbiæ*, SCUDDER. ‡ *Linyphia.* § KOCH and BERENDT. See also THORELL's "European Spiders." || SIR WILLIAM DAWSON—"Story of the Earth and Man," page 55.

3. But man's physical nature is by no means the most important part of him. He is a rational and moral creature as well. It may seem strange that there should be any need to emphasize or even express the fact that man stands alone in the world as a moral being. Yet in our generation this has not only been doubted, but vigorously denied, and it is needful for us here at least to allude to the fact. I do not enter into the interesting and undoubtedly difficult question as to the exact difference between human intelligence and animal instinct. It is enough here to say that the ripest utterance of philosophy declares that the lower animals cannot form those high ideals which constitute the peculiar characteristics of man: the ideas of necessary truth, or moral good and infinity, culminating in the idea of God. There is no ground for believing that any of the lower animals have a sense of good as good, and of binding obligation, of a sense of evil as evil, as deserving of disapproval.*

Even Mr. Darwin, much as he has done or attempted to break down the barrier between man and the inferior creatures, is compelled to acknowledge that we have no reason to suppose that any of the lower animals have the capacity of comparing their past or future actions or motives, or of approving or disapproving them. "Therefore," he continues, "when a Newfoundland dog drags a child out of the water, or a monkey faces danger to rescue its comrade, or take charge of an orphan monkey, we do not call its conduct moral." †

When poor old "Jumbo" interposed his bulky body to rescue the baby elephant, and thus was stricken by the Canadian Railway train that caused his death, the action was one which excited a thrill of admiration and sympathy. Whatever motive may have stirred the massive creature to this act of affection, we cannot attribute it to moral ideas. Such an act is separated by an impassable gulf from that of the noble engineer who, from a sense of high obligation in the discharge of his respon-

* President McCosh—"Christianity and Positivism," page 359. See also chapter V. of that seed-bed of pertinent and lofty thoughts.
† "Descent of Man," page 111.

sible trust, ventures his life to save an endangered train;
from that of the physician who in the discharge of his
duty to God, to humanity, and to science risks his life
again and again in efforts to rescue the victim of contagious disease from impending death; from that of the
mother who, in holy consecration to her children's welfare, toils, sacrifices, suffers day after day, year after year,
that her offspring may be nurtured not only into vigorous
physical life but into moral purity and faith. Whatever
may be the difference between these two classes of actions,
we know that in those of the animal there is no sense of
good as good, of evil as evil; no sense of obligation to
a higher Power or to any idea of duty and moral righteousness. Goodness is a law determining the relations
between things, relations which have to be realized by
free-wills.* Thus it follows that among innumerable
forms of organized being in the world, there is but one
representative of moral life. No being save man con-
templates a general law of life, making its fulfillment a
deliberate end of action; no being save man possesses a
conception of duty or "oughtness." No animal con-
templates a general law of conduct, or intelligible rule
of life applicable for the government of the order to
which it belongs; no animal subordinates physical impulse at the bidding of such a law; no animal aims at
the perfecting of its nature under a general conception
of the excellence of its own nature as dog, horse, or ape.
Therefore we conclude that man alone of all living
beings known to us in this world is a moral being.†

4. Further, the power of reasoning intelligence, the
sense of God and of right and wrong, reverence, duty,
and conscience, all these appear to have been as vigorous in man at the beginning as they are to-day.‡ So
far from there being evidence that man at the outset was
a chattering ape-man, or a human-like savage uttering
inarticulate sounds, with no thought of God except a

* NAVILLE—"The Problem of Evil" (Godet). † CALDERWOOD
—"Science and Religion," page 278. "The Relations of Mind
and Brain," page 504. ‡ RAWLINSON — "Origin of Nations,"
page 10.

wild fear of Nature and a blind wonder at the strange things occurring on all hands around him, the contrary is the case. What is the testimony of History?

The evidence appears to be that there is a special tendency in religious conceptions to run into developments of corruption and decay. We have found in the most ancient records of the Aryan language proof that the indications of religious thought are higher, simpler, purer as we go back in time. At least in the very oldest compositions of human speech which have come down to us, we find the Divine Being spoken of in the sublime language which forms the opening of the Lord's Prayer.* Babylonian documents of early date tell, similarly, of art and literature having preceded the great deluge, and having survived it. The explorers who have dug deep into the Mesopotamian mounds, and ransacked the tombs of Egypt, have come upon no certain traces of savage man in those regions, which a widespread tradition makes the cradle of the human race.† When we are in search of our purest forms of moral truth, our sublimest ideals of duty, and our loftiest forms of reverence and praise to God, we do not turn to modern religious developments such as the Book of Mormon, or the fanciful worship of Comte and the Positivists, or to Herbert Spencer's "Data of Ethics," or the theories of Michael Bakunin and the Nihilists. We go further back. We go back to the very earliest and oldest; and the nearer we draw to the dawn of human life the sweeter, the simpler, the loftier do we find the conceptions of God and right.

The religion of our Lord Jesus Christ, which is confessedly the one perfect presentation of moral purity and excellence, is, as He Himself declared, but the fulfillment, the outflowering, the enlargement and development of the law and the prophets. Mount Sinai and the Mount of Beatitudes, the Ten Commandments and the Sermon on the Mount, are widely separate in time, but are linked together by community of thought, and are generically one with the precepts of religion and right-

---

* DUKE OF ARGYLL — "The Unity of Nature," page 520.
† RAWLINSON.

eousness which ruled the life of Abraham, Noah, and the patriarchs.

Not less significant is the fact that everywhere in the imagination and traditions of mankind there is preserved the memory and the belief in a past better than the present. It is a constant saying, we are told, among African tribes that formerly heaven was nearer to man than it is now; that the highest God, the creator himself, gave formerly lessons of wisdom to human beings; but that afterwards he withdrew from them, and dwells now far from them in heaven. All the Indian races have the same tradition; and it is not easy to conceive how a belief so universal could have arisen unless as a survival. It has all the marks of being a memory and not an imagination. It would reconcile the origin of man with that law which has been elsewhere universal in creation—the law under which every creature has been produced not only with appropriate powers, but with appropriate instincts and intuitive perceptions for the guidance of these powers in their exercise and use.*

II. Our lesson leads us, in the second place, to consider that Legal Perfection which is bestowed in the act of Justification through the soul's Faith in the Lord Jesus Christ.

Whatever may be our view as to the degree of perfection originally possessed by man, we shall not differ widely as to the fact that a large portion of the human race is sunken in a low depth of iniquity. This is well expressed by the sharp contrast drawn in one of the passages chosen as our text. Israel faithful and Israel fallen are thus figured:—

7 Her nobles were purer than snow,
   Whiter they were than milk. * * *
8 Their visage is blacker than coal;
   They are not known in the streets.†

"God made man upright, but they have sought out many inventions."‡   "All we like sheep have gone

---

* THE DUKE OF ARGYLL—"The Unity of Nature," pages 542-3.
† Lam. iv. 7.   ‡ Eccl. vii. 29.

astray."* These are Scripture expressions which declare to us what history and human consciousness affirm, that man is now separate from that ideal of holiness which it is possible for him to conceive and which he knows that he may realize. You are walking in the forest, and find in your pathway a riven oak. You did not see the falling bolt nor hear the crash of the thunder, nor witness the shattering of this forest king, but you know it was smitten by lightning. The destroying bolt has left its own testimony. Look now at this ruined man! You did not see him destroyed, but the traces of destruction are manifest everywhere upon him, and you know that some time he was riven by the lightning stroke of sin.

Most of you have frequently been reminded of a poem entitled "Beautiful Snow." Every year as the winter sets in it becomes a theme for banter and jest by the paragraphers of the public press. Yet the poem is by no means as well known as the universal knowledge of its title would seem to signify. That title is very deceiving,—it calls up a vision of the simple beauty of the snow-fall, but in point of fact there is very little of such charm in the poem itself. It is a sad and dolorous strain, the burden of which is well expressed by the words of Jeremiah's Lamentations which have just been quoted.

> How the wild crowd goes swaying along,
> Hailing each other with humor and song!
> How the gay sledges like meteors flash by—
> Bright for a moment, then lost to the eye,
> Ringing, swinging, dashing they go
> Over the crest of the beautiful snow :
> Snow so pure when it falls from the sky—
> To be trampled in mud by the crowd rushing by !
> To be trampled and tracked by the thousands of feet,
> Till it blends with the filth in the horrible street.
>
> Once I was pure as the snow—but I fell ;
> Fell, like the snow-flakes, from heaven to hell.
>
> *   *   *   *   *   *   *   *
>
> Merciful God! Have I fallen so low ?
> And yet I was once like this beautiful snow.†

---

* Isa. liii. 6.   † JAMES W. WATSON.

It is the degradation of the human family that we are called upon to contemplate no less than its exaltation. Sinful dispositions and habits, allied with adverse circumstances, their usual consequences, have wrought through long periods to crush man down and efface the Divine image wherein he was created. The cruel, immoral, bestialized savage is not the original man, but the degradation of the original. Had savagery been the primitive condition of mankind, it is scarcely conceivable that he ever could have emerged from it. Savages left to themselves continue savages, show no signs of progression, stagnate, deteriorate. There is no historical evidence, says Rawlinson, of savages having civilized themselves; no instance on record of their ever having been raised out of their miserable condition by any other means than by contact with a civilized race. The torch of civilization is handed on from age to age, from race to race. If it were once extinguished, there is great doubt whether it could ever be relighted.*

Here in the spiritual sphere it is even as naturalists have proved it to be in the material world, the germs of life when once obliterated from any space, can never by spontaneous generation be restored. Life is brought in from without, it never is born from within. A death-smitten space, if it shall bloom once more with vital beauty, must receive its germs from some other force or will than that which lies within itself.

The Bible scheme of redemption presents God as the external Force, the Divine Will seeking to restore our race from a lost condition. Heaven has labored through the ages to inspire man with desire to regain his moral standing; and thus animated we behold him struggling up, fostering the hope and aspiration for heavenly things, sometimes gaining the heights and again plunged into the depths; now walking on the highway of holiness, and again plunged in the mire; floundering helplessly or soaring loftily, but amidst all changes and discouragements struggling upward toward God by the help of God.

---

* RAWLINSON—"Antiquity of Man Historically Considered," page 26.

It has been announced by Heaven, and recognized by man himself, that this restoration cannot be attained by self-help. " Come now," we read, " and let us reason together," saith the Lord. " Though your sins be as scarlet, they shall be white as snow."* " Purge me with hyssop and I shall be clean," is the cry of the penitent Psalmist unto God; " Wash me and I shall be whiter than snow!" " Create in me a clean heart, oh God, and renew a right spirit within me."†

The old Testament starting-point for this work of redemption seems to be the presentation of God as a Being of perfect holiness. Men, we know, never rise higher in moral excellence than the deities whom they worship. It would have been strange, indeed, if the worship of such corrupt, quarrelsome, and licentious divinities as composed the Pantheon of Greece and Rome should have produced any other effect upon the life of their votaries than that moral corruption which history declares. To effect and maintain purity of morals on the part of the Hebrews it was necessary that their God should be presented to them as one of Infinite Holiness. This attribute accordingly we see everywhere represented and conveyed in the requirements of the Ceremonial Law.

Cleanliness, it has been said, is next to godliness. In one sense it is certainly true. The thought of moral purity associates itself closely with bodily purity. When the Israelites came up out of Egypt to receive from Jehovah a law, a church, a theology that should lift them into a high position as a nation, it was taken for granted that knowledge of and belief in God as a Holy Being must lie at the foundation of all progress toward personal purity in man. But how should that idea be conveyed to and kept prominent before a people who had long been debased by a condition of expatriation, bondage, social and religious communion with the gross idolatries of Egypt? No doubt this question lies at the base of the grand system of object-teaching presented in the ceremonial law of Moses.‡

Observe how the idea of physical purity was intro-

* Isaiah i. 18.   † Psalm li. 7–10.   ‡ Philosophy of the Plan of Salvation.

duced into the ordinary laws of health. Ceremony was associated with moral ideas. Contact with any unclean thing, with the dead, with bone, with contagious diseases, rendered the individual unfit for religious service and set him aside from the congregation of the people. Frequent washings were associated with worship; the beasts that were naturally or by experience most repugnant or injurious as human food were put under the ban as unclean meat. No unclean thing, no clean beast if marred in any wise, could be offered to Jehovah as a sacrifice. All offerings were without blemish and without spot.* Priests were required to be physically perfect men.† Externally they were clothed in garments of finest white linen on which no stain was tolerated. Frequent ablutions were compelled in all their approaches to the altar and in their conduct of Divine worship.‡ In this manner, advancing along the thought that in the human mind the idea of cleanliness lies very near to godliness, the Hebrew was led to regard sin as a moral impurity, most hateful to God, who at the same time was held before him in all this symbolism as a Being of Infinite Holiness.

Above all, this thought was held before the Hebrew by the sacrifices of the altar. A Holy God cannot suffer sin to go without punishment or propitiation. Sin must be atoned for. This fact preserved within men the sense of sin's impurity; it preserved that sense of justice in dealing with sin without which righteousness cannot exist; it maintained the duty of every soul to rise out of sin daily into a state of purity. If you say the condition of the Hebrew offerer of sacrifice was only one of legal holiness, even if admitted, one will see that the sense of forensic purity before God was well calculated to lift up the soul to an ideal; to encourage one to attain in fact his status in law. But there can be no doubt that something more than this resulted from the sacrificial rite. It was God's ordinance for bestowing upon the penitent an impulse towards the higher life as well as the sense of a legal or formal purity.

---

*See Leviticus generally, especially chapters xi–xvi. † Lev. xxi. 17–21. ‡ Numb. xix. 7–22.

Let us not dwell longer here. These sacrifices of the law of Israel were only types and shadows of that one Perfect Sacrifice which was to come. The people of those early generations walked upward along the ages towards that sublime Figure lifted upon the cross of Mount Calvary. The Church of the Old Testament moved towards the Rising Sun of a Perfect Faith whose rays touched and bathed indeed that cross of Golgotha, but left only its great shadow stretching backward, within which the ages ever moved. Yet as they neared the summit, the shadow shortened; and when at last in the fullness of God's own time the True Israel, the Holy People stood on the brow of Calvary and laid their hand upon the Cross of Jesus, lo! they had passed from beneath the shadow! for the perfect day had come and the sun shone in the zenith. Henceforth the Cross shall cast no shadow! Human hopes are realized, human faith is perfected, shadows and types have ceased, because Jesus the Lamb of God, the one Sacrifice for sin, has been offered upon the altar of the Cross once for all.

This is the point to which we are come to-day. Here let us rest. Faith in the Lord Jesus Christ, according to the appointment of God's scheme of redemption, rescues the soul from the guilt of sin. God pardons for Christ's sake those who receive the work and offering of Jesus as made for them, but the gracious gift does not stop there. It is impossible for men to receive Jesus Christ by faith without also receiving the Holy Ghost within them as the germ of a new spiritual life. Salvation means something more than a formal pardon, something more than the criminal's acquittal or his discharge from the judgment of law. It means the bestowment of a germinal life of holiness which shall develop until the believer's being shall be possessed therewith, and he become in fact what he is in law, purified before the eternal God. Justification is the sinner's legal purification, it purges his record before the law. Sanctification is the actual imparting to the sinner of the germs of purification, insuring for him the ingrowth and outgrowth of a character and life which shall be made perfect in the holiness of heaven.

As disciples and followers of Christ we are called to-day to the conflict with sin. It is ours to stand for whatsoever things are pure, lovely, and of good report. Man has fallen. It is ours to raise him. This is a lost world, but, thank God! it is also a found world since Christ has died. It is our duty and privilege to bring the knowledge of this gracious truth to the ears of the erring. Most men, like bottles in the glass blower's hand, are blown into shape by the breath of other men; and some are vessels to honor and some to dishonor; some are as the toper's flask, some as the dandy's perfume bottle; some as the apothecary's vial to bear healing medicine to the sick. Oh, you who deal with the plastic metal of mortal and immortal souls, take heed how you breathe within them and upon them the breath of an influence that shall shape their destiny for all time and eternity!

But be assured, there can be no power with you to shape men into purity of life until you yourself have cleansed your soul at the fountain of all holiness. If you would be a true knight of virtue you must first receive from the Divine Master's hand the stroke and signet of your knighthood. Will you kneel before him here and now, and yield you to the high chivalry of holiness, body and soul, for time and eternity? Two ways open before you, the service of Christ in purity of heart and life, or the service of self in sinful continuance in evil. The course of your life will inevitably be directed by the nature, inclination, and desires of your heart. Buzzards fly to a carcass. They will soar aloft in the air, most beautiful creatures of motion, looking like angels in the upper sky, so gracefully do they move upon their spiral courses. But let the sight of a carcass on the plain below catch the eyes of the graceful things, and at once they swing passionately downward and revel in the body of uncleanness and death. It is their nature—they are buzzards!

Bees fly to honey! All day long they hum and flutter over beds of flowers and blossoming vines, passing by whatever of unloveliness may lie in their flight to settle always within the cups of nectar-bearing flowers. Bees to the flowers! Buzzards to the carcass! Spiritual honey-bearers or moral scavengers? Which is the better object in this God's world of ours? And which part, O brother, will you choose?

While the pendulum swings the clock will speak out, tick-tock from the wheels; ding-dong from the bell. It may speak a false hour, but it will speak. Life is that clock. While the pulse of life beats on, man will speak notes of guidance and truth, notes of guidance and error. True or false, one or the other, life shall give its voice into the world. What shall it be? May the Divine Master so lay his hand upon the delicate wheels of your being that they shall ever keep time to the movement of the Heavens, and voice forth to the world and show forth from the dial of your daily living a heart and life in unison with the Sun of Righteousness.

Perhaps I am speaking to some one to-day who is deeply conscious that his soul is stained with sin and needs a Saviour for purification, but who is plunged in deep despondency. "Alas!" you cry, "my hope is perished. I am lost. My sun has gone down. It is night with me!" Well, yes, it is night, but with the night up come the stars; and soon also the moon, full and fair, bathing the world with its silver glory. Then, by and by, lo! in the east show the purple streakings of dawn; and see! there is the day-spring from on high, the up-risen sun, once more, and the world is rosy and bright. So human hopes rise and set; they give way to lesser lights, sometimes to greater; sometimes to darkness. But they keep on and on, and man never ceases to hope. Sweet hope! when nights have ceased to darken, when stars and moon yield no more radiance, when the orb of this earthly day shall rise and set no more, then in the realm of eternal hope we shall bathe our souls forever in the light of heaven, whereof the Lamb is the light, a steady, sweet, glorious shining that shall never waver nor lessen, but shall widen as the years of eternity roll.

LECTURE X.

———

The Rainfall.

"He shall come down like rain upon the mown grass."—Psalm lxxii. 6.

THE RAINFALL.

THE allusions to rain in Holy Scripture are very frequent, as one would expect with so common and important a natural phenomenon. It is used to express figuratively the thoughts of inspired writers, in a double sense, according as it is viewed from the standpoint of the disadvantages, dangers, and losses which it sometimes involved, or the blessings resulting from it. For example, God is represented as a covert from the rain into which the soul has fled when the storm beats upon him.* The overflowing shower is an emblem of the Divine judgment upon sinners,† and Divine wrath descending upon the godless is represented under the emblem of falling rain.‡ A sweeping rain is an apt figure of a needy man who oppresses his poor neighbor,§ and the continual drop, drop, dropping on a rainy day beomes in the Proverbialist's mind a fitting figure of a contentious woman.‖ Our Saviour uses the beating rains and floods that gather in the dry beds of streams after heavy showers, to represent the temptations, griefs, and cares which break upon the souls of men, destructively in the case of those who "without foundation" have built their faith upon the sands, but vainly in the case of those who have reared the structure of their eternal hope upon the everlasting rock of Christ's truth.¶

On the other hand, rain is frequently used as the emblem of all that is blessed and desirable in both temporal and spiritual things. The coming of the "former" and the "latter" rains is constantly viewed in Scripture as the realization of all the hopes of the agriculturist. When we remember that Palestine was substantially an agricultural country, even more of a farming community than the United States, we can readily see how much

*Isa. iv. 6. † Ezek. xxxviii. 22. ‡ Job xx. 23. § Prov. xxviii. 3.
‖ Prov. xxvii. 15. ¶ Matt. vii. 25.

(179)

this meant. In the song of Moses "which he spake in the ears of all the Assembly of Israel" his Heavenly doctrine is represented as dropping as the rain.

> My doctrine shall drop as the rain,
> My speech shall distill as the dew;
> As the small rain on the tender grass,
> And as showers upon the herb. *

The outgoing Word of God in its descent upon an expectant people, and the triumphant and joyful acceptance of the same, is represented in Isaiah as the rain that cometh down and watereth the earth and maketh it bring forth and bud, while all the mountains and hills, glad at the refreshing showers, break forth into singing, and the trees of the field clap hands.† Job represents the eagerness with which his retainers and neighbors awaited his coming in the day of prosperity as like the eagerness with which the farmer looks for the fruitgiving rains.‡ In Solomon's Song the ceasing of the heavy winter showers and the beginning of spring when buds are opening, and flowers blooming and the fragrance of blossoming grapevines fills the air, is an emblem of that period in the soul's history when one is born into the new life, and all heaven and earth seem to be rejoicing in sympathy therewith.§ These are some of the lessons which the inspired writers have enfolded within the phenomenon of the falling rain. We shall have something to do with them hereafter; but the lesson which we have to learn to-day from the rainfall is the Manifestation of Divine Power in the coming of Jesus Christ. The lesson will perhaps best be indicated by reading the whole passage from which our text is taken.

> 1   Give to the king Thy judgments, O God,
>   And Thy righteousness unto the king's son!
> 2   Let Him govern Thy people with righteousness,
>   And judge thine afflicted with justice.
> 3   Let the mountains bring peace to the people,
>   And the hills bring peace by righteousness.
> 4   Let him judge the poor of the people,
>   Let him save the children of the needy,
>   And break in pieces the oppressor!

---

* Deut. xxxii. 2. † Isa. lv. 10, 12. ‡ Job xxix. 23. § Canticles ii. 11–13.

5 May they have Thee in fear while the sun endures
   And while the moon shineth,—to all generations !
6 May He come down like rain on the grass of the meadow,
   As showers, as downpouring rain upon earth.
7 In His days may the righteous ones blossom unhindered,
   And fullness of peace, till the moon be no more ;
8 May He have the dominion from sea to sea,
   And from the river to the ends of the earth.*

The beautiful imagery of this Psalm presents to us a
picture of the coming of the Christ to exercise his dominion upon earth.   The descending rains renovate the
whole surface of the land and exercise a sovereign influence upon the vegetable kingdom; they quicken
seeds to life, develop grain and fruits, reclothe fields,
vineyards, and forests, and spread blessings everywhere
for the children of men.   So in the vision of the prophetic Psalmist should it be when Messiah should come.
He would dominate the souls of men; society should be
renovated; the world should bend to the yoke of his
thought; from the Mediterranean to the utmost seas,
and from the Euphrates to the ends of the earth, his
spiritual sceptre should extend and bless the children of
men.   This then is the thought upon which we are to
dwell, the power of Christ in renovating society.

I. The prediction of the Psalmist has been fulfilled.
The manifestation of Jesus in the world has been with
Mighty Power for the Subjugation of our race.   We are
not thinking of physical power alone, the might of war,
the strength of numbers, the potency of wealth, commerce and culture, but of the power of Purity and Love,
of Religious Truth and the Spiritual Life.   We shall
presently trace some striking examples of this Christ
Sovereignty over men; but let us first turn to the book
of nature for such facts as may lie hidden within the
metaphor of the Psalmist, and which may show us what
an idea of power the rainfall is competent to express.
"Unto the place," says the wise Preacher, " whence
the rivers come, thither they return again."†   In other
words, the waters of the Amazon, Mississippi, St. Law-

---

* Ps. lxxii. 1–8.   † Eccl. i. 7.

rence, of all the great rivers of America, Europe, and Asia, are lifted up by the atmosphere, and are continually flowing in invisible vapor streams back through the air to their sources among the hills.

Moreover, these invisible channels through which they flow are so regular, certain, and well defined that the quantity thus conveyed one year with the other is nearly the same, inasmuch as the amount of water discharged annually by each river is, as far as can be judged, nearly constant.   In view of this general statement we may form some conception of what a powerful machine the atmosphere must be; and though it is apparently so capricious and wayward in its movements, we see further that it gives evidence of order and arrangement, that it performs its mighty office with regularity and certainty, and is therefore as obedient to law as is the steam-engine to the will of its builder.   Indeed, as Lieut. Maury has remarked, it too is an engine.   The South Seas themselves with their vast intertropical extent are the boiler for that atmospheric engine, and the northern hemisphere is its condenser.*

Let us pass from this general statement to particulars, for which I am indebted to one of our own citizens, Mr. John Birkinbine, engineer.   Not to weary you with statistics and details, I will limit my illustrations to facts concerning the rainfall over the surface of Philadelphia alone, which is equal to about one hundred and twenty-nine and one-third square miles (accurately 129.373 square miles).   According to observations at the Pennsylvania Hospital, the average rainfall over the area of Philadelphia for fifty-seven years was forty-five and nineteen hundredths inches or three feet and seven hundred and sixty-six thousandths (3.766).   The average amount of rain falling upon the city is therefore equal to nearly one hundred and two billions four hundred and twenty-five millions of net tons weight.   This is about thirteen times the weight of the output of anthracite coal in the State of Pennsylvania during the year of our Lord 1886, that output having been thirty-three millions of gross

---

* Lieut. Maury—"Sailing Directions," vol. I., 1858, page 21.

tons. It is more than seventy-five times as much as the greatest annual production of iron in the State, which was nearly five and three-quarter millions of gross tons.

Descending from the annual rainfall to the estimate of a single heavy rain, we have these startling facts: On August 4th, 1885, there was a rainfall of four and forty-six hundredths inches. That means a downfall of more than ten billions of gallons upon the area of Philadelphia, weighing forty-two millions of tons. That single rain therefore deposited on the area of our city a weight of water greater by over twelve per cent. than the total amount of anthracite coal mined in 1886, or more than one-half of the weight of the total crop of corn, wheat, and oats in the United States during the same year.

The automatic recording water-gauge connected with the office of the Water Department at Thirteenth and Spring Garden streets, Philadelphia, showed that on the morning of November 18th, 1886, fifty-two hundredths or about one-half an inch of rain fell in nine minutes. Such a rainfall over the area of Philadelphia is equivalent to a flow of two hundred and ninety thousand cubic feet per second, which is fifteen thousand feet per second more than the average flow of water over the Falls of Niagara. Think of it, a little summer dash like that sets loose upon our roof-tops and streets a greater stream than pours from the mighty cataract of Niagara. Well may the street contractors bless the helpful rain that supplements their lagging efforts to fulfill their obligations to the city. Yet more may suffering citizens bless the healthful showers that sweep our streets, flush our sewers, purge our gutters, and bring us blessings of health and purity.

If you are not wearied with these immense sums, permit me to take one further example from the facts procured for us by our patient engineer. The total weight of water in the atmosphere surrounding the whole earth is estimated at the enormous figure of fifty-four thousand four hundred and sixty billions of tons. Of such a weight we can form no conception, much less realize how it can be held in suspension, and moved back and forth through the channels appointed for its distribution and circulation. But that problem, as we have seen, has been solved by the Almighty Mind and Power back of all nature's operations, and some elements of the forces which enter into the solution we are able at least approximately to determine. It is probable that the greatest proportion, perhaps five-tenths, of this vapory ocean within the atmosphere, is confined within a stratum or belt reaching to the height of six thousand five hundred feet above the level. Let us, however, assume the average height to which the vapor that is distilled upon Philadelphia as rain must be elevated from its source in the ocean, lakes, and running streams, to be ten thousand feet. Let us further take the familiar standard of thirty-three thousand pounds raised through one foot of height per minute as equal to one horse-power. We shall then reach the conclusion that to raise the amount of water contained in *one inch* of rainfall over the area of Philadelphia to a height of ten thousand feet requires nearly *four millions of horse-power*.

Have you any idea of the force represented in this sum total? It is greater than the total amount of steam and water power employed in all the manufacturing establishments of the United States as reported at the last census. So that the entire manufacturing industry of the republic has not sufficient power connected with it to raise in one day the water represented by *one inch* of rainfall upon the area of Philadelphia. This means that the whole steam and water power of the United States, if working together to that one end, could not furnish more than twelve per cent. or one-eighth of the force necessary to elevate the amount of rain which has fallen in *one day* over the area of Philadelphia.

Take another comparison. If we go back to that November dash of rain during which a little over one-half inch of water fell in nine minutes, we find that to raise an equal amount in the same time to the height of ten thousand feet, would require the development of three hundred and twenty-nine millions horse-power! In other words, the entire force which the cataract of Niagara could produce in *nine hours* would be scarcely sufficient to elevate to cloud level the water which fell on the city of Philadelphia in *nine minutes.**

I confess that when I first read these figures I was filled with amazement at the vast amount of power exercised by the sunbeams—for it all amounts to that—in pumping up vapor of water into the clouds, and the equally vast power which is represented in the natural force or forces that reduce this vapor of water and cause its precipitation upon the face of the earth. Yet why should we be surprised? At whatever point we may touch nature we shall find that it gives forth like facts to careful observation, intelligent thought, and the skillful hand. But I must pass now from these statistics, to those great spiritual lessons towards which our thoughts are tending, and for which alone these facts are here of paramount value to us. Are we to suppose that the Psalmist who used the rainfall as a figure of the dominion of the Christ, knew what vast ideas of force were covered up within his metaphor? Not at all; doubtless the inspired writers were often but dimly conscious of the great truths which they uttered in types and shadows, in parable and figure of speech. But nevertheless, the truth lay within their imagery and was known to the Divine Mind. History unfolded the meaning as the years rolled on, and we to-day may see better even than the prophets saw the sublime facts that lay concealed within their words. With our fuller view of the natural force expended by the rainfall and knowledge of the History of Christianity, we may here affirm that the Psalmist's prediction as declared under the imagery of the descending rain has been more than fulfilled. It was a new manifestation of power made by the Lord Jesus Christ, the power of religious· life, the power of an immortal hope, the power of holiness in the soul. The world learned through Christianity as it never had conceived before the kingship of the simple truth, the potency of purity, of love, of all spiritual ideas to sway the thinking and lives of men, and so in the end to bring nations into obedience to the sceptre of the Divine Teacher. We turn to History for examples of this fact.

---

*See a paper by Mr. John Birkinbine in "Franklin Institute Journal," vol. CXXIII., No. 735.

1. Christianity showed its power by revolutionizing society as to the nature and standing of woman. The bonds of a thousand generations fixed in the customs, laws, religion, and perhaps more strongly still, in the passions and avarice of men, were broken by the new power manifest in the Church of Christ. There was not a nation of the ancient world, with the single exception of the Hebrews, among whom women, as a class, held an honorable position, or in any wise approached companionship with man. Solon, the wise Greek, viewed woman as a household drudge, with whom rational intercourse and friendship were impossible. Aristotle regarded women as intermediate between freemen and slaves. The greatest of Hellenic philosophers declared that state radically disordered in which wives should claim to be equals of their husbands. Plato even went so far as to suggest a community of wives on the ground that children so brought into life would be wholly devoted to the state. Grecian women purchased the right to frequent public lectures, and associate on terms of equality with artists and scholars, only at the costliest price conceivable—their virtue. At Syracuse no free woman was allowed to go out after sunset except for immoral purposes. A woman was regarded always as a minor and never free. Pericles said that her glory was that no one should speak to her. Such was the standing of women with that people who were peerless in art, letters, and philosophy.

The same opinions and customs substantially prevailed among the Romans. It was a fundamental conception of the law at Rome that woman should never be independent. The legal status of the wife was that of a daughter, the sister of her own children. Her property became her husband's. Her consent was not necessary to the marriage of her daughters. The husband had at least a qualified power over her life for even petty offenses. She could not after his death be the legal guardian of her own infant children. Habitual and contemptuous distrust of the sex was in the very life of the governing classes. It ruled custom, shaped statutes, and entered with depraved and dominating force the highest minds.* She was the slave and toy of man, rarely his friend and companion, and never received honor, as Christian women count honor, except in the case of the vestal virgins. With the laws and customs of society thus hardly discriminating against her, it is not strange that the cruel foot of the strong sex had trampled her moral and intellectual nature into the very mud of an unspeakable social impurity, the cruelest wrong of all, and the most fatal in its consequences to the nation.

If Rome and Greece, foremost of the pagan nations in point of civilization, maintained this attitude towards women, you may readily conceive what was her position amongst the other nations of the world at the time that the Son of God became incarnate. What was the attitude of Christ and his apostles towards women? We know that "The Women Friends of Jesus" were among his most trusted and beloved followers. They were honored with his friendship, they received equally with their men friends the lessons of saving truth and wisdom which he spake. His attitude towards the sex was always and everywhere one of helpfulness and equality. His utterance upon marriage and divorce was a law of emancipation, and drew a protecting barrier around wifehood and motherhood. It sealed the sanctity of marriage. It proclaimed with divine sanction the law of monogamy, the right of one man to one wife only— the right of every wife to her husband alone.

This position was maintained by the apostles of Jesus. St. Paul was the most conspicuous champion of womankind among the founders of Christianity. He declared her equal with man before Christ. He labored for her conversion equally with that of man. The first converts made by him in Europe were women. He gave them a place in the Church as fellow-laborers, sharers even of the offices of the Church. The names of Lydia, Phœbe, Priscilla, the elect lady, and numbers of others mentioned in the New Testament with honor and applause show how Paul and the primitive Christians, in

---

* DR. STORRS—"The Divine Origin of Christianity Indicated by its Historical Effects," pages 148, *sqq.*

obedience to their Master's law, were revolutionizing
the ideas and customs of the pagan world concerning
the nature and standing of woman.

Indeed this action was the logical result of a fundamental principle of Christianity, viz., that spiritual powers are more than, or at least equal to mere physical
force; that the standard of one's position before God
and in the Church is neither sex, nor wealth, nor culture, nor social standing—but spiritual estate and attainments. Before the tribunal of Christian law there is
neither male nor female, bond nor free, Jew nor Gentile,
barbarian nor Scythian—all are one in Jesus Christ.
Women therefore were honored, loved, and respected,
because they possessed gifts of heart and mind equally
with man, although they were not equal in point of bare
physical force. This germinal thought, which at once
lifted society beyond the standard of mere brute force,
and fixed for the ideal of humanity a spiritual and intellectual character, operated inevitably to the exaltation
of womankind. All this seems very simple and easy as
we state it here. Christianity has educated us to regard
these principles as the simplest social axioms. We take
them as a matter of course. We can hardly conceive
how it had ever been or ever could have been otherwise; yet it was not without a mighty struggle that the
religion of Jesus Christ slowly permeated mankind,
weakened and at last broke the fetters of female oppression, and lifted woman to the place where Christ had
appointed and would keep her, side by side with man,
both in the Church of the Living God and "the Church
that is within the house." Think how much was involved in this! It is absolutely certain that under every
state of society the mind of women must shape the
character of childhood. As the child is but the "father
of the man," a degenerate mother means degenerate
children, degenerate society, a degenerate race. But
woman exalted, refined, purified, means the placing of a
regenerating and saving force at the very fountains of a
nation's worth. This Christ has done for women, this
He has done for the world.

It is not strange that in all ages of the world Jesus of

Nazareth has counted among his most devoted followers those who have received from his hands such inestimable blessings. Surely if ever Christianity is threatened by lax laws concerning the Sabbath, by laws that break down the sanctity of marriage relations, by the progress of scepticism and irreligion, woman's voice should be the first to raise the cry of alarm, and woman's hand should first advance the standard of Christ and rally to its defense. It is not strange that among the warmest friends of Foreign Missions are Christian women, whose hearts go out in tender pity towards their sisters in pagan lands still oppressed by customs and laws such as degraded the nations in the days of Jesus. "Woman's work for women" is wrought by a lofty love for Jesus, by a sense of gratitude for what He has done for them, and by the profoundest sisterly sympathy with those whose bonds are yet unbroken, and who never can feel the joy of deliverance until the mighty power of Jesus shall come down for the renovation of society like rain upon the wilderness.

2. Nothing perhaps gives us a better idea of the moral condition of a nation than the character of its general amusements. The pleasures of Rome for many years were excited by scenes of slaughter. The Roman gladiatorial combats stand well nigh alone and unequaled in human history for ferocity. The Coliseum, pictures of whose ruins are in many of your homes, which is the most imposing and characteristic relic of pagan Rome, was simply a theatre for the slaughter of human beings as a pastime, an amusement not only for the populace, but the noble men and ladies of high rank. These gladiators were trained athletes, captives of war, for the most part, who fought each other to death in the arena with net, dagger, lance, trident, and swords ground to the finest edge and point. At the triumph of Aurelian eight hundred pairs of gladiators fought. During the games of Trajan ten thousand men thus fought. Even female gladiators contended with each other. Sea battles were arranged, as by Cæsar, Augustus, and memorably by Claudius, who sent two fleets with nineteen thousand

men upon them to a desperate contest on Lake Fucinus, for the mere amusement of the throngs of spectators covering the surrounding shores.   Christians and other condemned prisoners were sometimes burned in shirts of pitch to illuminate the gardens, or were hung on crosses and left to be torn by famished bears for the amusement of the populace.   These horrible entertainments were varied by conflicts of wild beasts.   Under Nero four hundred tigers fought with elephants and bulls.   At the dedication of the Coliseum by Titus five thousand animals were killed.   " There is scarcely one element of horror," says Dr. Storrs, "which can be conceived in man's wildest dreams which was not presented as a matter of luxury to make complete the ' Roman Holiday ' at the time when Christianity entered the capital."*

Shocking as these. details must be to your sensibilities, I have only culled from authentic sources those which are least horrifying.   Remember now that these atrocities were not simply sporadic, occasional events, the result of some wild outburst of passion, prejudice, or bigotry. They were the habitual amusements of the people.   From the highest to the lowest they were indulged in and enjoyed to the full.   Amongst those who constantly witnessed them, and for whom seats were always reserved, were representatives of illustrious families, senators, judges, philosophers, poets, ladies of highest rank and breeding.   Even the vestal virgins in their sacred dress came there and sat in seats of honor to gaze upon the gladiatorial " shows."   The whole nation was mad after these scenes of blood.   Men and women, noble and base, all and all alike gloated over and glutted their cruel hearts upon deeds, the bare recital of which excites in us emotions of horror.   In holiday garb, surrounded by gay tapestry, amid festoons of flowers and statues of gods, while particolored awnings shone in the sun, and bright decorations fluttered in the wind, these women and men laughed, applauded, and shouted with joy to see these scores, hundreds, thousands of their fellow-creatures solely for the sport of spectators mutilating,

---

* "The Divine Origin of Christianity," page 259.

slaying each other in the space beneath them, until the arena ran red with blood!

The control of the civilized world was centered in the Empire of Rome. The destinies of Rome were in the hands of one man—Augustus Cæsar. He was at once commander-in-chief of the army, the head of the Senate abjectly obedient to his will, and the Pontifex Maximus of the state religion. The population of the capital city numbered two millions, one part of whom lived in misery, the other in almost boundless luxury. Well nigh one-half were slaves, and of the rest the greater part were either freedmen or their descendants, or foreigners. Bad as we know slavery to be from our own bitter experience with African bondage, it was far worse in Rome. Slaves were entirely unprotected. Males and females were exposed to nameless cruelties compared to which death by being thrown to wild beasts in the arena might seem absolute relief. Sick and old slaves were cast out to perish from want. The familiar story, which has been woven into well-known verses by one of our poets, of Parrhasius torturing to death a slave that he might have a model from which to put the true expression of a dying man upon his picture of Prometheus chained to the rocks of Mount Caucasus, is not bare fancy, but an apt expression of the actual condition of the relation between Roman masters and slaves. On the one side was uncontrolled cruelty and oppression, on the other unendurable hate, cunning, and corruption. The freedmen, who had often acquired their liberty by the most disreputable courses and had prospered in them, combined in shameless manner the vices of the free with the vileness of the slave. The foreigners poisoned the springs of life yet more by the corruption which they brought with them. The free citizens were idle, dissipated, sunken, engrossed mainly with the sports of the arena. They were mostly supported at the public cost, or were the clients, mere camp followers or paid retainers of great men.

Heartlessness towards the poor who crowded the city was a well-known feature of ancient Roman society. There was absolutely no provision for them. Hospitals were unthought of. Charity was a word yet unborn. To bestow alms upon the needy was regarded as only affording them the means of protracting a useless existence. The only escape that remained for these, and for all other miserables of the era, was self-destruction, and this was not only freely advised, but the terrible power was as freely exercised.

A few noble spirits of the times felt that this state of things was utterly hopeless. Society could not reform itself. Philosophy and religion had nothing to offer; they had been tried and found wanting. Seneca longed for some hand from without to lift up society from the mire of despair. Cicero pictures the enthusiasm which would meet the embodiment of true virtue should it ever appear on earth. Tacitus declared human life one great farce, and expressed his conviction that the Roman world lay under some terrible curse.*

Had religion no word to speak against such deeds? No! This oppression, impurity, and cruelty were wrought under the sanctions of religion.

Historians well know, although the people do not perhaps often think of it, that the deities of the nations among whom the Gospel was first preached, as Romans and Grecians, were notoriously selfish, cruel, and immoral. We dare not sully the ears of innocence by naming the character and service of some of their gods. Their worship was sin, a mania of lust; of their temples it could be said, " Her house is the way of hell, going down to the chambers of death." A great horror fills the soul as one thinks that these were the gods whom children and youth, young men and maidens, matrons and men were taught to adore.

The only religion on which the state insisted was the deification and worship of the emperor. Not only emperors, but their wives, paramours, children, and the creatures of their vilest lusts were deified. Nay, any private person might attain that distinction if the survivors possessed sufficient means. The most abject superstition dominated the fears of the populace. The

* EDERSHEIM—"The Life and Times of Jesus the Messiah." Vol I., page 258.

priests practiced unblushing impostures upon the people. Superstition and fraud went hand in hand with blasphemy, and one might read everywhere such sentiments as this inscribed upon the tomb of a child, "To the unjust gods who robbed me of life ; " or this on the tomb of a girl of twenty, " I lift my hands against the god who took me away innocent as I am." * The idea of conscience, as we understand it, was unknown to this seething mass of heathenism. Absolute right did not exist. Might was right.

We must keep before us this picture of the world to which Christ came, and we would have a just view of the meaning to the men and women of that era of such Scriptures as these: "The Son of Man is come to seek and to save *that which is lost !*" † " Pure religion and undefiled before God and the Father is this, to visit the fatherless and the widows in their affliction, and to keep himself unspotted from the world." ‡

Conceive, if you can, the coming of the Holy Evangel to such a people. Think how its presentation of an infinitely Holy God, who could look upon sin with no degree of allowance, must have been regarded. Imagine what a revolution in all their thinking upon the Divine and moral duty must have followed the acceptance of the doctrine and worship of a Saviour, who demanded Love, Kindness, Peace, Purity! The Gospel of Christ was not only a revelation, but a revolution. It emancipated Woman. It gave Childhood a holy status in society. It quenched in Brotherly Love the cruelty of the arena. It enthroned Purity in the home and Sanctuary. It lifted Religion from the mire, and reclothed her with Holiness and Authority. It built an altar for Faith upon the human heart, and amid the ashes of despair rekindled the Hope of a blessed Immortality. It conquered human prejudice and passions as they had never been subdued before, and that in their deadliest array within their strongest citadel. All this the Gospel did; and this it did by the Power of Jesus the Christ. Yes, from the midst of the wreck of the hoary and colossal in-

---

* EDERSHEIM—"The Life and Times of Jesus." † Luke xix. 10. ‡ James i. 27.

iquities of the age, the voices of Christ's foes might be heard saluting the Church rising in glorious form from out the ruins, and crying in the language of the apostate Julian, " Thou hast conquered, O Nazarene ! "

This is the faithful testimony of History. May we not stand justified in view thereof in saying that even from the standpoint of our modern knowledge of the immense natural force expended by the rainfall, the Psalmist's prediction of the power of Christ's kingdom made under the figure of the falling rain, has been more than fulfilled ? There are two practical lessons rising out of our theme that invite attention.

1. The first is a lesson of courage in the face of modern attacks upon Christianity. Christian men and women, standing here with hands full of these proofs of the power of our Holy Religion to sway nations and eras, will you lose courage before any foe of Christ? Will you be turned aside from the path of triumph which stretches across the ages past and leads forward into the conquests of coming time? Ah! it is said, "we must yield to the tendencies of the times." Yield? Who then is He who seized the tendencies of ancient Greece and Rome and swayed them here and there as the pilot turns his ship? Do you know His Name? Have you heard, have you felt His Power? Ah! you hear it said, "we must accept the laws of Progress!" Well, that colossal Figure who towers above every horizon of modern history, whithersoever we turn, and holds aloft the sceptre that has swayed forces which have set forward the race along the paths of its noblest action and destiny, He is the world's True Lawgiver! He alone holds the reins of safe advancement, and His are the chariot wheels that shall mark out for man the highway to his furthest and loftiest progress.

Do not be deceived! "The tendency of the times," "Law of progress," are vain phrases by which to forecast the future and determine your duty. There is a ship driving across the stormy Atlantic. Her prow is towards Europe. Now she is crossing the Gulf Stream, whose tendencies are towards the south. Will she turn her head from Europe, and follow the trend of the Gulf Stream southward? I trow not! On she goes. Now she has steamed into the storm belt. The winds are from the south-east, and they are sweeping up towards Labrador. Strong tendencies in that rough south-east wind towards yon north-west coast! Will the captain turn his vessel's beak from Europe, and follow those tendencies? Not he! There is a chart in the captain's room, on which is marked out the vessel's way like a line—a great parallel from port to port. There is a chart in the steering-room too, and the quarter-master at the wheel has his eye upon the course which the sailing-master has given him. "East. East-by-north. East-by-south. East!" So he reads, and steers the vessel along the parallel which the captain has marked for him.

"Law of progress," forsooth! "Tendencies of the times," indeed! Do not seek them in the winds, the waves, the currents of this storm-tossed ocean of life! There is our Divine Captain, and here are our chart and sailing directions. Christ is our Captain, and, oh! a mighty and all-wise Pilot has He been. He knows the way and all its turns and terrors. The winds and the waves obey His will. Peace, then, O troubled hearts; be still! His hand is on the wheel; the Bible is in your hands; consult and consider that as your sure authority and guide, and all will be safe. Christ and his laws override and direct all tendencies of nations and men, and aside from these there never has been and never will be any permanent progress.

2. Our second lesson is one of confidence in carrying our Lord's Gospel to heathen nations, and in using it as the sovereign remedy for the social evils of our own land. What has been done, can again be done. Jesus Christ is the Same yesterday, to-day, and forever. Human nature is changeless in its fundamental tendencies and wants. Simply, the conditions of mankind have changed. The old sorrows, the old sins, the old conflicts are here still. The old hard, world-powers and devils of self, on the one hand, and on the other the poor, the ignorant, and they that are out of the way; on the

one hand the cruel heart and heavy hand of Pride, on the other the wail of feebleness, the moan of heart-brokenness, the shriek of despair; these old, old forces, follies, miseries are all here and everywhere to-day where men live, struggle, die. And here, too, blessed be God! is " the old, old Story of Jesus and His Love!" Here is the Hand of Almightiness, clothed with the tenderness of Divine Pity, down reached to draw all men unto the Infinite Fatherhood. That old Story is as new, fresh, potent as ever. That Hand is still omnipotent to Save, and it is stretched out still. Have confidence in the Gospel to do the work of human Salvation! It is able—for He its Divine Author is Able even to the uttermost. Trust Him; use Him for others' saving; yes, O Sinner, and for your own! Reach up thy trembling handling from whatever weakness and loss to the Almighty Hand whose very wounds bespeak his yearning love, and suffer Him to lift you up and lead you on, out of this Wilderness into the World of Eternal refreshing and peace.

LECTURE XI.

Showers of Blessing.

"*There shall be showers of blessing.*"—EZEKIEL
xxxiv. 26.

SHOWERS OF BLESSING.

WHEN the Children of Israel were led out from Egyptian bondage, they had the hope set before them of a land of promise which should be enriched with the dews and rains of heaven. That portion of Egypt, the land of Goshen, in which the Israelites dwelt, was not an infertile land, as is abundantly proved by the ancient remains continually being uncovered therein, but its fertility was the result of irrigation. The waters of the Nile were made to do service in irrigating the soil, watering the plants precisely as the waters of the Platte and Arkansas rivers are made to serve a like purpose in Colorado to-day. The change from Egypt to Palestine was in this respect a very great one. From a land which was flat, sandy, and well nigh, although not wholly rainless, they passed to a country of mountains, valleys, hills, running streams, and regular seasons of rain.

In a country of so diversified surface as Palestine, one would naturally expect considerable difference in climate. From the sandy section in the extreme south to the rugged mountains of Galilee in the north; from the low plains of Jericho, which lie in the deep trench of the Jordan, to the lofty slopes of Lebanon and Hermon and the elevated hills round about Jerusalem, the contrast is very great as to elevation, and hence also as to climate. In considering the rainfall of Palestine allowance must therefore be made for these local variations in surface. Allowance must also be made, it is probable, for the great difference between the condition of Palestine at present and its ancient condition. The diminution of vegetation from the entire land, the disappearance of vineyards and wheat fields from the mountain slopes and valleys, but above all the denudation of the mountainous heart of the land of its forest growth, must largely have affected the rainfall.

(199)

Palestine is suffering to-day just as the United States is beginning to suffer, and in the future will suffer far more unless the foolish and wicked policy which permits the wasteful use—I might almost have said, the murderous slaughter—of our native forests, be soon stayed. With the disappearance of trees and vegetables, Palestine has become exposed in a greater degree than in early times to the evils of drought.* The maximum rainfall in the vicinity of Jerusalem is scarcely sufficient at the present time to justify the statements as to the fertility of the land which we have in ancient history.† The principal dependence of the inhabitants of Jerusalem for water for domestic uses is the rain collected in cisterns from the roofs and terraces of their houses, and the greatest diligence and care are required to secure enough for the public comfort.

With these allowances it may be stated generally, that in Palestine the whole period from October to March constitutes one continued season of rain without any regularly intervening term of prolonged fair weather. The rest of the year is comparatively rainless, and the land becomes dry and chapped. The early and the latter rains, therefore, of which we read frequently in Scripture, for which the husbandmen waited with longing, seem to have been the first showers of autumn which revived the parched and thirsty earth and prepared it for the seed, and the latter showers of spring which continued to refresh and forward both the ripening crops and the vernal products of the field.‡

The autumnal rains are the "former" early rains of Scripture, and usually commence about the beginning of November. They come mostly from the west or south-west, continuing for two or three days at a time, and falling especially during the night. The rains continue with greater or less severity during the entire winter, when the roads, or, more properly speaking, trails or tracks in Palestine become muddy, deep, and slippery.‡ As the winter draws to a close the rains

---

* STANLEY—"Sinai and Palestine," page 121. † WILSON & WARREN—"The Recovery of Jerusalem," pages 20–21. ‡ ROBINSON—"Researches," vol. I., 429. James v. 7. Prov. xvi. 15.

become less frequent, but occasional showers, very much like our warm spring rains, fall during the month of March, and even in the early April. These are the "latter" rains which are especially grateful and helpful in forwarding the growing crop and developing the ripening grain.*

I. We turn from these natural details that lie within the imagery of our text to mark the divine lesson which it enfolds: The Coming of Jesus Christ to the world has vastly increased Human Blessedness.

The blessings that follow the rainfall have been thus happily expressed by the Psalmist :—

> 9 Thou dost visit the earth and waterest her ;
> Abundantly dost Thou enrich her.
> The river of God was full of water,
> For thus Thou preparedst the earth,
> And providest for men their grain,
> 10 Watering the furrows of the land,
> Softening the ridges thereof ;
> Thou makest her soft with showers,
> Thou blessest the increase thereof.
>
> 11 Thou crownest the year of Thy goodness,
> And thy pathways drop with fatness,
> 12 The wilderness pastures drip,
> And the hills gird themselves with joy ;
> 13 The meadows Thou clothest with flocks,
> And the valleys are mantled with grain ;
> Everything shouts for joy,
> Everything everywhere sings.†

The sterility of the world in the chief elements of true happiness at the coming of Christ is fearful to contemplate. The masses of mankind were joyless. There was laughter, indeed—the laughter which is as the crackling of thorns under the pot;‡ the mournful utterance of a life whose very substance and vitality were being consumed in the fires of passion and vice. But of that peace which is as a river—deep, pure, silent, broadening toward the end, where life enters the limitless ocean of eternity— of that there was very little. Christianity gave to multitudes that peace, and brought the possibility thereof to

---

* ROBINSON—" Researches," vol. III., page 9.   † Ps. lxv. 9-13.
‡ Eccl. vii. 6.

all the race. It found society a parched and barren waste; it caused the wilderness to drip, the desert to blossom, and parched and barren hearts it mantled with the richest livery of hope. It gave beauty for ashes, the oil of joy for mourning, the garment of praise for the spirit of heaviness.*

It has been said, perhaps often thought, that the example of Christ has impressed upon the human race a character of over-sobriety; that Christianity has thrown a sombre hue upon men; that the life of ordinary persons cannot be as Christ's was, and if it were so it would blight the very sweetest blossoms of mortal life. What ground is there for such an opinion or assertion? There is none at all that one can mark out with any definiteness. It means nothing to point us to the lives and teachings of ascetics, hermits, monks, nuns, and sour-visaged and atrabilious representatives of the gloomy features of the religious life in whatever age, or under whatever form of Christianity. Do you tell me that these people express the true Christianity? No! Their religion is as little like the original as the mimic flowers that caterers carve out of turnips and carrots to garnish a baked fowl or a boiled ham, are like the dear old-fashioned pinks and pansies of our mothers' flower-beds!

Such forms of religion are rather a transfusion into the pure healthy blood of Christianity from the dark, superstitious, and doleful forms of pagan faiths. I do not mean to say that there was no brightness in paganism, especially as represented by the gods of ancient Rome and Greece. There was much of that; but on the other hand there was a great deal of gloom; much that sprang from and ministered to terror, fear, and all the baser passions and emotions of human nature; and it is that spirit and temper which has been introduced into Christianity, and thus has made it in the minds of many persons a religion of gloom. But there is no need to be deceived by spurious and alien ideas of this sort.

There is an old tradition that our Lord Jesus Christ was often seen to weep, but never to smile. I do not

* Isa. lxi. 3.

believe it ! Christ was one who loved little children, who took them in his arms and blessed them. He noticed their plays, for once he drew a metaphor from a merry group that "played wedding" with mimic pipes and dances to their playmates, who perversely would not laugh. Then they "played funeral," making the plaintive wailings of Oriental burials, but with equal but opposite perverseness the young audience refused to "lament." Did you ever know a man who loved little children to be after the fashion of a wooden image ? Can you think of one habitually fondling these dear buds of humanity and remaining smileless and grim as an automaton, or the waxen figures in a Jarley show? I cannot think it, and I do not believe it of Christ. I picture Jesus of Nazareth as a cheerful, mild, and pleasant, although serious and vigorous character; in short, an ideal man in all his manly and lovable qualities. Now, honest laughter and pure mirthfulness belong to manhood.

Moreover, the Gospels tell us that the holy Angels sang at Jesus' birth, and made the heavens above Bethlehem's plain ring with their hallelujahs. He Himself told us that there is joy in heaven over one sinner that repenteth. His picture of himself is that of a Shepherd who has found his lost sheep, and brings it home on his shoulders " rejoicing," and who calls his friends and neighbors together, saying, " Rejoice with me, for I have found my sheep which was lost !" He pictures to us the family of God, the Holy Father Himself as one who welcomes home a prodigal son with all the tokens of gladness and mirthfulness, bidding musicians and dancers to be hired, and a feast prepared, saying, " Let us eat and make merry ! for this my son was dead and is alive again; he was lost and is found.* It was meet to make merry and be glad." To the end of his days Jesus bore this cheerful spirit. When His feet were standing on the very brink of the River of Death, when He could reach out His hand and almost touch the cross of his Passion, we read this sentence, " Ye shall be sorrowful, but your sorrow shall be turned into joy." Again he said, " Ask

* Luke xv. 24.

and ye shall receive, that your joy may be full." Even in His last intercessory prayer, when He was pouring out His heart in the agony of desire to God ere He went across the brook Kedron to the agony of Gethsemane, He introduced this sentence, " But now I come to Thee; and these things I speak in the world, that they may have my joy fulfilled in themselves."*   Let this suffice.   It is impossible for us to think of such a Teacher as a smile-less, joyless man, or to believe that his Religion can be intended to throw shadows over human lives by darkening the light of gladness and silencing the voice of mirth.   Oh, no! "Speak ye comfortably to Jerusalem!" —that is the mission of Christianity.   "Comfort ye, comfort ye my people!"—that is the voice of the Christ ever crying in the midst of the desert of this world.

That the Primitive Church faithfully fulfilled this mission there is no doubt.   The Religion of Jesus brought balm to the wounded hearts and weary, burden-worn shoulders of an era when humanity was bitterly oppressed.   The voice of infinite compassion called not in vain, "Come unto me, all ye that labor and are heavy laden, and I will give you rest!"   The masses of the nations—"the common people," were covered by the terms of that Divine Invitation, and "the Common People heard Him gladly."   Alas! the Church and the Christian State have too often misrepresented their Lord and His Holy Religion, and have been oppressors not relievers of humanity.   But whatever have been the sins of some, the Many have never misread the Gentle Shepherd's Heart.   Men in every age have known that Jesus is the Friend of the Miserable, and have turned to Him for refreshing.   He has never failed them, but has come down like rain upon the meadow-grass to quicken dying hopes, and cause life's wilderness places to blossom and be fragrant with the sweetness of Sharon's Rose.

II. Let us turn our thought into a more practical channel and ask, how does Christ confer blessings upon men?   What is the gift that lies at the fountain head of

---

*John xvii. 13.·

all those streams which enrich human life? In other words, how may man obtain blessedness?

Our Lord Jesus Christ gave an answer to this question from the slopes of a mountain in Palestine, to which his reply has given the name, "The Mount of Beatitudes." The Sermon upon the Mount has challenged the attention of thinking men throughout the last nineteen centuries. It presents an unequaled summary of the great ethical truths upon which the system of Christianity rests. A reading of this sermon shows that the controlling motives of life, according to Christ, should be Holiness and Helpfulness. The sermon deals with human duty, first subjectively, presenting the spiritual graces which men should seek to cultivate, such as inward peace of heart, humility, meekness, purity, righteousness, mercy, firmness, and self-denial for the truth. In the second place it treats the subject objectively, that is, in its relations to the world outside of one's own heart. It urges the duty of active benevolence; it bids men become a blessing to their fellows, by illumining them with the light of truth—"ye are the light of the world;" by savoring them into healthful life—"ye are the salt of the earth." Thus, the Sermon upon the Mount may be resolved into a presentation, first, of those aims or ends which express an inward condition of soul; and, second, those which express an outward and beneficent relation to men. Such are in a few words the principles which may be taken fairly to represent the manner in which Christianity deals, or should deal, with the problem, How may men become blessed? We may obtain a juster valuation of these principles by exhibiting them in contrast with some of the prominent theories of the present day which deal with the problem of human happiness.

The apostle of modern theories of evolution is not Dr. Darwin, as most persons, perhaps, suppose, but Herbert Spencer. Mr. Darwin was a naturalist. Herbert Spencer is a philosopher; and to him, more than any thinker among English-speaking men, is to be charged the perversion of evolutionary theories into an agency destructive of Christianity. Mr. Spencer says,* "No

* Data of Ethics, page 46.

school can avoid taking for the ultimate moral aim a desirable state of feeling, called by whatever name—gratification, enjoyment, happiness." Again, he says, "If we call *good* the conduct conducive to life, we can only do so with the implication that it is conducive to a balance of pleasures over pains." Says an American writer of the same school,* "morality or goodness is not the prize of life. That prize is happiness, and morality only furnishes the negative conditions." Says Miss Bevington, the English positivist: "Every one else knows and affirms, and no positive moralist attempts to deny, that virtuous conduct is only to be achieved at all for the sake of what lies beyond it."—That is to say, for the sake of the happiness which it produces.

Again, let us contrast the great aims of life announced by Jesus in the Sermon on the Mount with the doctrines of Nihilism, which are to-day in whole or in part receiving the assent of multitudes of our fellow-men. The late Michael Bakunin, the father of Nihilism, said: "Brethren, I come to announce unto you a new gospel, which must penetrate to the very ends of the earth. This gospel admits of no half measures and hesitations. The *Lie* must be stamped out and give way to the truth." I almost hesitate to continue the quotation, but when Satan comes in among the sons of God it is well for us at times to hear what he has to say, that we may know not only how to answer, but to avoid him. "The first lie," says Bakunin, "is God. The second lie is right * * * might, my friends, forms the sole groundwork of society, and when you have freed your minds from the fear of a God, and from that childish respect for the fiction of right, then all the remaining chains which bind you, and which are called science, civilization, property, marriage, morality, and justice, will snap asunder like threads. Let your own happiness be your only law. But in order to get this law recognized, and to bring about the proper relations which should exist between the majority and minority of mankind, you must destroy everything which exists in the shape of State or social organization—our first work must be the

---

* Quoted in the Nineteenth Century Review by Mr. Mallock.

destruction, the annihilation, of everything as it now exists * * * Take heed that no ark be allowed to rescue any atom of this world which we now consecrate to destruction—now we Nihilists say, no law, no religion—Nihil!"* Nothing!

Surely, in view of these contrasts and comparisons, which show us unmistakably the superiority of our Lord Jesus Christ as a moral teacher, we will not be disposed to turn away from Him to any other, If, then, we put the question, How shall man be blessed? we can do no better than accept what Christ has taught, namely, that man shall be blessed, first, by cultivating a holy life, second, by devoting his life to the blessing of others.

1. Consider for a moment the first of these paths to blessedness, securing a holy life. "Blessed are the pure in heart." There is an old saying, "Virtue is its own reward." I have seen it more than once held up to ridicule, and yet it is profoundly true. Virtue, which is but another name for holiness, has to be pursued for its own sake, not for the sake of the happiness which may result. Of course, one is glad to receive whatever happiness may ensue, but virtue should be practiced because it is right. This is a great fortification against temptation. Is one assailed by popular clamor that would urge him into evil courses, that would force him upon a path contrary to conscience and righteousness, by threats that if he do not hearken to the voice of the mob his social or political prospects shall be blighted, his happiness threatened? Surely it is an anchorage to a soul blown upon by such a tempest, to be able and willing to say, as Henry Clay once said so nobly, "I had rather be right than President." We might have learned such a lesson even from a pagan philosopher. Was it not Cicero who said: "Socrates is my friend, Plato is my friend, but more than either my friend is TRUTH?"† Surely it does give strength to one whose faith and virtue are assailed by inducements to unrighteous dealings, held out through prospects of large gains in business, to

---

* Quoted from MR. CUNLIFFE OWEN's paper on Nihilism in the Nineteenth Century Review, January, 1880. † Socrates amicus, Plato amicus, sed magis amica veritas.

be convinced that purity is better than prosperity, that
unsullied manhood is better than happiness; that it
shall profit a man nothing if he gain the whole world
and lose his own soul. Surely it does fortify the tempted
soul to be able to appeal from the false and unfriendly
judgments of men to the judgments of Him whose righteousness never faileth; to turn aside from the perishing
crowns of this world to that great reward, that unfading
crown, which is in reserve for those who walk in garments of white, keeping them unspotted from the world.
In short, blessedness, according to the creed of Christ,
consists primarily in the attainment of a pure heart; it is
a question of what am I? not of what have I?

2. The second source of blessedness which Christ
holds out is beneficence, the act of blessing others.

"Ye are the salt of the earth," He said to His disciples.
Your life must consist in active seasoning of all untrue,
unkind, and corrupt aims, ideas, and acts; in continually
saving those who without your influence would surely
perish. "Ye are the light of the world," he said. Your
duty is to stand as a lamp in the midst of darkness, illu-
minating the passer-by and shedding radiance upon the
homes within the circuit of your shining. In such actions you shall find true happiness. If ye know these
things," said the Master, "happy are ye if ye do them."

Christians sometimes fail of blessedness because they
do not see its close relation to being a blessing.

A parishioner once sought advice of Dr. Alexander.
He was under a cloud, and could find no comfort in the
discharge of religious duty. The Doctor said to him:
"Do you pray?" "Yes, I spend whole nights in
prayer." "How do you pray?" "I pray," was the answer "that the Lord would lift the light of his countenance upon me, and grant me peace." "Go," said Dr.
Alexander, "and pray God to glorify His name, and to
convert sinners to Himself." The prescription met the
case. The man found blessedness in bestowing it.

Canon Liddon has remarked in one of his sermons that
love is greater than knowledge, and that he who can
make love grow among men deserves a higher benedic-

tion than he who only brings to them intellectual enlightenment. Speaking to an academical audience in England, he said, "As compared with knowledge, love is a stronger thing, and its worth more practical as an abstract existence. To enwrap other men, perhaps multitudes, in the flame of a passionate enthusiasm for private or public virtue is better than to analyze in the solitude of a study rival systems of ethical and political truths." This is a true Christian philosophy, yet there is no need to separate knowledge and love, for Christ has both to give. Christ enkindles and bestows at once the love of truth and the love of man. This is his great gift, his benediction to the world. This, as He Himself declared to the Roman knight, Pilate, in the judgment hall, is his true royal mission, given Him by his Father, a real token of His earthly kingship. "To this end was I born. For this end came I into the world that I might bear witness to the truth."

Go forth, then, Christian people, in obedience to the spirit and word of Jesus, to bless a miserable race with all the spiritual gifts of God, and with the hope of immortality. Mankind needs this. You need it. You have found Christianity a source of moral strength in conflict with sin and necessities. Its support has nurtured you, inspired you to endurance and action. It has blessed your life, helped you to your highest successes, rescued you from most threatening perils. Let the blessing be passed over to others in the name of Him who is the giver of every perfect gift. To-day the Church and world understand better, perhaps, than ever, that Jesus Christ came among men as a Friend. By that Holy Name which you bear I urge you to be true to the mission of Christianity, and give all the forces of your life to broaden the zone of human happiness, and limit and contract to its very minimum the belt of human misery and sin.

Salvation is free! Yes, it is, thank God! Water is free. How it bubbles from the mountain spring, and laughs down the mountain sides, making musical notes as it ripples over rocks, runs under ferns, and finds its way to the flowery meadow. There is not a bird twittering from the boughs that overhang it, not a squirrel barking on the branches above it, not a beast in all those tangled woods, nor creeping thing, that may not come and quench its thirst at the mountain brook. There is not a flower, shrub, or reed along the banks, or blue-tinted flag, or waving tuft of grass with banner of green leaf "hanging half-mast high," that may not send down its rootlets, or bend down its head, and freely drink. The stream sweeps onward to the river, and the river courses by yon teeming city. There is not a child or woman or man who may not go down to its limpid currents to drink, or bathe, or take the waters freely, even to satiety, for domestic and personal use. Water is free! What under heaven is freer, unless it be the air?

Stop a moment! Go to the gate of our beautiful Park; enter the Fairmount water-works, and look at the splendid machines whose mighty whir and thug are forcing the water—free water—of the Schuylkill through scores of miles of mains and pipes into all the factories, shops, churches, hospitals, and homes of Philadelphia. Water is free! But—when you pay your yearly water-tax you observe that it takes a good deal of money to deliver free water to your doors!

We do well to speak of the freedom of salvation, the freedom of the blessed offers of Christ through the Church, but forget not that the *machinery* by which the Water of Life is to be borne to the thirsty and impure is *not* free, but, on the contrary, is very costly. Therefore it is becoming that those who are the children of God should yield of their substance liberally, that "free salvation" may be brought to those who most are in need of it. God has given you power; social power, intellectual power, physical vigor, the mighty force of sympathy—heart power; yes, "It is He that giveth thee power to get wealth." * Use all these Divine gifts as stewards of God in Christ, remembering well and always that here, day by day, in this life as well as in the Day of Final Judgment, you must "Give an account of thy stewardship."

There is also a lesson here for those who have never

---

* Deut. viii. 18.

yet allied their lives in faith with the Son of God.
Surely the knowledge of the Divine Goodness should
lead you to repentance. Ought not the blessings of
Christ to stir you up to grateful action? God certainly
expects that result. In one striking passage in Isaiah,
in which the Lord describes His purposed blessings
under the metaphor of showers of rain, He declares
that the result shall be a consecration of men to Him, a
solemn devoting of their lives to His service, a holy joy
and pride in the fellowship and name of His spiritual
children.

> 3 I will pour water on him that is thirsty,
> And floods upon the dry ground;
> I will pour my Spirit upon thy seed,
> And my blessing upon thine offspring.

> 4 And they shall spring up among the grass
> As willows by the water courses.

> 5 And one shall say, "I am the Lord's!"
> Another shall call by the name of Jacob,
> Another subscribe with his hand, "To the Lord!"
> And surname himself by the Name of Israel.*

Has not your Heavenly Father a right to expect like
issues from his goodness toward you? Does He not expect such? Will you disappoint such loving and reasonable desires? He is not far from any one of you, and
He stands offering you all the blessedness of a purified
life, a pardoned soul, and Paradise at last. Will you accept his offer? Will you believe, and be safe and happy
eternally? How *can* you darken your soul against the
light and vision of this merciful Saviour and His offered
blessing?

One summer evening, while stopping in a beautiful
suburban home not far from our city, I was told this
story by one who had lately been an inmate of the house.
A maiden some sixteen years of age had all her life been
the unconscious victim of a blemish in her eyes that
hindered perfect vision. A surgical operation was finally
agreed upon, and successfully made. The girl was kept
within the house until her eyes gathered full strength,
and was permitted gradually and sparingly to go out-

---

* Isaiah xliv. 3–5.

doors. It so happened that some time elapsed after her recovery before she went into the open air after nightfall. One evening she rushed into the parlor, with face aglow with excitement. The joy of a great discovery illumined every feature. "Oh, come!" she exclaimed, "come out quickly to the lawn, and see what beautiful things have appeared in the sky!"

Her friends hastily followed her out of doors, wondering what might have occurred. They saw nothing! "What do you mean?" they asked the maiden.

"Look!" she said, pointing eagerly heavenward, "don't you see those bright things up there? They are there —and there—sparkling all over the sky!"

"My dear child," one who loved her said softly, "those are *the stars!*"

Yes, the stars, which she had never seen before! Friends could hardly take in the fact that for all the years of her life the dear child had been moving through God's world with a limited vision, seeing only what lay close around her, utterly oblivious that there were stars, hosts of stars, all over the sky, and all so very beautiful. How strange it seemed!

I think of something far more strange—ay, and pitiful! Oh, souls of men, heaven is full of shining lights that God has hung out to charm the pathway to His eternal home, to lure you upward, to show you how far eternity exceeds time in beauty, how far heaven rises beyond earth in value and glory. Yet, O my friends, your eyes are still withholden! You do not see, you do not comprehend, you will not look, and suffer your soul to be filled with the glory of heaven and God. Oh, for the hand of Him who opened the eyes of the blind when He walked this world, to touch your soul and give you sight of these realities! He *is* here!—verily here, near you, close beside you, willing to fill your life with the blessings of His grace, blessings which everywhere overhang you and only await your acceptance. Kneel before Him! Pray Him to anoint your eyes with eye-salve, that you may see! Then lo! the heavens and the earth, the present and the future, will break forth before you, radiant with the quenchless stars of immortal hope

LECTURE XII.

The Bow in the Cloud.

"And the bow shall be in the cloud; and I will look upon it, that I may remember the everlasting covenant between God and every living creature of all flesh that is upon the earth."—GENESIS ix. 16.

THE BOW IN THE CLOUD.

It sometimes happens during a morning or afternoon shower that the sun bursts forth from behind a cloud while drops of rain are yet falling through the air. If, at that moment, the observer stands with his back to the sun he will see upon the opposite heavens, beneath the passing rain-cloud, the beautiful phenomenon known as the rainbow. The physical origin of this lovely creature of Nature was unknown to the ancients, but has been explained in modern times by students of the laws of optics.

In order to understand this explanation, several facts must be taken for granted. First, sunlight is a mixture composed of seven heterogeneous kinds of light known as the primary colors—red, orange, yellow, green, blue, indigo, and violet. These indeed may be reduced to three, which according to Professor James Clark Maxwell are vermilion, ultramarine, and emerald green.*

Second, certain objects known as prisms have the power of decomposing sunlight into these primary colors; and when thus separated in their order they are commonly called the solar spectrum.

Third, the fact that the spectrum appears as we see it, the colors arranged one above another in the order named, is due to their different degrees of refrangibility or capacity to be broken from a direct line when passing through the prism. The ray that is least broken, red, will be outermost, and so on in order until that which is most deflected, violet, will be at the other extreme of the spectrum.

Now a rainbow is a circular spectrum. What are the prisms which have produced it, and how is it produced? The spherical drops of water falling out of the rain-

---

*See Contributions to Science, page 473, in Life of James Clark Maxwell, with diagram.

cloud become in fact prisms, within which the rays of light are separated into their primary colors. A ray falls upon the outer surface of the drop, is refracted or broken from the direct line as it passes through, is then reflected from the opposite inner surface back to the convexity nearest the observer, and passing out of the drop is once more refracted and so falls upon the observer's eye as a single color of the spectrum. The eye is so placed as to receive but one of the colors from any one drop, but from the other falling drops it receives the remaining colors.

Let us divide these innumerable drops into seven vast army corps. Each corps will include the drops which produce one of the seven primary colors, and the uniform of that corps shall be red, green, blue or other color according to its order. You must see that all the individuals of this army corps will be mustered together in one great line of parade stretching around the sky. For since every ray of any one color, red, for example, when passing through its raindrop prism is broken from the direct line at the same angle of refraction, all those rays must occupy the same relative position to the horizon, and so the myriad of red points joined one to another will appear as an extended line before the observer. Next to this line of red will stretch the battle line of that army corps which wears the orange uniform; and so on through all the seven corps of colors, until at last we shall see the whole united host mustered rank on rank in beautiful and orderly dress parade over the black background of the receding cloud.

It would be impossible, perhaps, in a popular discourse like this, to explain the mathematical principles upon which the various colors are so disposed as to form a circular spectrum. It will be enough to state that the appearance of parallel rays of homogeneous light thus reflected and refracted, would naturally be that of a bright circle whose centre is opposite to the source of light, and whose radius is, for raindrops, about 42° 2'.* Second, the different kinds of homogeneous light which

---

* Art. "Light," Encyclopædia Britannica ; Ed. ixth.

make up sunlight, would together produce a circular spectrum of which the less refrangible rays are on the outside. Third, we have an infinite series of such arrangements superimposed upon one another, the centre of each individual being at the point diametrically opposite the point of the sun's disk which produced it. Thus the immense number of falling raindrops, receiving the immense number of passing sun-rays, produce an immense number of colored images which are blended into one band or ribbon of color stretching around the sky. As the primary colors are seven, there will be seven of these circular bands arranged one above another in the natural order of their refrangibility.

Sometimes two distinct bows are visible, one within the other. The inner one is called the primary bow, and is the brighter of the two. The primary bow is due to rays falling on the outer portion of the drops which suffer two refractions and one reflection before reaching the eye. The secondary bow, which is the fainter of the two, is due to rays falling on the inner portion of the raindrop and suffering two refractions and two reflections. In the primary bow the arrangement of the colors is the same as in the solar spectrum. In the secondary bow this order is reversed.

Rainbows differ in intensity of brightness, which fact is produced by the overlapping of the colors. This is occasionally so greatly exaggerated that only faint traces of color appear. This may happen, for instance, when the sun shines on raindrops in the lower strata of the atmosphere through clouds of ice-crystals in the higher strata. By reflection from the faces of these crystals the source of light is spread over a much larger spherical angle. The rainbow is then much broader and fainter than usual, and nearly white. The size of the drops of rain also produces modifications in the intensity of color. Bows formed by moonlight are called lunar rainbows, and are rarely seen.

The lunar rainbow, which is a very beautiful phenomenon, differs from the solar simply in the source and intensity of the light by which it is produced; and, as in all cases of feeble light, the distinction of the colors is very difficult. In fact, except under the most favorable circumstances, the lunar rainbow rarely shows colors at all, giving a pale ghostly gleam of apparently white or yellow light, but with full moon and other favorable circumstances it is easy to assure oneself that the colors are really present.

In Bible narrative the Bow in the cloud is introduced to us as the sign of God's covenant to preserve the earth from the destruction of another universal deluge. The circumstances of its introduction into the course of sacred history are briefly these. The waters had wrought their work of judgment upon the antediluvian world. Mankind had become so corrupt that the hope of a future of purity and noble development was nearly extinguished. Outside the pale of one family the race seemed hopelessly insalvable. By an act of Divine surgery the element of fatal disease was separated from the element of life and cast away upon the waters of the flood. Noah and his family were preserved in an ark of gopher wood, which outrode the deluge and was finally lodged upon Mount Ararat. The first act of the patriarch after his deliverance was one of worship. He chose victims from the clean beasts in the ark, and offered amid the debris of the drowned world a sacrifice of thanksgiving and adoration to the Eternal God who had spared him and his. This act of piety was most acceptable to God, and thereupon he made a covenant with Noah not only for himself and his posterity but for all the animals associated with him. In this covenant he guaranteed the permanence of the order of Nature; "Seed time and harvest, cold and heat, summer and winter, day and night shall not cease."*

"And God said unto Noah, This is the token of the covenant which I make between me and you and every living creature that is with you for perpetual generations. I do set my bow in the cloud, and it shall be for a token of a covenant between Me and the earth."†

Thus at the very time when man most needed assurance it was vouchsafed to him. All his ideas of the stability of Nature had been swept away, or at least greatly

---

*Gen. viii. 22.   † Gen. ix. 12.

shaken by the terrible event which had just occurred. How could he with any heart enter upon the work of rebuilding destroyed homes, restoring the desolate earth? What confidence could he have that in the future his life and works should be preserved from the overwhelming judgment that had reduced mankind to a single household? That assurance came in the promise which Jehovah made to Noah; and the token of that promise, in accordance with the unvarying method of divine dealing with man, was so chosen as to preserve the covenant in perpetual remembrance. In this case the covenant sign was most beautiful and significant.

It has been widely supposed that the rainbow was created after the deluge for this purpose. Its appearance has therefore been regarded as a miracle. There seems to be no ground for this opinion. There is certainly nothing in the text that compels such a view. Indeed, the language may indicate the contrary,—"I do set my bow in the cloud." "My" bow, is language that leaves in our mind the impression of a previous existence and possession, not a new creation. "I do set," (or as it properly reads, I have set), is language which may indeed favor the popular understanding, provided we give to the word "set" one of its ordinary meanings. But in the Hebrew the word translated "set" does not necessarily signify made or placed for the first time. It properly means to appoint, to set apart. This sense survives in the English word *set* by which the Hebrew is translated. We speak of a set time, meaning an appointed time. We speak of one's setting apart an object for a special purpose, meaning simply that we appoint or consecrate an object already existing to a new end or sacred purpose. I have often heard the expression "set the day," used as equivalent to "name" or "fix the day," especially in reference to weddings. We may thus believe that Almighty God called the attention of Noah to that which he had often seen before; saying, in effect, I have set apart this my bow in the cloud to be henceforth a token to you of the covenant which I have made.

Of course it is obvious that if rain had existed, as undoubtedly it already existed before the time of Noah, there must also have been a rainbow. The theory that up to that period the cradle and home of the human race was watered by mist alone as was the original Paradise, I think untenable. There never could have been a time when falling raindrops coincident with the shining of the sun would not have produced the bended bow upon the clouded heavens. The interpretation of the word "set" as above given is that which is now all but universally received; and it may be said that it has not been forced upon exegetical science as some interpretations have been by the progress of physical science, since it was well known and commonly received among ancient Jewish Rabbis, among them the distinguished and learned exegete, Maimonides.

I. The first thought that meets us as we look at this Bow of God in the Cloud is that Nature is a Symbol of the Divine.

1. This truth is liable to serious abuse. There are men who make a religion of the natural; men who exalt nature above the throne of God; men who use the love and knowledge of the natural as a lever to lift out from their own thoughts and those of their fellows the old faith in the eternal verities of Heaven. With others "communion with Nature" (as the phrase goes) is considered a sufficient substitute for the communion of the saints. If a Sabbath day, bright with the glory of spring, invites to fields and woods, such men will satisfy their consciences for the neglect of public and private worship of God and the religious duties of the Holy Day by saying: I can worship by watching the sea waves rolling upon the beach; by listening to the voices of birds, the music of insects, and the rustle of winds among forest trees; by walking through green fields or climbing mountain slopes and filling my heart with the freshness and beauty of the landscape.

This reasoning is plausible, but it is false. The altar and sacrifice of Noah *preceded* the Bow in the cloud; they were the cause, not the consequence of that covenant of which the rainbow was the external pledge.

This is still the lawful order: first, the spiritual service of sanctuary worship, then the confirmation of physical works; first, the voice of God at the altar, then the echo thereof in material nature; first, God's self, then His symbol. I am firmly persuaded that the love of nature can never be truly helpful if it shall banish from the soul the nobler devotion to God. Men must be taught to love Nature in subordination to Him who is the Lord of all. They are to know that while religion is natural, the natural is not religion; that religion is beautiful, but the beautiful is not necessarily religion. Nothing can take the place of religion in the human soul. It is an inexorable law of men's highest development, " Seek first the Kingdom of God and His righteousness, and all these things shall be added unto you." No man can safely reverse that order.

2. This is our warning against the abuse of the thought that Nature is a symbol of the Divine. We must think also of how to utilize the thought. The rainbow in the cloud is beautiful. No heart can fail to be touched by the charm of its external loveliness. But that beauty is greatly enhanced when one sees behind it the living thought of Him who stretched it beneath the cloud, and who made it a token forever of his merciful purpose towards men. This presents very forcibly to our minds what possibilities of spiritual helpfulness may lie within all natural phenomena. We are not to think that all material creatures rank equally with the rainbow in symbolizing divine truth. God has himself set for us a meaning within the Bow, and that fact makes it pre-eminent as a symbol. But there is nothing which God has made that does not express objectively some thought of His. The wealth of divine benevolence, power, taste, wisdom, and skill as these lie locked up within the treasuries of natural worlds, is being uncovered day by day. It is our privilege and duty to possess this wealth and reveal it to others. But we must always insist for ourselves as well as our fellows that knowledge and enjoyment of the creature should never take the place of knowledge and enjoyment of the Creator. God is greater than His

works. To know God's handiwork is indeed the enlargement of one's personal life. But to know God Himself is "life eternal." *

These sentiments have animated some of the noblest spirits among the captains who have led the hosts of modern science into paths of natural discovery. They have felt that "the secrets of the Lord are with them that fear Him." † Professor Hentz, the father of American Araneology, was a man of singularly devout spirit. He never entered his study-door without stopping a moment in silent prayer beneath a picture of the All-seeing Eye which he himself had made. Indeed, the constant pressure of his forehead against the door while in the act of silent devotion left an indelible mark.‡ It was thus that he prepared himself to question the mysterious oracle of Nature whose utterance seemed to him to voice the Word of God.

The late Professor A. A. Hodge has related this incident: It was my inestimable privilege as a boy to be a student of that great Christian philosopher, Professor Joseph Henry. I was his assistant in the laboratory when he made a series of experiments which established the possibility of the electric telegraph. He was a very reverent man. I shall never forget how when he had completed his arrangements, and the moment had arrived when he would put nature to her crucial test, he bowed his uncovered head and said, "I have asked God a question; let us await his answer."§

I remember a striking sentence in the eulogy upon Professor Henry which I heard pronounced by Professor Mayer at the Boston meeting of the American Association for the Advancement of Science. The speaker was drawing a parallel between Joseph Henry and Michael Faraday, and said: "They both loved science more than money, and their Creator more than either."‖

---

* John xvii. 3.　† Ps. xxv. 14.　‡ NICHOLAS MARCELLUS HENTZ, M. D.—"The Spiders of the United States," page 11, Preface. Biographical Notes by EDWARD BURGESS. § The anecdote was told in Dr. Hodge's "Popular Lectures on Theological Themes" (1887); but I do not find it in the printed lectures. ‖ I quote from memory.

In view of such facts, what contradiction can there ever be between true science and exegetical theology? Science is but the exegesis of God's revelation in nature; the minute unfolding and classifying of his works; even as Theology is the interpretation and systematizing of the truths of his Word. One should protest in behalf both of Revealed and Natural Theology against any effort of godless savans on one extreme, and short-sighted divines on the other, to put the Bible and science in hostility. They are one, and of One. What God hath joined let no man put asunder!

I welcome the man of science with his carefully gleaned facts into the domain of theology. Whether his field has been the highest of God's works, man himself, or the very lowest, the insignificant radiates and molluscs, they all throw light upon the First Great Cause, the Infinite Creative Mind—the God whom we adore. Not the smallest fact is without its value in our common search after God; even the driest details of science have their counterparts in the "jot" and the "tittle" of the Bible student, the intricacies of Hebrew points and roots, of Greek particles and accents. If at times our supposed facts seem to clash, it is no more than is seen among theologians and scientists as separate classes whose facts and deductions we know often enough have joined issue, science with science and theology with theology. Moreover, on both sides supposed facts have often proved to be the merest fancies, and certain deductions the wildest theories.

It would be an iniquity for which there could be no reparation, I had almost said no forgiveness, were the Christians of this generation to allow a divorce between natural science and revealed religion; to hand over the realm of nature to the undevout man of science, and silence thus the voice that calls Christ's own disciples from "Nature up to Nature's God," and through Nature's God to Nature. The study of nature especially belongs to the Christian; a renewed heart is a necessary qualification to the highest attainments in that field; for it brings the mind of the inquirer into sympathy with the mind of the great Designer; the pupil with the

Author of all; the apprentice with the Master Architect and Builder of the material universe.

To the undevout nature is simply a workshop; to the Christian it is a voice; to the scientist who strives, waits, plods, and pries, she grudgingly yields up rich knowledge of her wonderful construction and powers. To the saint she opens at once the inner chamber of her most hallowed mysteries and speaks of her Creator God. But when the saint is also a man of science there are ten thousand tongues, mute to others, with which she whispers the Goodness and Greatness of the Almighty. May God speed the day when Faith shall lend new zeal to Science; and Science shall give new strength to Faith! Then shall be established the true relation between the science of God's created things, and the science of God himself. Then shall every natural fact in God's worlds, like the Bow in the cloud, become for man a sacrament, a material sign of a spiritual truth, a token tangible, audible, visible of the Divine Thought that lies therein or under it.

II. Another thought which the Bow in the Cloud brings to us is that God has covered with the protection of his covenant the inferior creatures of the earth.

The rainbow is not only a sign of God's purpose to protect men from universal destruction by a deluge, but guarantees like protection to the fowl of heaven and the beasts of the field. It is not to be supposed that the knowledge of this fact is possessed by the brute creatures, but they have the benefit of the fact through the knowledge which man possesses. It is needful that man should emphasize to his own thought the truth which Heaven has here revealed.

We may not admit the community of man and the lower orders, as asserted by advocates of the philosophic theory of evolution, and may not therefore hold that God's covenant covers man and beast on the ground that they are of common origin. Yet certainly there is a community of interest and destiny which is manifest in many ways. The domestic cattle and fowl, for example, are close sharers with man in the incidents and accidents of life. The earliest stages of human development in civilization are marked by the establishment of flocks and herds.* The faithful, patient, and laborious brute friends and servants of man have largely contributed to his successes and advancement in all ages and races. Cold and heat, hunger and thirst they share in common with their masters; they suffer when he suffers; their content is enlarged as his happiness increases.

This last at least should be the rule. "The merciful man is merciful to his beast." He recognizes the right of the dumb creature also to the possession of earth. What! Has the brute rights? Yes! The Magna Charta of animal rights is older than any mere human charter, for it is written in the flaming colors of the Bow of God's Covenant upon the cloud of God's heaven, by the hand of God himself. The sanctions of religion unite with human interests and the claims of kindliness to vindicate the right of God's dumb creatures to fair and merciful treatment by men. We may rule them, but not tyrannize over them. We may use them, but not misuse them. We may train them for our service, but not abuse them in our service or for our sport. We may even exercise the last and highest prerogative of sovereignty and slay them, but must spare them needless suffering.

It is somewhat difficult to find a word for the feeling which is here described. "Humanity" expresses kind treatment to our fellow-men. One can scarcely venture to apply the word to kind treatment of beasts; yet I do not think it an incongruity that some American organizations for protecting animals from cruelty are known as "Humane" Societies. Certainly no man of humanity can be unkind to a brute. No man who is persistently cruel to the lower orders will rise to the height of kindliness towards his fellow-men. Nay, no man who abuses animals can well mount to a high order of manhood in any respect. Thus closely, at least, we are bound together in community of nature, interest, and destiny. We may allow the Holy Scriptures to suggest the word which we seek. It is written, "A righteous man regardeth the

* Gen. iv. 20.

life of his beast."* Kindly regard for the beast, then, if not humanity, is righteousness. Surely it is an act of righeousness to cover with the hand of human authority and protection those helpless creatures whom God has committed to us for our proper use, but whom He has not withdrawn from beneath his own providential care.

Yes, providential care! That covenant of mercy towards beasts which God established with Noah, and of which the Bow in the Cloud was the sign, was reaffirmed by the Author of the Christian religion. Said the Lord Jesus Christ: "Are not two sparrows sold for a farthing? and one of them shall not fall on the ground without your Father." † I like the definition of God's providence which is familiar to a multitude of children in Great Britain and America, and which the children of the Pilgrim and Puritan fathers knew well—"God's works of providence are his most holy, wise, and powerful preserving and governing all His creatures and all their actions." ‡ Think of it! from an Archangel to an ant; from the order of a Lincoln that elevates to freemen four millions of slaves, to the first frail spinning work that lifts the baby spiderling into the air—the Divine providence extends with wise and loving interest and control. Verily, such Christian teaching should compel from its disciples a cordial sympathy with God's dumb creatures, and all who would interpose between them and human cruelty the spirit of that Protecting Covenant which bent above them in the days of Noah. I wonder that some one has not suggested to such societies that among the symbols of their seals and heraldic devices the rainbow might be introduced as a most fitting and beautiful emblem.

One can scarcely touch this subject without alluding to vivisection. The term is applied to a form of experimenting by physiologists and naturalists which requires the cutting and mutilating of living animals. The alleged purpose of such experimenting is, for the most part, the protection of human life. The effects of medi-

* Prov. xii. 10. † Matt. x. 29. ‡ Westminster Shorter Catechism. Question 11.

cines upon the animal system, the successful modes of treating certain diseases or accidents, these and such like problems men have attempted to solve in the laboratory by experimenting upon domestic animals.

Now, I think it must be granted that the custom cannot be wholly condemned. The higher interests of man, the protection of human life, the amelioration of human misery, the solution of problems that may bring life, health, and happiness to vast numbers of the human species—surely these are ends of such value as to justify the sacrifice of dogs, rabbits, and cats. Just in so far as humanity demands the sacrifice it seems to me that it may be made. But the sacrificial knife should never be drawn save by a consecrated hand upon a victim sacredly devoted. In other words, he who is engaged in vivisection should be careful to bring to it the purest motives and the most merciful methods. It cannot be doubted that there has been much cruelty, most unjustifiable cruelty, wrought upon helpless brutes in the name of medical and natural science; experiments which brought torment to living creatures have been made time and again, not to verify facts, for these have already been sufficiently established and fortified, but simply to gratify the curiosity of students. The work of vivisection has often fallen into heedless hands. Young men, and men of irresponsible positions, have taken it up without due consideration of the rights of dumb creatures, whom they torture in their tyro-efforts to imitate the experiments of men of character and genius occupying responsible positions. Herein lies the chief danger of this modern mode of experimentation. While I do not declare against vivisection itself, when practiced under righteous and humane restrictions, I must declaim with all my heart against the radical abuses of it. Surely it ought to stay such abuses to remember that all the creatures of God are spanned beneath that covenant sign of his protecting mercy banded on the clouds above Ararat and repeated in every Bow in the Cloud since then.

There is another point to which I may allude, viz, the needless cruelty inflicted oftentimes in collecting specimens of living things for private and public cabinets. The fact that a man wants to enrich the treasures of a collection of beetles, butterflies, ants, spiders, or other creatures of sea and earth, does not justify him in inflicting cruel pains upon the lower creatures whom he covets for his museum. There are few specimens really required for the use of man that may not be collected by methods that give painless death. The naturalist may rightly think that as a priest in the temple of Science and in behalf of Science he can sacrifice the life of the inferior creatures that inhabit the world with him. It may be said that this life exists in such excess, is exposed to such constant inroads from all quarters, and withal is so comparatively unimportant, that one may well anticipate the inevitable doom by taking the life which scientific progress requires. But I prefer to base the act, when required by legitimate science, upon that dominion which God has given man over inferior animals, even to the taking of life. That sovereignty must be exercised as one shall answer to God. And in its exercise no pain should be inflicted upon any creature which it is possible to avoid. Every man should hold himself under the highest obligations to spare all needless sufferings, and limit destruction to the necessities of the case.

A public speaker always ventures upon dangerous ground when he attempts to criticise anything relating to human dress, especially the dress of ladies. But there is one point to which our subject directly tends that in spite of these possible dangers ought not to be passed by. One can readily conceive a conjunction of circumstances something like this—a pastor looks from his pulpit through a church window, and sees a rainbow spanning an eastern cloud—the symbol of God's covenant to protect the fowls of the air. Returning thence his glance to his own congregation, this pastor might behold all the colors of that rainbow reflected into his face from the nodding feathers of wings, torn from beautiful fowls of heaven and birds of the air, to decorate the hats, bonnets and cloaks of the children and ladies in the pews! Now, I do not enter upon the question how far it is lawful for us to use our right over the life of birds and beasts for the purpose of clothing and adorning the human person. We may consider it settled that such acts are lawful when required as contributions to the protection and comfort of our bodies. But even if we regard as unsettled the question of our right to use such objects for purely ornamental purposes, we must admit that there is an extreme against which it is our duty to protest, and it seems to me that we have not simply verged upon, but have overpassed that extreme. It has come about that thousands and tens of thousands of the beautiful plumage birds of our country, our noble water fowl and bright-hued wood birds, are slaughtered every season by the paid hunters of milliners and exporters of bird skins. Even the song birds, the sweet companions of our summer hours, whose modest plumage one might think would protect them from such assaults, are not spared, but are slain along with the rest in the confidence that human art and dye stuff can render them suitable objects for the milliner's use. We are in danger, in actual danger of having our native bird fauna exterminated. The melody, good cheer and sweetness which would thus be lost to our life surroundings are considerations of high moment. But apart from these, the material interests of the country would suffer in this loss by destroying one of those natural checks upon the inroads of insect life which preserves for us the balance of nature, and so is an important factor in agricultural economy. As long as ladies indulge this taste for decorating their persons with the wings and bodies of birds, just so long will the importers and jobbers in milliners' goods keep their enginery of destruction in cruel and murderous play upon the "fowls of the air." Will the ladies continue this indulgence? Shall the cry of alarm raised by naturalists, and by such an organization as the Audubon Society for the protection of birds and by the kindly hearted friends of animal life, be heard in the parlors and homes of American women? Surely the gentle hearts of our Christian maids and matrons, who are so ready to respond to the calls of mercy, will hear this plea of the suffering birds, and, remembering the rainbow token of God's covenant to protect both beasts of the field and fowls of the air, will rise in revolt against a fashion which has in it no claim of necessity, but which is stained a thousand times over with the blood of slaughtered creatures of God! Will you, fair maid, will you, kind matron, give your example and voice to an act so truly godlike?

III. A lesson which the Bow in the Cloud is especially designed to teach, is the truth of God's Covenant Faithfulness, and that Peace of mind which results from trust therein.

The promise to Noah is that nature's order shall be preserved, and the inhabiters of earth never again be destroyed by a flood. The Rainbow was made the sign of that promise. Every appearance thereof brings to man its reaffirmation. It shows on the vast scroll of the firmament like the broad seal of State upon a parchment, and is the signal and token of God's promise and troth. Indeed, it may be said that every season-change brings to us the same manner of confirmation. " Seed time and harvest, cold and heat, summer and winter, day and night," * with every recurrence, are proofs to us in continued series that God is making his promise sure. These have not failed to the world of men. Nature's fixed order goes on, Heaven's guarantee to earth of an unbroken covenant of natural blessings.

This should bring confidence and hope to mankind. God's hand is on the world, and He will control it for good to the heirs of his promise. " The voice that rolls the spheres along hath made the promises." Let us trust the promises and be at peace! This is the lesson which the Rainbow has always brought, and doubtless was intended to bring to man. It has been beautifully emphasized by more than one of our English poets.

> " When thou dost shine, darkness looks white and fair,
> Forms turn to music, clouds to smiles and air :
> Rain gently spends his honey-drops, and pours
> Balm on the cleft earth, milk on grass and flowers.

---

* Gen. viii. 22.

" Bright pledge of peace and sunshine ! the sure tie
Of thy Lord's hand, the object of His eye !
When I behold thee, though my light be dim,
Distinct, and low, I can in thine see Him
Who looks upon thee from His glorious throne,
And minds the covenant betwixt all and One." *

The following lines are from Campbell's poem :—

"When o'er the green undeluged earth
    Heaven's covenant thou didst shine,
How came the world's gray fathers forth
    To watch thy sacred sign !

" And when its yellow lustre smiled
    O'er monntains yet untrod,
Each mother held aloft her child
    To bless the bow of God.

"How glorious is thy girdle cast
    O'er mountain, tower, and town,
Or mirrored in the ocean vast,
    A thousand fathoms down !

"As fresh in yon horizon dark,
    As young thy beauties seem,
As when the eagle from the ark
    First sported in thy beam.

" For faithful to its sacred page,
    Heaven still rebuilds thy span,
Nor lets the type grow pale with age
    That first spoke peace to man." †

Man's life is within the protecting covenant of God.
Surely this is a truth well calculated to bring peace to
the heart. God governs man and all things around him
in accordance with an appointed order, and He seeks to
bring man himself into obedience to that order. In such
knowledge and obedience his heart must surely have
rest. His life does not drift at haphazard, but is guided
by beneficent law. That log floating along the current
you say is drifting. Yonder balloon scudding through
the air you say is drifting. That downy seed of dandelion or thistle rising from the parent stalk and floating

---

* HENRY VAUGHN—"The Rainbow."   † THOMAS CAMPBELL—
"To the Rainbow."

across the meadow is drifting. Not so! The log on the current, the balloon in the sky, the seed upon the meadow breeze are all carried forward by laws as fixed, wise and benevolent as those that guide the stars and planets in their orbits. If drifting means a work of simple chance, you cannot apply the word to such acts as those. Much less can you use it of human souls under the hand and government of God the Creator. In Providence there is no such thing as drifting. However it may seem to our eyes, the unseen Hand Divine surely directs all our ways. Every vision of the Bow in the Cloud should confirm us in the belief of this truth, and strengthen our trust in Him who is governing the worlds over us and for us in accordance with the promise which he has made of preservation by order and law.

The winning yacht " Coronet," according to the log that was telegraphed to us a few days ago, passed through a terrible storm which severely tried and indeed threatened the existence of the vessel. But after awhile, says the log, the yacht passed into a centre of calm, and then the men had much needed rest. That is a curious fact with these hurricanes that blow across the ocean. There is always an outlying, swirling, tossing, death-threatening margin of storm. Once past that and within there is a centre of quiet. Ah, how like the storms of this life, an ocean beaten up by the gales, yeasting, frothing, roaring and heaving with storm-driven waves! Yet, ever there is a restful centre; it is the bosom of our God, and there we can always find rest.

Let us remember, too, that always the light of loving help speeds to us more swiftly than the bolt of our sorrow.

> And see what joyous greeting
>   The sun through heaven has shed,
> Though fast yon shower be fleeting
>   His beams have faster sped.
> For lo ! above the western haze
>   High towers the rainbow arch
> In solid span of purest rays ;
>   How stately is its march !*

---

* KEBLE—" The Christian Year." 25th Sunday after Trinity.

I was once traveling on a Union Pacific train across the great western plains when we were overtaken by a storm. Off to our right the rain descended with such fury that it obscured earth and sky. The ragged margin of the rainfall reached as far as the railway and beat against the windows of the cars. On the opposite side of the train the sunlight poured through the windows with summer intensity and brightness. The result was that for several miles we sped along under a rainbow. It was indeed a striking picture of the mingled storm and sunshine of this life of ours. At one moment of our pilgrimage there is gladness, at another grief. Nay, in the same moment there will be on the one side the buffeting of care and adversity, and on the other the sweetness of love and success. But above all this commingling of storm and sunshine it should never be forgotten that for every soul there may be, and there should be that bended Bow of God radiant with the promise of a hope whose beginning brightens this life and whose eternal continuance is the glory of the life immortal.

He who has learned the lesson to rest upon God amidst the tumults of this life may be assured that there shall come for him after life's stormy day "the Saints' Everlasting Rest." Longfellow has beautifully suggested this thought by following the drops of a summer rainstorm in their circuit through the fountains of the earth and the water-courses, up again to the cloud on which the bow of God is setting :—

> For his thought that never stops
> Follows the water drops
> Down to the graves of the dead,
>   Down through chasms and gulfs profound,
> To the dreary fountain-head
>   Of lakes and rivers under ground ;
> And sees them, when the rain is done,
>   On the bridge of colors seven
>   Climbing up once more to heaven,
> Opposite the setting sun.*

Yes, it is when the sun is setting that the the rainbow oftenest appears; and it appears upon the black

---

* LONGFELLOW's Poems—" Rain in Summer."

thunder-cloud out of which the sharp showers and the forked lightnings have just emptied themselves, and as the cloud is rolling away beyond the horizon. Beautiful symbol of immortal peace! When death's dark cloud has overswept this life and passed away forever beyond the horizon of experience—lo! above the open coffin and the closing grave, far above, upon that vaulted sky into which the soul has passed, the bridge of colors seven is spread for us, and over it we pass into the un-fading glory of our God.

LECTURE XIII.

The Rainbow around the Throne.

"And there was a rainbow round about the throne like an emerald to look upon. * * * And in the midst of the throne, and round about the throne, four living creatures full of eyes before and behind. And the first creature was like a lion, and the second creature like a calf, and the third creature had the face as of a man, and the fourth creature was like a flying eagle. And the four living creatures, having each one of them six wings, are full of eyes round about and within : and they have no rest day or night, saying, Holy, holy, holy, is the Lord God, the Almighty, which was and which is and which is to come."—
REVELATION iv. 2, 4, 6, 7.

THE RAINBOW AROUND THE THRONE.

John's vision of the Divine Glory of which this text is a part cannot be understood without reference to Ezekiel's vision of the wheels.* The two prophets evidently had in view the same objects; or, if the statement be preferred, their minds were similarly impressed by the Holy Spirit in witnessing and declaring the glory of God. What was the vision of Ezekiel? Briefly stated, the priest-prophet at Chebar beheld a thunderstorm rolling out of the north; its massive clouds were radiant with vivid lightnings and resounding with thunders, an emblem of judgment and divine anger. From the midst of this sublime tumult there arose four Living Forms, strange composite creatures—symbols of the cherubim. They had the general likeness of a man. They were four-winged, two pairs of wings were outspread above them touching at the tips, and two served as drapery to their bodies. They were four-faced, bearing the features of a man in front, of a lion on the right, an ox on the left, and that of an eagle behind or opposite the human face. They were eight-armed, two human hands being placed beneath each face and the wings. In the midst of these Living Forms, intertwining among and outflashing from them, were glimmerings of fires, as of torches, and flashes of lightning. Beside each one was placed a wheel whose felloes extended heavenward, high and dreadful, and were filled with eyes round about—the emblems of action, intelligence, progress, omnipotence. Above the heads of these Living Forms was stretched a crystal firmament; above the firmament a throne as of a sapphire stone, and upon the throne a Likeness as the appearance of man. The throne was girdled about with amber fire, and around the Human Form was "as the appearance

---

* Ezek. i.

of the bow that is in the cloud in the day of rain."
This, adds the prophet, was "the appearance of the likeness of the glory of God."

In the vision of St. John, the order of description is
reversed. Ezekiel begins with the cloud-base and so
passes upward to the supporting columns of Living
Forms bearing aloft upon their expanded wings the
domed firmament, and having beside them the animated
wheels as of the very chariot of the Lord. Thence his
vision rises to the sapphire throne with its issuing amber
flames, to the Manlike Form upon it, and last of all, to
the overarching rainbow. On the other hand, John's
glance is first at the throne, at Him who sits upon it and
the rainbow bending above it. It is noticeable that the
thought of Ezekiel passes in orderly sequence from the
base to the summit of his visional object, surveying every
detail in succession. On the contrary, after the first
glimpse of the throne and its Occupants, John's attention passes from one object to another, not in orderly
succession but from point to point overleaping intervening objects and then returning to cover them.

Nevertheless we can arrange the succession without
any difficulty and trace the resemblances and differences
between his vision and Ezekiel's. There are the lightnings
issuing from beneath the throne. There are the four
Living Forms, except that they are not combined in one
person but each represents a separate personality; moreover, the calf-face has taken the place of the ox, and
the cherubim are six instead of four-winged. The crystal firmament of Ezekiel appears to John as a glassy
crystal sea. The wheels of Ezekiel disappear, although
the eyes upon the felloes of the wheels are transferred to the wings of the cherubim. But in their
place John sees, first the symbol of the Holy Ghost,
seven burning lamps, which are the seven Spirits of
God; and second, the twenty-four thrones on which
are the twenty-four crowned Elders robed in white.
The storm-clouds with their lightnings which formed
the basis, the chariot-bed, so to speak, of Ezekiel's
visional appearance do not appear in John's; but in
their stead we have the voices of worship, offered by the

cherubim, echoed and enlarged by the elders, the angel choir, and the hosts of the Redeemed in heaven and on earth. More noticeable still, there appears upon the throne a Figure standing beside the sitting Figure of Him who was "like a jasper stone and a sardius." This new Figure is that "as of a Lamb that had been slain." Bending above all, in John's vision as well as in that of Ezekiel's, there is the "rainbow round about the throne."

The lesson which I would have you learn from the Rainbow as it thus appears in these visions is this: Creation is subordinate to God, is united, harmonious and active in His government and service, and the whole dome of nature and Providence is covered with the Covenant of Divine Mercy renewed and perfected in Jesus Christ. This is a series of truths which are bound in one sweet lesson by the beautiful emblem which God appointed in the days of Noah as the symbol of His promise of life and peace. In the course of this lecture, we shall consider these truths in detail.

I. We learn, first, the truth that Creation is subordinate to God.

The cherubim of Ezekiel remind us of those that guarded the gates of Paradise to maintain the decrees of God against erring man, lest he should further violate the natural conditions of his creation. They stand guarding the throne of God, silent and seemingly wrathful, if so we may interpret the intertwining lightnings and torch-fires, like repelling fiery serpents. But on their expanded wings they bear up the crystal firmament that supports the throne. They are the pillars of Divine government in Nature. The cherubim of John's vision are like Ezekiel's in form, but different in their active relations; they are not silent but vocal, and, in full sympathy with the Redeemed who chant their salvation song, they themselves cease not day and night to lift up their Trisagion hymn, "Holy! Holy! Holy!" But, in their passive relations they are one with Ezekiel's cherubim, for they bear up the crystal pavement upon which the throne of Divine government is reared. It is thus that we come to take these living forms to represent the sub-ordination of the universe to God. They are personifi-cations of natural power employed in God's service, " as standing on the highest step of created life, and uniting in themselves the most perfect created life."*

The Old Testament has many beautiful examples of this truth as it lay in the minds of the inspired writers. The universe was to them the creation, the handiwork of God. It existed not only by the Divine Will, but in continual obedience to and dependence upon it. The Psalter and the Book of Job especially abound in such references. That splendid poem of Nature the 104th Psalm may be consulted in this connection, and those passages in Job which record Jehovah's answer out of the whirlwind. I render into English verse a few stan-zas from the latter.

JEHOVAH'S ANSWER TO JOB.†

I.

(Then Jehovah answered Job out of the storm, and said :)—

2 Who darkeneth God's decrees by witless words ?
3 Gird up thy loins now with thy human strength :
  I will inquire, and do Thou answer Me !

II.

4 When I laid Earth's foundations, where wast thou ?
  Declare it, if thou knowest how that was done !
5 What architect its plan computed ?—say !
  Or who hath laid on it the measuring line ?
6 On what foundation are its pillars sunk ;
  Or who hath laid the corner stone thereof,
7 What time the Morning stars together sang,
  And all the sons of God shouted for joy ?

III.

8 And who shut up the sea with double-doors,
  When it brake through, and issued from the womb ?
9 When I put round it, for its raiment, clouds,
  And thick mists as the swaddling clothes thereof,
10 And measured out its boundaries for it,
  And bars and doors decreed for it, and said :
11 Thou shalt come hitherto ! No further come !
  Here be the rising of thy proud waves stayed !

---

* BAHR—" Symbolik," i. 340.   † Job xxxviii. 1-21.

IV.

12 Hast thou in all thy days bid forth the dawn,
   Or caused the dayspring once to know its place ;
13 That it may seize the fringes of the earth,
   And shake the wicked out, as from a rug?—
14 May change the Earth's dim outlines into form,
   As signet-ring the face of plastic clay ;
   And Nature stands forth from obscurity
   Appareled in the lovely robe of Day?
15 Then from the wicked is withheld their light,—
   For night is light to them !—and in the act
   Of violence the upraised arm is stayed.

V.

16 Hast thou e'er reached the well-springs of the sea,
   Or gone to the foundation of the deep?
17 Were e'er the gates of Death unveiled to thee,
   And didst thou see the gates of Hades' realm?
19 Hast thou observed the compass of the earth?
   Speak, in so far as thou dost know all this !
20 Which is the pathway to the Home of Light?
   And Darkness—whither lies its dwelling-place,
21 That thou should'st guide each to its utmost bound,
   And know the paths back to the house thereof?
   Ah ! thou must know it ! for thou wast then born,
   So very great the number of thy days !

II. There is something more than a simple Subordination of Natural Forces taught in this vision of St. John. We learn that in the plan of God all Nature is in Harmonious Service with God.

Seraphim and cherubim, angels and archangels join with mankind and the animate world and with all inanimate nature to advance the Divine Glory. The whole universe of intelligent and material creatures is represented as built into and enclosed within one mighty temple of glory beneath the all-enclosing dome of the rainbow which overarches the throne. In order to get this thought of harmonious service we will need to inquire into the meaning of the strange Living Forms in the vision—emblems of the Cherubim.

Undoubtedly these forms, as Layard has suggested,* were familiar to Ezekiel and to the people whom he addressed, inasmuch as they are conceptions which belong to the common treasury of Oriental symbolism. They appear in the temple of Jerusalem. They were

---

* LAYARD—"Nineveh," ii. 448; "Nineveh and Babylon," ii. 643.

among the most familiar art objects in Assyrian and
Babylonian temples and palaces. They are seen in the
sphinx and other Egyptian forms, and in the griffin or
eagle-lion of Greece. It would be useless to attempt
here a discussion of their varied symbolism. It will be
enough if we see in them the united types of the
highest forms of Nature, spiritualized and engaged in
harmoniously supporting the throne of God and contributing to his service.

It is curious, to say the least, that the animal types
which form the composite symbol of the cherubim, are,
by even the latest students of Zoology, placed at the
head of their respective natural families. The lion leads
the noble and familiar Felidæ or Cat family, the first of
the order of Carnivora.* The ox stands at the head of
the family of Bovidæ, or hollow-horned ruminants as
they are termed, including the oxen, buffaloes, antelopes,
sheep and goats.† The eagle leads the raptorial birds
in rank, standing at the head of the family Vulturidæ of
the order Accipitres.‡ Man himself, of course, is the
highest of all the creative forms of Earth. Surely, it
could not have been by mere chance that such a combination as this should have been taken from among the
creatures to mirror forth the Divine Creative life in
visible glory. At all events these animal types could
not have been better chosen to exhibit the manifoldness
and fullness of creative life.

It is not without significance, also, that these high
types of the inferior orders are so closely associated by
Ezekiel and John with man. We see this composite
figure, which represents the highest order of angelic intelligence, rising out of and compounded, so to speak, of
eagle, lion, ox, and man. What does this mean? Is there
not here a startling suggestion of something very much
like the theory of modern evolution? Indeed, I wonder
that some Christian evolutionist has not made use of this
imagery to declare an ancient and Scriptural recognition
of the development hypothesis. For the manner in

---

* WRIGHT—"Animal Life," page 74. † WALLACE—"The
Geographical Distribution of Animals," vol. ii. page 222. The
Classification of Sir Victor Brooks. ‡ WALLACE, *Idem*, 345.

which this association may be sufficiently explained from another standpoint, I must refer to my last Lecture upon the covenant made with Noah for himself and the lower creatures. However, it is certainly true that there are natural forces and faculties which man, on the animal side of his nature, bears in common with the noblest orders of beasts. Strength of the ox, courage of the lion, activity of the eagle, parental affection and self-devotion in all, are traits which belong to our humble friends of the brute creation, and which have received the highest expression in man.

In man, did I say? The saying can only be limited by the comparatively narrow confines of this life. The living forms whom we are considering are proofs of this. The ruder forces, basilar powers of Nature that have such fitting representatives in the ox, lion, and eagle, must in some sense enter into the nature of the cherubim themselves. Why not? Broadly speaking, zoological life may be compared with a pyramid at whose base lie the lowest forms, creatures of the water that possess the most rudimentary organs and simplest functions. Type on type of higher organism rises until the classification ends in man. He is the perfect organism, so far as human observation extends. But, confessedly, there is a vast interval between him and God the Creator. Is this interspace vacant of correlated forms of life? Is there nothing living to bridge the void between humanity and Deity? Yes, there are the angels! Science has not yet discovered, but Revelation has uncovered them; and there is nothing contrary, but much in harmony with the facts and theories of science in the revelation. A distinguished naturalist, whom I have more than once quoted, has said: "The grand law of 'continuity,' the last outcome of modern science, which seems absolute throughout the realm of matter, force, and mind, so far as we can explore them, cannot surely fail to be true beyond the narrow sphere of our vision, and leave an infinite chasm between man and the Great Mind of the Universe! Such a supposition seems to me in the highest degree improbable." *

---

* WALLACE—"On Natural Selection," page 372.

Our pyramid then may not and does not end in man. Man is simply the fleshly termination thereof. The edifice of life goes on through those mysterious ranks of being known to us as angels, until it ends at the very pillars of the Divine throne in the highest grade of angelic being, the cherubim themselves.

Nor is it contrary to the truth to express this continuity of life from the earth side upward by a symbolism drawn, first, from inanimate nature, as the clouds and rainbow, and next, from the highest orders of animals and from man. Moreover, the physical qualities which such creatures as the eagle, ox and lion personify are certainly possessed by those angels whose life history we read, though in too brief glimpses, in the Holy Bible. Their swiftness of motion, lofty courage, strength, supreme powers of destruction as the executors of judgment in the Divine government,—these and such like traits appear in the angels of Sacred history. They are not impalpable impotencies—mere ideals. They are forces; they are thrones, principalities, powers. They touch and move the fountains of Nature. They call fire from the rock and dews from the air, as in the case of the angel who appeared to Gideon.* They hold in their hands the forces that throb and glow in earthquake and volcano, as in the case of the angels who procured the destruction of Sodom and Gomorrah.† They control the mighty forces of disease and death, which they are commissioned to use, as in the judgment of pestilence sent upon the Israelites in the days of David,‡ and the pestilence which slew the first-born of Egypt,§ and the destruction of the Assyrian host, so vividly described by Byron.‖

> The Assyrian came down like the wolf on the fold,
> And his cohorts were gleaming in purple and gold;
> And the sheen of their spears was like stars on the sea,
> When the blue wave rolls nightly on deep Galilee.
>
> Like the leaves of the forest when summer is green,
> That host with their banners at sunset were seen;
> Like the leaves of the forest when autumn hath blown,
> That host on the morrow lay wither'd and strown.

* Judges vi. 38.   † Gen. xix. 22, 24.   ‡ II. Sam. xxiv. 16.   § Exod. xii. 23.   ‖ II. Kings xix. 35.

For the Angel of Death spread his wings on the blast,
And breathed in the face of the foe as he pass'd;
And the eyes of the sleepers wax'd deadly and chill,
And their hearts but once heaved, and forever grew still.*

In the New Testament we read of an angel putting forth physical exertion, as when one rolled away the stone from the door of our blessed Lord's sepulchre. Throughout the entire book of Revelation we see angels move through the vision of the exiled apostle in numberless missions of providence and grace. They see, they eat, they speak, they sing, their voices are heard by human ears, their touch is felt upon human hands, as when they led Lot and his family forth from Sodom. In short, they command material forces and achieve material results. When they appear their bodies resemble a human form. Nor is there any indication in Scripture that these bodies are not real and only assumed for the time and then laid aside. For myself I believe that they are material, though of a form of matter of which we as yet can form no true conception, but which some day, perhaps, in the progress of a sanctified science, we shall be able to understand if not discern. That the angels do not all possess human form is manifestly the opinion of Ezekiel and John, as we learn from their description of the Life Forms by which the cherubim are represented. At all events their life history, so far as the Bible gives it, accords with the fact which these cherubic symbols express, and shows them united in sympathetic and harmonious service of God with man and the inferior animals and with all creation.

2. There is another significant fact in the symbolism of these cherubic emblems that must now be noticed: they are embodied in wings. That is to say, the wings are not only stretched above them constituting the framework of the firmament at whose four corners they stand, but they cover and, one might say, compose the whole lower part of the body. What is the significance of wings? Undoubtedly they are a spiritual emblem of the highest significance. According to the Greek tradition,

---

* LORD BYRON—"The Destruction of Sennacherib."

the beautiful human bride of Cupid who was at last endowed with immortality, was conceived in mythology and art under the form of a winged maiden, or at other times as a butterfly, which bore the same name. The insect, most frequently the butterfly and moth, breaking from its unwinged chrysalid state into the imago or winged form, has been regarded as symbolizing the same truth. The outspread wings, as an emblem of the Divine protection, are one of the most common Egyptian emblems, appearing continually over the gates of tombs and temples. In Scripture usage we find these protecting wings in the beautiful blessing of Boaz to Ruth, " A full reward be given thee of the Lord, the God of Israel, under whose wings thou art come to take refuge."* The Almighty speaks of having borne his people as on the wings of eagles,† having brought them out of Egypt as an eagle carries its young ones upon its wings. " Hide me under the shadow of thy wings," is the cry of David,‡ in the hour of distress, and the sweetness of this refuge he expresses in the words, " How precious is thy loving kindness, O God! and the children of men take refuge under the shadow of thy wings." §

The accuracy of observation, the delicate sympathy with nature and the beautiful, the genuine poetical spirit and taste of the ancient bards and inspired prophets have never been more truly illustrated than in their choice of such a symbol to express such spiritual truths. There is certainly no object in nature that challenges higher admiration for wonderful structure than the wings of a bird, and were there no other than that, it seems to me that it alone would be enough to demonstrate the power and presence of an Infinite Mind.

Any one who has watched the flight of the meadow lark as it arises from " the dewy weet," and sings in the upper air ; or who has followed the spiral course of the hawk or eagle rising higher and higher until it beats its wings against the very gate of heaven ; or who has followed the strong flight of sea birds, gull, albatross or Mother Cary's chickens over the crests of tempest-driven

* Ruth ii. 12.   † Exodus xxi. 4 ; Deut. xxxii. 11.   ‡ Ps. xvii. 8.
§ Ps. xxxvi. 7.

waves, must have felt a strange uplifting of soul, a long-ing to share such perfection of motion, a yearning to mount up on wings as eagles. I can remember that as one of the strongest emotions of my boyhood as I lay upon the grassy hillsides, and watched the flight of birds.

Often have I sat at my father's door watching in child-ish absorption the flight of martins, swifts and swallows as they skimmed the air for insect food in the gathering shades of evening, and counting with eager interest those that stayed their flight to perch on the ball, the rod and harp-shaped weather-vane crowning the village church opposite our home. And often did I wonder, admire and wish that I too could fly, like those weird birds, and stand upon the pinnacle of the church steeple and fling myself with joyful abandon from it, and skim away upon outstretched wing over street and rooftop.

Perhaps there are few children who have not felt the same emotion, and it is sympathy with such a spirit that merges easily into those spiritual aspirations which lift the soul above the grosser things of life to high and pure communion with the things of heaven. A bird upon the wing is a physical expression of the very poetry of mo-tion, and is a perfect symbol of a soul's aspiration for the higher life.

Wordsworth in his address to a sky-lark thus sweetly breathes this sentiment :—

> I have walked through wildernesses dreary,
> And to-day my heart is weary;
> Had I now the wings of the faery
>   Up to thee would I fly.
> There is madness about thee, and joy divine
> In that song of thine.
> Lift me, guide me, high and high
>   To thy banquet place in the sky.*

The same poet speaks of the same bird as a

> Type of the wise, who soar but never roam,
> True to the kindred points of Heaven and Home.

Our sacred hymnology has many traces of the same symbolism, some of our most familiar hymns being

---

*WILLIAM WORDSWORTH—"Address to a Sky-Lark."

quite based upon them. For example, we have Sea-grove's hymn :—

> Rise, my soul, and stretch thy wings,
>   Thy better portion trace ;
> Rise from transitory things
>   Towards Heaven thy native place.

And there is also the favorite hymn of Isaac Watts :—

> Give me the wings of faith to rise
>   Within the vail, and see
> The Saints above—how great their joys,
>   How bright their glories be.

We are now prepared to understand the significance of the wings which form so large a part of the Living Forms both in the vision of Ezekiel and St. John. The nature-powers of intelligence, strength, courage, and action symbolized by man, ox, lion, and eagle are repre- sented as spiritualized by means of the wings that sus- tain, encompass, and rise above them. The thought that comes to us is that these types of nature are devoted to the spiritual service of God. They are separated from their animal life and consecrated to the highest uses. The whole symbol beautifully expresses to us the thought of Nature as purified, spiritualized, and devoted to the worship and glory of the Holy God.

How much the world needs to learn this lesson!

We are approaching the last decade of the nineteenth century, a century that has been characterized above all by two great social phenomena. The first is the won- derful manifestation of spiritual power and philanthropy. This is exhibited in the revival of religious work among the laity; in the high valuation of childhood; in the organization of Sabbath-schools; in the founding of Christian missions; in the consecration of the Church and its substance to the evangelization of heathen na- tions; in the introduction of woman's influence and efforts as a potent factor in the world's work and duty; in the establishment of those magnificent institutions of charity that have done so much to relieve human misery; in the advancement of mankind to a higher plane of personal liberty, free thought and free government. All this is the result of the religious and moral element of society, vitalized by the seven Spirits of God, filled with the restless activity of the Living Forms before the throne, and animated by the lofty and merciful spirit which breathes through the beautiful symbol of the overspanning rainbow above the throne.

Side by side with this great moral force there has moved through the century the spirit of modern science. Scientific thought has been possessed with the restless activity and numberless eyes of the wheels of Ezekiel's vision. Heaven and earth, sea and air have been sought out, searched into, and have uncovered their mysteries as never before. Mankind has been continually startled by marvelous developments of physical science, and the practical results which have issued therefrom. There are some questions which, as we draw near the close of the century, urge themselves more and more upon our thought: Shall these two mighty forces, the religious and scientific, diverge or unite? shall they join in fratricidal conflict, or clasp hands in loving fraternity in the service of humanity and the worship of God? Are these two forces maintaining harmonious development and progress? Is not the scientific outrunning the religious? Is not the material overshadowing the moral? Have we not had already too much science, or if you please so to put it, with our much science have we not had too little of that moral preparation without which science cannot be a blessing? In this generation we behold numberless gifts and endowments, the hard earnings and possessions of science, go to societies who are often in whole or in part "too low morally and intellectually to know how to make the best use of them."* As a result we have seen these scientific endowments become curses rather than blessings.

Take examples. The art of distillation taught by science is a blessing in the mechanical arts and medicine, but it has become an overshadowing curse through the drinking habits of the day. The moral nature of man is not able to control his own appetite, and the moral

---

* WALLACE—"Natural Selection," page 330.

tone of society cannot rise to the point of facing and suppressing the enormities of the drink-evil. We are brought face to face with the humiliating facts that men are expending for intoxicating drinks millions of money where they spend thousands for the cultivation of their minds and the elevation of their homes. Science has given us rum, and rum has given us poverty, pauperism, crime. Science has uncovered to us the art of distillation, and the art of distillation has bestowed upon the world, along with a modicum of blessing, an amount of sorrow and wickedness which is truly incalculable. Few homes have not felt the blightings of this curse. Few hearts have not been wrung by it with agony; while the home and the state have been burdened with expenses which far outweigh all other ordinary expenditures of the family and society.

Yet we cling to our drink-traffic and keep our unclean streets, our unadorned walks, our cobble-stone pavements, the very worst perhaps that the world has ever seen, with the single exception of the corduroy roads of pioneers' days; we cling to the drink-traffic, and keep our crowded jails, penitentiaries, almshouses, orphanages. We cling to our drink-traffic, preferring to spend millions of money in manufacturing criminals, miserables, paupers, rather than stop the traffic and spend our money in beautifying our city, and blessing our fellows. Yes, we *prefer* it!—for, society elects it.

Again, gunpowder and that more recent explosive, dynamite, are gifts bestowed by science upon society, and is it not a question—nay, I may venture to say that it is not a question at all—whether society is ready to receive them? In our country we have spent millions of money to explode gunpowder through death-dealing missiles upon the red men of the West; and we have spent tens of millions only to educate and Christianize them. Glance at Europe! See marshaled on every border vast hosts of soldiers, armed with weapons of war, the highest products of mechanical science. Hear the ring and clatter of factories and arsenals, directed by the highest scientific skill, busied in preparing yet more perfect, that is to say, yet more destructive agencies against human life, limb and property. Have these gifts of science been bestowed upon societies quite prepared to receive them? Or, is there no known higher use to which these unnumbered millions of gold, and these priceless thousands of men, with all these high attainments of science and art can be put, than to devise and prepare modes by which human beings may destroy each other?

We need take no other example. It is a serious reflection for society, while science continues to pour her new discoveries into our lap, whether this be an unalloyed blessing? Certainly, at least, we dare affirm that it never can be so unless morals, religion, purity, truth, and nobility of heart and life keep pace with scientific discoveries. The man who divorces science from religion is an enemy of his kind. I assert it without hesitation, and on such grounds as that which I have here disclosed. The thought has been admirably expressed by a French lady, Madame Adam, in a recent English review :—

"You must have moral as well as material good. A government which aims only at the one and forbids the other is a bad government. The science which forces itself, absolute and unintelligible, on the ignorant, is not one whit better than the obscurantism which tries to force itself on the enlightened. When science claims to be all-sufficient, she makes an empty pretension. She is but one fold of the veil of Isis—the fold that sweeps the ground.

"It is the business of the man of science to observe the conditions of matter. It is the business of the priest and the moralist to observe the conditions of spirit. Each of them seeks to utilize a given force for the material or moral benefit of man. If the scientific man has sometimes to remind the priest of the conditions of physical existence, the priest in his turn has to remind the scientific man of the conditions of moral life." *

Christian women and men, what have you to say towards the solution of this problem? What will you

---

* "Paul Bert's Science in Politics," by MADAME JULIETTE ADAM. Quoted from the "The Contemporary Review," January, 1887.

do to bind into harmony these two living forces, religion and science? What will you do to prepare the world by the gift of religion for the gifts of science? The duty is before us, the struggle is upon us. The demands for action, for prayer, for unceasing supplication at God's throne, and quenchless energy in the propagation of Divine truth, are everywhere upon the blast, and they besiege our ears with calls that might well awaken the dead. If our souls be dead to the momentous issues of this conflict, may God awaken us to-day! If the world shall fail to discern this duty, and shall sleep on, shall dream on in fancied security, leaving an unsanctified science to join with unsanctified commerce, unsanctified industry, and an unsanctified press to materialize mankind and destroy morals and faith from the earth— alas, alas, the final conflagration, the wreck of society, the ruin of the civilizations of the past cannot be far away!

III. We have come to the last truth in our lesson: the whole Dome of Nature and Providence is covered with the Covenant of Divine Mercy renewed and perfected in Jesus Christ.

Let us catch up for a moment the thread of these prophetic visions of which we have been thinking.

Ezekiel's first glance is at the wrath-charged thunderstorm. Thence it travels upward toward the lightning-surrounded Living Forms to the theanthropic Form upon the throne, ending in the overarching rainbow "like the hanging out from the throne of the Eternal of a flag of peace."* John's vision begins where Ezekiel's ends— with the rainbow emblem which, however, bends above an additional Form, that of the atoning Lamb who is in the midst of the throne. The apostle's glance travels downward, and finds instead of Ezekiel's pedestal of thunder-clouds and lightnings, the family of God in heaven and earth, angelic and saintly, hymning a doxology to the Creator of the universe, and the Redeemer of all souls. One cannot but see even from this imperfect analysis of the two visions that the eye of John has noticed the

---

*FAIRBAIRN's "Ezekiel."

changed conditions of the Church of God. It is fixed
upon a period far in advance of the time of Ezekiel. It
recognizes the vast progress made in the history of redemption, the introduction of new elements, as the
Mediator, and the joyful hymns of the reunited children
of God, a family made one in the Sovereignty of grace.
The old nature-emblems are still there, the Living
Forms, the crystal expanse of firmament, the rainbow
overarching the throne. They carry with them, too,
much of their old meaning, but there is come to them a
new force, a sweeter and profounder sense.

John's vision reveals to us just beneath the rainbow
dome with its message of safety and peace, the person
of Jesus, "the Lamb as it had been slain." The dome,
the summit of this visional temple of the new worship,
is the rainbow. The base, the floor, is not the storm-
charged clouds fearful with lightnings, as in the vision
of Ezekiel, but a group of living, holy, joyous beings,
the united family of God, the family of heaven and of
earth engaged in holy service. The Living Forms lift
up their Trisagion hymn, "Holy! holy! holy!" The
crowned Presbyters raise their doxology, "Worthy art
thou, O Lord our God, for Thou didst create all things."
Then there is silence. The vision undergoes a change.
The Lamb is seen in the midst of the throne clad with
the seven spirits of God, the emblem of the Holy Ghost.
Now the Living Beings and the crowned Elders strike
their celestial harps and lead the choir of the universe
in their new song, while the heavenly temple is filled
with the incense of the prayers of saints. Hark! This
is the song which they raise: "Worthy art thou, for
thou wast slain and didst purchase unto God, with thy
blood, men of every tribe, and tongue, and people, and
nation, and madest them to be unto our God a kingdom
and priests; and they reign upon the earth." Now the
innumerable company of angels, ten thousand times ten
thousand and thousands of thousands, and every created
thing which is in heaven and on the earth, and under
the earth, and on the sea, and all things that are in them
are heard raising their voices in mighty chorus, saying:
"Unto him that sitteth on the throne and unto the Lamb

be the blessing, and the honor, and the glory, and the dominion forever and ever! And the four Living Creatures said 'Amen!'" The song rises aloft through the whole animated Temple of holy beings and echoes under that rainbow dome which speaks in every band and color concerning the New Covenant of Mercy, the Covenant which is in the Blood of the Atonement, by which the world of believers is forever saved from the deluge of Divine wrath. The Rainbow marked that bright day when the Covenant of Peace dawned upon a destroyed world. The Rainbow shall crown that Blessed Day when in the full fruition of the Covenant the whole Ransomed Church shall join with Creation in the jubilee of finished Redemption.

Could anything more forcibly and clearly present to us, in symbolism at least, the truth that in the ideal creation, all things, visible and invisible, shall join in harmonious praise of God through Jesus Christ the Lord? To-day we seem to be far away from that blessed consummation. To-day, as the Apostle Paul has declared,* "we know that the whole creation groaneth and travaileth in pain together until now." "For the creation was subjected to vanity, not of its own will, but by reason of him who subjected it." But on the same page that declares this manifest truth we have the sweet utterance of the "hope that the creation itself also shall be delivered from the bondage of corruption unto the liberty of the children of God. For the earnest expectation of the creation waiteth for the revealing of the sons of God.†

When shall that glad day come? When shall all the forces of nature, and all the discoveries of science, and all the faculties of the human mind together bow in humble worship before Christ and render praise for final redemption? Shall that day ever come? Surely it shall come! May God grant that we, each one in his place, may do our best to further its coming! Thus we may be sharers in the final glory and blessedness of that service of universal worship which forever shall ascend in the temple of the Highest beneath the rainbow dome that covers the throne of God and the Lamb.

---

* Rom. viii. 22. † Rom. viii. 19.

LECTURE XIV.

———

The Angel and the Rainbow.

"And I saw another strong angel coming down out of heaven, arrayed with a cloud; and the rainbow was upon his head, and his face was as the sun, and his feet as pillars of fire, and he had in his hand a little book open."—
REVELATION X. 1–2.

THE ANGEL AND THE RAINBOW.

THE tenth chapter of the book of Revelation contains material upon whose explanation I do not even venture. It will satisfy the requirements of this lecture if we consider the holy being described in our text as an angelic minister in a divine livery, that is, presented in the natural symbols which represent the Lord Jesus, and sent forth with the Gospel. He appears clothed with a cloud, an emblem in the Scriptures of something exalted, heavenly, spiritual, mysterious, and therefore Divine. His face is as the sun, a symbol of majesty and Divine truth. His feet are as pillars of fire, emblems of that purity with which the Holy Church and all holy ministries should touch the earth and move among men.

"And the rainbow was upon his head." Undoubtedly we must regard this head-dress as the coronet or crown of the angel. The rainbow is his diadem, and the lesson which the symbol teaches is, manifestly, that the angelic ministries are crowned with mercy to men. That covenant of Divine compassion and preservation, by which mankind is inspired with eternal hope, is surely the very crown of the Revelation of God; its symbol is therefore worthy the loftiest angel to wear, worthy the noblest spirit of earth to accept, for it expresses the sublimest attribute of God Himself.

In paintings and sculptures upon the tombs and temples of Egypt royal personages are depicted by artists as crowned with the uræus, a poisonous serpent. Egyptologists have thought this to be an emblem of the swiftness and deadliness of royal power. Thus the Pharaohs hedged themselves about with terror. How sharp the contrast between these ancient kings of earth and our heavenly King Jesus! He is, indeed, Divine, Omnipotent, All-glorious, but he crowns his majesty with compassion towards the lowly, the ignorant and them that are out of the way.

These characteristics belong to all who are appointed by God angels or messengers of good will towards men. We may give to this figure the widest interpretation. We see here something more than the ministry of holy angels continually exercised for God among saints; more than a type of that sacred ministry by which in succession of the ages the holy Evangel is disseminated whether by word of mouth or written scroll. We see here a type of all agents and instruments whatsoever that stand forth in the eye of heaven as messengers of truth; a type of everything that is or shall be a lawful carrier to men of messages of light and help from any quarter of Heaven or any point of God's universe.

In this view of St. John's vision, the strong angel crowned with the rainbow, who is seen speeding with fiery feet through the heavens bearing a written roll or book, typifies not only a Christian Church and ministry, but Christian Art, Science, and Literature. All these have been and ought to be angelic messengers bearing an evangel of holiness and good will. Alas! they have not always been such. Such they are now only in part. The good has ever been perverted by evil. The livery of heaven has always been seized to clothe Satan therewith; the very angels of light have been dragged down to become messengers of darkness and corruption, so that over Art, Science and Literature, sacred and secular, aye, over the pulpit itself, the holy angels of God have been compelled to lift up the sad wail, " How art thou fallen from heaven, Star of day, son of the morning !" * It is from this broad interpretation of the mission of the angel and the rainbow that our discourse shall proceed.

I. Our first and principal lesson therefore is that the Purity, Majesty, and Strength of God as presented in the Gospel and represented by all Angelic Ministries, are dominated by Divine Mercy.

---

* Isa. xiv. 12.

The messenger of heaven is crowned with the rainbow. The fitness of this natural symbol as a token of heavenly mercy and human hope has been universally recognized. It stands almost alone among atmospheric phenomena as wholly separated from the thought of discomfort and pain, loss and death to the human race. Nature, for the most part, like the Roman god Janus, is two-faced. When gazing upon one face we see radiant smiles; looking upon the other we behold frowns. From the one face go forth utterances of gladness and beneficence, from the other voices of terror and destruction. To-day we gaze upon the clouds with admiration of their beauty and gratitude for their fruitful showers; to-morrow they gather in black masses that utter terrifying thunders and flash forth lightings to destroy. The rains and rivers bring us blessings, but their floods at times blight as with a curse. The winds are our helpful servants, but they beat us with the terrible tornado and desolating storm. The snows greet us with many forms of beauty and beneficence, but they carry in their bosoms the elements of death. Even the sunlight, harbinger of love, the source of unnumbered blessings, beats upon the world in the fierceness of a tropical summer, smiting men by day. But the rainbow is a creature of simple beauty. It is lovely without a trace or suggestion or possibility of harm. It is seen when the storm is sinking out of one horizon while the sun appears in another. It is the emblem of storms that have passed. It speaks of hope; it charms by its varied colors and stirs within the heart no sentiment but admiration, gratitude and praise.

This has been the universal sentiment of the race. "Look upon the rainbow," says the son of Sirach in the Apocrypha, "and praise Him that made it. Very beautiful it is in the brightness thereof. It compasseth the heaven about with a glorious circle, and the hands of the Most High have bended it."* The ancient Greeks and Romans regarded it in the same light. Iris was the goddess of the rainbow, and was represented as

---

* Ecclesiasticus xliii. 11–12.

the daughter of Thaumas, Wonder, and Electra, Lightning, and the granddaughter of Ocean and Earth. She was the messenger of Jupiter, king of the gods, and of Juno his queen. She lived among the other deities of Olympus, which she only left for the purpose of conveying divine commands to mankind, by whom she was looked upon as a guide and adviser. She traveled with the speed of the wind, always from one end of the world to the other, could penetrate to the bottom of the sea or even to the Styx, the place of the dead. It was her office to charge the clouds with water from lakes and rivers, in order that they might go forth in gentle fertilizing showers. She was represented as a beautiful virgin with wings of varied hues, clad in robes of bright colors and riding on a rainbow; at other times with a nimbus on her head on which the colors of the rainbow were reflected.*

Homer thus alludes to this goddess in the course of his description of the armor of Agamemnon in which " the king of men " arrays himself for battle :—

> "Three glittering dragons to the gorget rise,
> Whose imitated scales against the skies
> Reflected various light, and arching bowed,
> Like colored rainbows o'er a showery cloud
> (Jove's wondrous bow, of three celestial dies,
> Placed as a sign to men amidst the skies)." †

In the same Book Homer represents Iris as the messenger of Jove, exercising her office at the close of a thunder-storm in bearing a divine command to Hector in the midst of the battle between the Grecian and Trojan troops.

> "But Jove descending shook the Idæan hills,
> And down their summits poured a hundred rills;
> The unkindled lighting in his hand he took,
> And thus the many-colored maid bespoke :
> 'Iris, with haste thy golden wings display,
> To godlike Hector this our word convey.'"

By the Germans the rainbow is called Bifröst, the Living way ; and Asen-brücke, the Bridge of Asen.‡ The

---

* MURRAY :—" Manual of Mythology," page 162. † " The Iliad," Book xi., POPE's translation. ‡ DELITZSCH.

ancient Hebrews looked upon it as a great band, joining heaven and earth, and binding them both together, as the Greek ἶρις comes from εἶρω, to tie or bind.* They made it, therefore, the sign of a covenant, or of a relation of peace between God in Heaven and the creature upon the earth. It carried to their minds a thought similar to that of the heavenly stairway or ladder of Jacob's dream, which united the throne of God to the stone pillow upon which the sleeping exile rested his head. It is thus that we are led up to the conclusion that the rainbow diadem of this angel messenger teaches us that all true angelic ministries to men are dominated by the Divine Mercy.

1. We see this first and especially in the Personal Ministry of Christ.

The crowning attribute of God is compassion. The New Testament, indeed I might say the whole Scripture, is the presentation of Jesus Christ as the Saviour. His incarnation, the germinal principles of his religious teachings, and his holy sacrifice for man, are presented in the four Gospels. The subsequent sacred books record the founding of the primitive Church, and the development and application of the principles which Christ taught by the apostles whom he commissioned. Everywhere the central truth is the manifestation of Divine love in the life and death of Christ. "God commendeth his love toward us," exclaims St. Paul, "in that, while we were yet sinners, Christ died for us."† "Herein is love," writes St. John, "not that we loved God, but that he loved us, and sent his Son to be the propitiation for our sins."‡ This is in entire harmony with what our Saviour Himself taught: "God so loved the world that He gave his only begotten Son, that whosoever believeth on him should not perish, but have eternal life."§

This glory of Christ is associated with his human life and office. In the life and death of Jesus all other revelation is corrected, completed, crowned, and man beholds

---

* KNOBEL. See LANGE, Gen. ix. *in loc.* † Rom. v. 8. ‡ I. John iv. 10. § John iii. 16.

the Almighty not simply as a Force, but as a Father. Christ shines in the light of heavenly mercy, for he interprets mercy unto men. He displays to the world the thought of a Pardoning God. The eternal Throne is illumined by that conception. It fills all heaven with radiance. It lights up the coldest chamber of earth. Yes, Christ shines in bodily presence before us the radiating source and centre of man's noblest conception of the Deity. He is God manifest in the flesh. He bridged the gulf between Jehovah's throne and footstool with his own sinless humanity, and over the bridge man passed as never before, and, beholding the Father, exclaimed, " I have seen God face to face, and have been preserved!"

I do not say that this was a discovery, but it certainly was a rediscovery. The Jews had the truth of the Fatherhood of God, but they had retired it from popular view. They were interpreting the Good Father to the people of Christ's day as a task-master; an "austere man," reaping where he did not sow.* Thus they had driven men to doubt and impiety, to bury their talents in the earth, and defy the coming judgment. Jesus restored the old view of God as a Patriarchal Judge. He stood amid the splendors of the earthly sanctuary and called God, "Abba, Father!" Since the days of the Shekinah the Jewish Temple on Mount Moriah never knew a brighter effulgence.

The Greek and Roman ideas of God had fallen into a deeper gulf of theological error than the Jewish. It has been remarked that in the Homeric representations of divinity and humanity, what most strikes us is that whereas the human characters are in their measure winning, attractive and heroic, the divine characters are capricious, cruel, revengeful, sensuous.† The revelation of God in Christ to such minds was something more than a revelation. It was a revolution! How profound a revolution it is impossible for us of this day and generation to conceive. It is the glory of Christ among men that as the Son of Man he held forth both the holiness and the Love of the divine Father. In Christ's

---

* Luke xix. 21.   † DEAN STANLEY—"Christian Institutions," page 300.

human life that glory was, indeed, veiled within a cloud as he moved among men, but still it appeared. Its rays were continually breaking through in the miracles of healing and divine benevolence that he wrought, symbols and foretokens of that blessedness which his fuller civilization has brought to the sons of earth. We see him walking on the sea, manifesting thus his power not only, but symbolizing the truth that in coming days the spirit of his civilization should triumph over nature, bridge the seas with ten thousand hulls, flash human thought underneath the ocean's waves, and, seizing everywhere nature's mightiest forces, bring them in subjection to the lofty thought of divinely-cultured mind. We see him raising the dead, manifesting thus his power, indeed, but setting forth also a symbol of the truth that life should be made more sacred, and unnumbered multitudes saved from the grave by the spirit of that divine Charity which he would engraft upon learning and science.

Through all these scenes of his earth life he was as the sun moving amid the clouds of morning which his rays had not yet scattered. He waited thus for the crowning act of his offering upon Calvary, the culminating commendation of God's love.

2. We are taught the same lesson concerning those kindred ministries to men—Science, Art and Literature. We confine our thoughts to Literature, which is well symbolized by "the little book" that the angel bore in his hand. The symbol is very apt as representing the modern magazine, and especially the daily journal, which is often a veritable βιβλαρίδιον (biblaridion) or booklet, both as to the amount and value of its contents. That is indeed a mighty messenger, whose force can hardly be measured by even angelic mensuration, which comes to the world on the wings of the printing press. Do I see aright when I behold its type in this angelic ministry? Do I take too lofty an ideal when I declare that the function of the press is to sweep the world as with purifying fires, under the high coronation of goodness and truth?

There is no subject that will better repay earnest consideration and discussion than the ethics of journalism. The functions, privileges and responsibilites of the daily press in particular need to be defined. The definition is somewhat complicated with other questions of great importance to society, as for example the "liberty of the press;" but the common welfare is deeply involved in right conclusions upon these points. The opinion which seems to prevail, among newspaper proprietors at least, is that the daily journal is a commercial enterprise solely, and is only amenable to the laws, responsive to the influences, and subservient to the conditions controlling all other business. Its chief function is held to be reportorial; that is, to communicate to its purchasers the events transpiring in the world, particularly in the community forming its immediate constituency.

The ideal newspaper, according to this standard, is simply a purveyor of news, good and bad alike. It reflects, as from a mirror, upon the public at large those incidents which occur in detail throughout the various parts of society. It turns a many-faced camera upon the events of daily life, and catching them upon the sensitized plates of a reporter's brain, reproduces the united impressions and places them in the market at a fixed price. It claims that what the public wants is "news," and that its own responsibility is ended when the public is furnished with what it desires. Further than that it has no responsibility at all, except to see to it, as any shrewd business man would do, that its operations are conducted upon careful and honest commercial principles, and are made successfully. Whatever may be said of this ideal, it must be admitted that, as a matter of fact, a large proportion of our leading journals are apparently conducted upon these theories. Let us briefly examine them.

In the first place, let me say that no man, or men, who claim to speak to or for the people, can put themselves upon the basis of simple private enterprise. It is not in human nature to permit this; it is not in the constitution of society; it is not in the purpose of God. The instincts of communities, their intuitive perception of what is right and safe, cry out against such a position. Every pastor of a church in this city might set up for himself and his people the plea: "We are simply an assemblage of private individuals, bound together by common consent, to worship God according to our consciences, and procure for ourselves and families the instructions of a qualified teacher of the Sacred Scriptures, who will also exercise among us other sacred and comforting functions of the gospel ministry. The State pays us nothing, and it has absolutely no concern with us and our pastor as long as we conform to law. We attend to our own business; what have we to do with the public, or the public with us?"

But society would decry such an utterance, and though the claim seems to have the color of justice, society would be right in decrying it. Even in this land, where there is no established religion, the pulpit is under the most solemn restraints, and has high obligations and responsibilities to the public at large, which no wise and good man for a moment would deny. The very position of the minister, even though he be the private pastor of an individual and private church, is such that community will always demand from him a measure of responsibility and a standard of private behavior and public action, which it could not ask from others. If you say this is unjust, I must answer that the instincts of society are usually just and right, and in this case we must declare that the voice of the people is the voice of God.

A similar standard obtains in the case of the public orator, the lecturer upon the rostrum and platform; indeed, of all who stand before their fellows to voice sentiments that may mould men and control the thinking, the conscience, the behavior of the masses. Now, there are few agencies that speak to men in these days in such numbers and with such potent influence as public journals. Can they escape from that responsibility which rests upon others in like positions? They cannot! They ought not to ask for, they ought not to be permitted such deliverance! The public says, and rightly says, and should continue to say, "Will ye or nill ye, ye must pass under the high and solemn responsibility of those who set themselves, or who are set by others in the place of prophets and guides of the people. At the peril of your souls, at the peril of the judgment of History, and the High Assize of Eternity, ye must exercise that prophetic calling! Woe unto you if ye be false prophets! Woe unto you if ye be blind guides!" This then is our first principle—no individual, no organ, no association which is essentially a creator and director of public opinions and morals can be safely regarded and treated as a *simple commercial agent*, for these functions are in the nature of a public trust.

Undoubtedly the newspaper has its commercial side, as every agency of good must have. It is a law of literature as of the gospel that they who are its voices to men must live thereby; but there is a vast difference between living by the preaching of the gospel, and preaching the gospel simply for a living. I mark the same difference in the moral attitude of every man who is a voice to or for the people. He is to be honored who lives by literature, but he is unworthy of his high vocation who pursues literature under whatever form simply for the gain thereof. I do not, I cannot believe that the great army of gifted men and women whose vigorous and incisive intellects are devoted wholly or in part to journalism are the authors of, or can rest easy under such a bare commercial theory of the functions and sphere of the press. Surely, it is the echo of the counting-room, not of the editorial chair! It is not "the silver tongue," but the silver dollar that speaks thus. Alas that money should ever have power not simply to recompense, but to command intellect!

There is no more pitiful figure in history than that of Balaam, the mysterious prophet out of the East, as he stood above the hosts of God in that memorable soul-struggle which Scripture records.* The bribe of honor and wealth was at his hand if he would utter a curse instead of a blessing upon Israel. The noble element within him, the divine, the true, struggled for victory. His judgment, his conscience, his feelings were all with the tented army of the true God whose faces were toward the gates of Canaan. "How goodly are thy tents,

---

* Num. xxii.–xxiv.

O Israel!" involuntarily he exclaimed. But Mammon, self-love, "the rewards of divination" struggled vigorously on the other part. Alas! the victory was not with noble spirit, lofty intellect, commanding genius, high attainments. There on those mountain heights these gifts of God struggled in vain with the spirit of evil and ignominy.

That old conflict is renewed in the bosom of many a gifted man to-day. Could my words reach those bright, vigorous and most promising intellects who supply the brain-force of journalism, I would say to them: The price of divination is indeed great. But no earthly guerdon is as worthy as the gift itself which you possess. This endowment of God to speak with words of power, vocal or printed; to thrill the soul; to awaken emotion; to excite thought; to arouse lethargy; invigorate weakness; guide ignorance; mould character; inspire conduct; shape destiny—this is the endowment of the true seer, the vates, the diviner. This power is yours. Do not sell it for paltry gold! Keep it pure, true to God, religion and humanity. Though the counting-room should say "Stand and deliver;" though the whole world should cry "Stand and deliver," do you refuse to deliver this gift of heaven to befoulment by a policy that would put the sacred gift of divination upon the market, to be sold in the shop and huckstered and cried on the street on a level with the wares of the fakir. Do not mistake me; it is not the selling of the journal that is ignoble but the selling of the *man* who makes the journal, the selling of the principles that make the man!

The second principle which I advance is that there are limits to the right of people to know and of the press to communicate knowledge.

The messengers and ministries that bear the written book and printed page must be dominated and circumscribed by goodness, truth and holiness. Indeed, on what principle of natural right and justice can one declare that he has claim to all knowledge—any more than to all land? Such an idea is communistic, and there is a communism of knowledge which carries a grave error and a serious peril.

There is knowledge which is not power, but rather weakness. There are facts that corrupt and enervate the mind. There are things that men are better far for not knowing. The night-life of a great city; the transactions of our slums and centres of moral impurity; the life which is lived by human creatures down in the muddy sediment of this great stream of humanity—surely these have no claim to be known by the masses of humanity. I raise the contention that they are not subjects for the ordinary legitimate enterprise of journalism. Enough that they must be known by those whose office it is to suppress the powers and purify the centres of corruption. Knowledge, illicit knowledge was the destruction of our first parents. It dragged them down from their exalted estate, and sent them forth from Eden banished and fallen. No Scripture could possibly be more appropriate here than St. Paul's command to the Romans: "But I would have you wise unto that which is good, and simple unto that which is evil."*

It is to be feared that to-day, in the perverted taste for information that had better be locked up within the secret records of police courts, society shall once more be banished from its Eden of purity, and wander shame-faced and fallen throughout the earth. If that sad day comes, it will come largely under the leadership of a public journalism which has espoused the false ideal against which I have animadverted, and degraded itself to sell illicit news and popular opinions at a cent or two cents a copy.

There are indeed times when the suppression of abuses and correction of hidden evils require that the worst features of society should be exposed to the public gaze. And there are newspapers who with noble fearlessness and wise discretion make themselves the worthy pioneers in disclosing these secret vices, and advocating their correction and the punishment of offenders.

It would be impossible for us to fix the limits within which either the pulpit, the platform or the press should confine such revelations of criminal life. But that there is a limit, cannot be doubted. Certain I am at least

---

* Rom. xvi. 19.

that to print such disclosures simply for the sake of the sensation produced and the gain harvested thereby, is as unworthy in the press as it would be in the pulpit. To do it as a part of the bounden duty and lawful work of one who is called to prophesy in behalf of good and against all evil, is as praiseworthy in the press as in the pulpit.

There is a theory of journalism which asserts that the purpose of the press in its revelations of all wickedness is to convict the community of sin and awaken it to righteousness. This, at least, throws over the revelations the mantle of a worthy motive and mission. Even thus, we must declare that it is perilous in the highest degree to break down barriers and guards, and allow all manner of public prints to glean with unsparing hand from the criminal life of a vast city, and spread the gleanings with unfettered license before the eyes of young and old, experienced and inexperienced, pure and impure alike. There is no power in the simple revelation of sin, in the disclosure of wicked deeds, to turn souls to righteousness. If that were so, the "Police Gazette" might become a very gospel—more powerful for good than any pulpit. On the contrary, it is usually the case that familiarity with vice hardens the conscience, breaks down sensitiveness of the nature against evil, thus preparing a way for it. Only those who have within themselves the living principle of a holy life, whose characters are strong, who are braced and bolted down to the ways of virtue, who are proof against assault, can without contamination come in daily contact with the ways and words, thoughts, sentiments, and policies of the unclean.

Revelations of sin never should stand alone. They are never influential for good when so standing. There is no impulsive power towards righteousness within them; no expulsive power as towards sin, no attractive power towards heaven. Something more, something positive is required for that. The voice which cries, "Repent! repent!" must also say, "The Kingdom of Heaven is at hand!" The exhibition of human loveliness as perfected in Jesus Christ, the disclosure of Divine love as incarnate in Jesus Christ, these are forces that expel sin, and urge toward holiness. The life and gospel of Christ, the morals, the intentions, the sequences of Christianity give men a sense of sin, teach them their imperfection, clarify and correct their false ideas of life, and open up before them the pathway of deliverance from evil. It is not enough to show men that they are floundering in the slough of sin, you must also show them that there is a life of holiness and happiness which is better, and to which it is possible for them to attain. There must come along with the revelation of sinfulness the correcting power of human sympathy and human help.

These are general principles; they apply to all ministries that go forth among men for good. They apply to the press, and I hold it to be truth that those newspapers and magazines that hold up before the people most prominently, persistently and attractively the beauties of human life, the beauties of nature, the glories of honesty, of honor, of righteousness, of truth; those newspapers that habitually pour upon human minds the light, sweetness and blessedness that may be garnered everywhere around us, are those who, by furnishing lofty ideals, do the very most to convict men of sin and deliver them therefrom. We cannot, therefore, accept the theory, that a legitimate function of journalism is to print unlimited reflections of the night-life society, even though it shall do it with the noble motive of convicting the world of sin, and leading it to righteousness. The mirror must be turned toward heaven! Yes, chiefly towards the pure, bright sweet heavens of God; and must reflect upon society the image of God and of the godlike.

It would indeed be a grateful assurance could we apply to the future of journalism, as was recently done in closing a public address by a prominent journalist of Philadelphia,* the words of the Psalmist:† " The Lord gave the word, great was the company of those that published it!"

---

* Mr. Talcott Williams.　† Ps. lxviii. 11.

II. Let us turn, in the second place, to mark the manner in which Heaven's Angelic Ministries are Received by Mankind.

It is pitiful to think that the angel of the Gospel, crowned with his symbol of mercy and peace, has so often been rejected by men. Yet there always have been those who joyfully have received the holy message and thanked God for the messenger. There are two words often used in this nineteenth century: "Experience—experiment." They are heard in halls where a spurious Nature-worship is rendered by a blind priesthood to the god of analysis and synthesis. They will not believe in a soul unless they can experiment with it. Very good! It is a good word,—experience. It has long since been received into the very bosom of theology. We have our treatises on religious experience, and there is no word better known among evangelical Christians than "experimental religion." A "Christian experience" is in fact the only or chief test of fitness for Christian fellowship in most Protestant communions. It is claimed by a great multitude, whom no man can number, that they have drawn near through Christ unto God; have experienced renewal of their inner life, an uplift of their natures toward Heaven, a widening of hopes, a kindling of aspirations which they never knew before; that they have tasted of the joys of the Lord, have been in communion with the Spirit of Holiness. They can say and do say with the great doctor of the Gentiles, "We know whom we have believed."

Call up the witnesses! Who are they? From modern times back to the earliest they stretch a living link, binding the garden of Eden with these closing decades of the nineteenth century: Clark Maxwell, Henry Wilson, Agassiz, Garfield, Logan, Lee, Stonewall Jackson, Joseph Henry, Michael Farraday, Isaac Newton, Milton, Mathew Hale, Fabricius, Linnæus, Erasmus, Calvin, Knox, Luther, Savonarola, Huss, Wycliffe, Paul, Moses, Enoch, Abel, which was the son of Adam, "which was the son of God." These all walked with God. They felt the change of the new life. They "experienced religion." Their testimony surely is worthy to be received on this as upon

other points, and that testimony must pass for proof that
there is reality in religion, that communion with God is
a fact based upon experiment.   I could bring to you to-
day an hundred witnesses whose testimony would be received in any congress of savans upon any one of the
various points of Natural or Physical Science, in which
they are experts, without the slightest hesitation.   These
witnesses with one consent will agree upon these facts
which I have stated.   They have experienced them.
With them it is a matter of personal experiment and observation.   They know the realities of the soul-life, the
possibilities of communion with the eternal God, and the
power of the world to come.   Who will reject their testimony?   On what grounds should their testimony be
rejected?   These clear-minded, careful men who ponder
every fact with discriminating judgment, cannot be given
credence upon one line of facts and denied it in another
concerning which they are equally competent and confident as witnesses.   No! the facts of the spiritual life are
facts.   The world has been full of witnesses thereto since
ever the world was; and still as the Angel of the Gospel goes forth with the " little book " believers and witnesses spring up to affirm their experience of its heavenly power.

Why should so many reject the Testimony?   I often
wonder: Are they defective on the spiritual side of their
natures?   Have they persisted in withholding belief and
acceptance until their will-power in that direction has
ceased?   If so, such men should have little weight as
witnesses in any question of religion.

The difference between the blue light at one end of the
beautifully-colored spectrum band and the red at the
other, is nothing more nor less than a difference almost
identical with a difference between a high note and a low
note upon the piano.   The reason why one end of the
spectrum is red and the other blue, is that in light as in
sound we have a system of disturbances or waves; we
have long waves and short waves, and what the low notes
are to music the red waves are to light.   The disper-
sion of light, whether effected by refraction or diffrac-
tion, is simply the sorting out, and arranging in regular

succession, of the various light tones in the order of their wave-lengths.

We can now recognize the strict analogy between the world of sound and the world of light. Ears are tuned to hear different sounds—some people can hear much higher notes than others, and some people can hear much lower notes than others. In the same way some people can see colors to which other people are blind; indeed, the more we. go into this matter, and the more complete we make our inquiries, the more striking becomes the analogy between these two classes of phenomena.* Is it so, indeed? Are there those to whom the beauty of the rainbow is but an empty name? Yes, many of us know such persons. Would it not be a most foolish act to set the "color blind" to judge the merits of painting? If a man lack the natural gift of spiritual insight, or have deliberately extinguished his own spiritual vision, is he a trustworthy guide for you or any soul in the most solemn and important of all decisions? I trow not!

There are eyeless fishes in Mammoth Cave. What if they with their atrophied sense of sight could be permitted to hear and understand the experience of the great-eyed dwellers of the deep sea? We might fancy the latter telling of the wonders of sunlight as it is seen in the waters of the ocean; of the beds of coral; of sea anemones, flowers of the great deep; of rocks and sounding breakers, boiling surf and rolling waves; of icebergs, and rivers of the sea like the Gulf Stream; of great ships, of forests buried beneath the waters, and green fields above them; of all those wonders of organic and inorganic life which abound in and around the ocean and its depths.

Our eyeless fish, listening with incredulity, ridicules the deep sea creature's experience, declaring out of its own consciousness, judgment, observation and experience that such things as it had heard never could be— never! Well, pass from this fable, to suppose one who

---

* J. NORMAN LOCKYER—"The Chemistry of the Sun." (1887.) Page 87.

has had no experience of things that belong to the spiritual world, whose eyes have never been opened upon the glory of Christ, the sweetness of faith and hope and communion with God, in the act of ridiculing the experience of a Christian, denouncing it as impossible, chimerical, absurd, because, forsooth, these things had never been known as a part of his own soul's experience!

III. We have now thought first of the Nature of Angelic Messengers, and second the Recipients of their Ministries. Let us turn a closing thought to the Purpose thereof.

Undoubtedly that purpose is to give men immortal life with God. The little book which the angel with the rainbow brings out of heaven to the world is that gift of Jesus Christ in which life and immortality have been brought to life. The rainbow crown which surrounds the angel's brow becomes in turn the coronal of believing men. That is indeed a gift, the soul's coronation with Divine love! Blessed is he who is thus set apart as a king and priest unto his God forever, whose life is girdled and glorified by the protecting covenant of Divine mercy!

Often, when a small boy, I watched the rainbow spanning the valley of the Little Beaver creek, on whose banks stands the Ohio village where I was born. I was told—and what lad has not heard the same enticing assurance?—that if I would go to the foot of the rainbow, yonder, where it just touched the earth, I would find a pot of money. I think it did occur to me to wonder why, then, my seniors did not go and get it? They were not usually so self-denying in the matter of youthful treasure-pots! But with the trustful simplicity of childhood I believed the assurance, and carried in my heart the resolve one day to secure that treasure as my own. Well do I remember the day when at last I mustered courage to undertake the task. No Jason ever set forth in search of Golden fleece with more hopeful spirit than I. Over fields, across the shallow water, up the rugged slopes of Pine Hill, beneath the. hemlock boughs,—only to find the withdrawing image further still away, and to stretch out my little empty hands towards the last dim tints that were vanishing from the sky. Poor weary-limbed toddler! what a disappointed heart did I carry home that day within my bosom!

Have I been wiser as a man than I was as a child? I do not know; but I have thought that after all, the old traditional trick of boyhood had within it a hidden truth. There *is* a treasure at the foot of yonder rain-bow for those who know how to find it, though, indeed, it is not to be found by pilgrimages over running streams and rugged hill-sides, in vain outgrasping after material treasures. I read the riddle differently now, and have tried to tell you what is that hidden wealth that lies within the circle of the Bow of God. Have you learned the lesson aright? Do you know the secret by the sweet experience of that peace which comes through the mercy of God in Jesus Christ? Thus interpreted, there can be no better wish for you than that you may retain the old childish longing for, and faith in the treasure of the rainbow. Oh, if our hearts could but keep fresh through all our days, the innocence, trust, hopefulness, and unworldiness of childhood!

> My heart leaps up when I behold
> A Rainbow in the sky;
> So was it when my life began;
> So is it now I am a Man;
> So be it when I shall grow old,
> Or let me die!
> The Child is Father of the Man;
> And I could wish my days to be
> Bound each to each by natural piety.*

Surely you all can wish that. By God's help try to make good your desires. Let every heavenly ministry vouchsafed to you, be used with intelligent faithful-ness. Thankful for the help which God gives you in His Church, His ministry, His ordinances, His word, His Sabbath—add day to day and decade to decade until all life from childhood to manhood shall be arched with the beauty of holiness, and your souls at last " over the bridge of colors seven " shall pass from earth to Heaven!

---

* William Wordsworth—" The Rainbow."

To mark the lives of friends, parishioners, readers, hearers thus growing in all womanly beauty and manly strength; to see characters developing sweetness, benevolence, patience, industry, unselfishness, love, every Christian virtue and grace—this is the highest reward as it should be the lofty purpose of every spirit who ministers living thoughts to living souls. The Pastor's holy pleasure in the ripening characters of these subjects of his ministry has well been expressed by one of the noblest of England's Christian poets.*

These in Life's distant even
  Shall shine serenely bright,
As in the autumnal heaven
  Mild rainbow tints at night,
When the last shower is stealing down,
  And ere they sink to rest,
The sunbeams weave a parting crown
  For some sweet woodland nest.

The promise of the morrow
  Is glorious on that eve,
Dear as the holy sorrow
  When good men cease to live.
When brightening ere it die away
  Mounts up their altar flame,
Still tending with intenser ray
  To Heaven whence first it came.

Say not it dies, that glory,
  'Tis caught unquenched on high,
Those saint-like brows so hoary
  Shall wear it in the sky.
No smile is like the smile of death,
  When all good musings past
Rise wafted with the parting breath,
  The sweetest thoughts the last.

* KEBLE—"Christian Year." 25th Sunday after Trinity.

LECTURE XV.

Lessons from the Spring.

"The winter is past, the rain is over and gone, the flowers appear on the earth, the time of the singing of birds is come, and the voice of the turtle dove is heard in our land. The fig tree putteth forth her green figs, and the vines with the tender grape give a good smell."—SONG OF SONGS ii. 11–13.

LESSONS FROM THE SPRING.

THIS piece of exquisite composition is an extract from the "Song of Songs, which is Solomon's." It is a description of that period of the year in the Holy Land which lies between winter and summer, and which by analogy may be called spring. In point of fact there are but two seasons in Palestine which are referred to continually throughout the Bible as summer and winter, cold and heat, seed time and harvest. This is the general division, although, of course, in a country so situated there is great diversity and variety of climate. We think of the United States as embracing an immense variety of climate and products. There is nothing specially remarkable, however, in such a fact considering the vast expanse of our domain. But when we think of Palestine as a little strip of land one hundred and fifty miles in length and forty miles more or less in width, it is a matter for remark that its climate should vary within that limited range from the cold snows of the summits of Mount Lebanon to the tropics of the valley of the Jordan. One may pass by a few hours' travel from the depths of winter on the mountains about Jerusalem to the palm groves and sugar fields of the Ghor at the head of the Dead Sea, and in the vicinity of Jericho. But we shall have substantial accuracy if we hold to the thought that the Holy Land is divided into the two seasons of a comparatively rainless summer and a winter that is marked by heavy rains. I have already alluded to this feature in the climate of Palestine in a previous lecture,* and it will only be required to state here that "the winter" of our text is this season of rain.

The winter rains commence about the beginning of November, and continue with greater or less constancy until the end of February or the middle of March.

* Lecture XI. : "Showers of Blessings."

They are a succession of severe showers or storms, with intervening periods of fine bright weather permitting the grain crops to grow and ripen. The climate during the winter months is very similar to that of the south of France, or the maritime districts of the north of Italy. When the season rains have ceased, and the winter is over and gone, the whole face of the earth, having been fed and prepared by the nourishing showers, is quickened by the warm sun into luxurious fertility. The grass springs up everywhere; the hills are covered with verdant olive trees; the fig trees and pomegranates, which grow in great abundance, push out their green figs and fresh leaves; and in the days of Solomon as now, no doubt they were everywhere intermixed with the vines which were in great luxuriance.* The flowers just forming into the grape diffuse far and wide that delightful fragrance which is familiar to all vine-growing lands in early spring.

We may suppose, without departing from reasonable probability, that Solomon drew his beautiful description from his own familiar pleasure-gardens. History has testified to the character, beauty and extent of these, and the great king has himself left record of his taste, which was indeed a prevailing passion among many oriental sovereigns of ancient times: "I planted me vineyards, I made gardens and parks, and planted them with trees of every kind of fruit. I made me pools of water to water therefrom nurseries of forest trees."† Here we have the natural groundwork of the allegorical description of Nature contained in the Song of Songs. Vineyards and gardens, pleasure-gardens, fruit trees, and water-pools are mentioned at various places in the Song. Josephus, in his description of Solomon's buildings, magnificence, and glory, relates that the king was a lover of horses and chariots, then remarkable objects in Judea, and that he drove in a high chariot, surrounded by halberdiers of his life-guard in gorgeous attire in gold-powdered hair. He often drove forth as early in the morning as daybreak, the most delightful period of

* BONAR—"Mission of Inquiry to the Jews," page 178. †Eccles. ii. 4–6.

Palestine in summer, to his lovely gardens, not far distant from Jerusalem.*

How fond Solomon was of Nature is manifest not
only by the statement concerning him † that he dis-
coursed concerning trees and cattle, birds, creeping
things and fishes, but by the manner in which these objects continually appear in his writings. In this Song of
Songs, for example, repeated mention is made of the
cedars of Lebanon, of cypresses, of palms, of lilies, and
the thorns among which they grow, of myrrh and aloes,
the camphire, mandrakes, calamus and cinnamon, and
other objects of the floral and vegetable world. He
speaks of horses, of sheep and goats, of hinds and roes,
of foxes, lions, and leopards; of the turtle dove, raven,
and generally of the singing birds. We can therefore
easily imagine the poet, the philosopher, the naturalist,
the sovereign, when the winter had well passed, driving
forth, before the heat of the sun had risen above the top
of Mount Olivet, to enjoy amid the natural beauties of
his enclosed garden the sweets of the spring time.

It is not strange that this awakening of the natural
world should have suggested to him the awakening of a
soul into a new life; that the glory which everywhere
was outbursting from the soil and swelling in buds and
blossoms from trees and vines; which was dotting the
face of hills and the breast of valleys with the lovely
forms of flowers; which was filling the air with the early
matins of song birds come back from their winter wan-
derings to build again among the branches; it is not
strange that sights and sounds like these should have
suggested to such a mind the mighty change which
passes over the human soul when it is born again under
the power of a living faith and sets forth in the midst of
the world the tokens of a new life.

I do not enter into the discussions which have so long
prevailed among Biblical scholars as to the nature and
purpose of this composition from which our text is
taken. I accept as substantially correct the view which
the Church has taken that the inspired author here purposes to set before our minds an image of the love which

* Josephus—"Antiquities," viii. 7, 3.   † I. Kings iv. 33.

exists between Christ and his Bride the Church; that, in this picture of the passing of winter and the coming of spring, there is depicted the sweetness which comes to a soul within the Church when the light of Divine love shines within it; when the Spirit of the loving God has rolled back the bitter season of unbelief, and through the falling teardrops of sorrow for sin struggles the first glint of a renewed nature. It is from this standpoint that I ask you to consider our subject to-day while we gather up a few of the lessons which are suggested by the return of spring.

I. First of all let us notice the Power which produces this change. It is not of man, but of God.

It cannot be said, when in the warm days of spring the vegetable world is stirred with its new life, that the sole causes of this change exist within the plants themselves. Undoubtedly the principle of a new life is within the seed. The capacity to be renewed is within the plant, but unless the showers had fallen, the sun had shined, the warm currents of life had flowed through the veins of mother earth, and the soil had contributed her nourishing strength, there would have been no change, no quickening, no new life. So it is with the human soul. Man is salvable. He is capable of being renewed in the image of Jesus Christ. That is to say, the germ of a holy life and a happy future lies within that essential nature with which he was originally gifted of God, and concerning which the Creator said, "It is very good." But those germs lie buried under the ruin of the fallen man, and are torpid with the benumbing influences of sin. In the deforested mountains of Pennsylvania groves of chestnut and oak spring up. The germs of the chestnuts lie hidden beneath the pine forests of the Alleghenies, but they would lie there undeveloped forever did not the axeman's hand clear away the mighty trunks of the overshadowing pines and let in God's sunlight, and the free circulating air, and the full rains of heaven. Then up spring the long-buried germs, and chestnut groves wave where once pine forests stood.

I am not seeking here to enter upon the question of man's natural depravity, or the extent of that depravity. I am simply asserting, what all theologians must declare, that for the practical purposes of man's salvation the truth lies as here I have put it. Let man's nature be what it may, the possibility of the new life must count as nothing unless the Spirit of God breathe like the winds above it, shine with the light of truth upon it, and descend thereon as showers of blessings. Without these operations of the Divine Spirit the beauty, joy, and fruitfulness of the new birth can never come to a soul. Its winter shall never be past; its May day can never dawn. Let us emphasize the thought that for this mighty soul-change we must look to God alone.

Can man produce a spring by artificial appliances? Can he send throughout Nature, by means of furnace-fires or steam-pipes, the thrill of life which bids the kingdom of plants leap into being and beauty? No! Man may make a hot-house, but he cannot cause a spring time. He may cultivate his little beds of flowers and banks of tropical plants within the narrow confines of steam-heated rooms covered with glazed roofs, and give our winter months a taste of artificial greenery; he may force sweet flowers and beautiful flowers from which all fragrance has been cultured, to grow in pots and yield untimely blossoms in the very face of winter snows. But what a small thing is that compared with those mighty and mysterious results which are wrought everywhere around us in the Spring! Who can fill the mountains with the glory of the greening forests? Who can cover the valleys with verdant grasses and dot them with the bright eyes of countless wild flowers? Who can array innumerable orchards with white blossoms of cherry trees and pink blossoms of peach and apple? Who can send the currents of vitalizing heat through the hearts of the hills, and push out upon the dogwoods their great white blossoms, sprinkle the meadow with violets and daisies, trail the sweet arbutus along fields and skirts of woods, and fill the air over the sunny slopes with that fragrance of blossoming vines which was so sweet to Solomon in the spring days of Palestine?

Ah! who can do this but that Omnipotent Force in Nature whom men call God? Yes, man may make a hot-house, but God alone can make a Spring.

How true is the metaphor when we pass with it into the spiritual realm! There are no human forces that can cause a change of heart. Civilization, culture, education, art, science—these may indeed clothe a life with some semblance of outward beauty; but if one would penetrate the soul to its utmost depths with regenerative forces; if one would permeate society through all its length and breadth with the power of spiritual life and salvation, he must call upon God, who alone is able to do this for man and for society. Let us then look reverently up to Him as the author of every good and perfect gift. "It is not by might, nor by power, but by my spirit, saith the Lord." "Which are born not of blood, nor of the will of the flesh, nor of the will of man, but of God."*

II. Second, the great season-change of the year teaches us a lesson of Encouragement and Hope in Labors for the Spiritual Good of Men.

How drearily the winter has dragged along! How often have we wearied as storm has succeeded storm! Will winter never be over? Oh, this dreary winter, will it never end? Such have been the queries and exclamations falling from many lips. The aged, the invalid and little children, shut up within their homes during the long cold months, have grown so tired and wished so eagerly for a change! Those who have had vigor to brave the storms have fought the battle with manful and womanly perseverance, yet they too have often tired of the struggle and longed that it might be ended by the coming of the pleasant spring. There are none who feel the pinch of winter so keenly as the poor.

> "For God only knows
> 'Tis a most bitter lot to be poor when it snows."

There sits the widow in her little room with her orphaned children, nursing the little fire kindled within her

---

* John i. 13.

little stove, frugally doling out the little shovelfuls of coal which she has bought in little bucketfuls at a time from the little retail shop around the corner. The wind rattles at the rickety window. The snow drifts through the broken glass. The streets are banked with windrows of soiled snow. The pavements are icy with frozen sleet. Work is scant, wages are low. Winter pinches hard and harder until life becomes well nigh a burden. Ah, we do not wonder that the widow and the orphan and the helpless poor grow weary over our tedious and severe winter, and wonder, Will it ever be over? Will the spring time ever come?

Have you never looked out upon fields banked with a snowfall a foot or more in depth, and streams bound fast in fetters of ice, and trees shaking their bare branches in the cutting air, and been conscious of a thought somewhat like this: Can it be possible that all these shall change to the verdure and balm of June? It is indeed a marvelous transformation, and yet as surely as winter comes, winter goes. The earth that is hardened like a stone by the frosts that lie far down beneath the surface shall be mellowed; the roots shall be unloosed from the grasp of the Frost King's icy fingers; the frozen streams shall be unlocked, and their fetters cast loose upon the crest of freshets swollen by melting snows; fields and forests shall be clad in verdure and made vocal with the hum of life; the winter shall be over and gone, spring shall come! Always since the earth began it has been so. Always while the world swings on its orbit it shall be so. Summer and winter, seed time and harvest, shall not fail.

We carry our metaphor into the spiritual realm, and find it here also true that sun and season prevail over all the discouragements, disappointments and obstacles of the spiritual conflict. The human heart is indeed hard, and lives are often blighted by the frosts of sin. The streams of charity and goodness become bound within the human heart in more than icy fetters, and the soul is barren of beauty and fruitfulness as are the meadows and woods in winter. But over all this dreary landscape there floats the promise of a renewed life. Trust that promise and keep a good heart! The souls around you who seem so impervious to the gentle influences of the Gospel, to the calls of God which you have sounded so often summoning them to a new life, they at last—believe it, O discouraged one!—shall experience the blessed change from death unto life. Sin is stronger than winter, and evil habits are mightier bonds than crystals of ice, but God is great. God is omnipotent, and He is able even to the uttermost. They who trust Him shall never be confounded, and He has promised to bless His truth to the deliverance of the sinner's soul.

We need to remember this lesson of the spring in view of the many discouragements that come to us in prosecuting the work of Christ among our fellow-men. We follow our missionaries in their self-denying labors among the nations of heathenism, oftentimes with a discouraged and doubtful heart. The winter has reigned so long, superstition and sins of paganism have permeated society so deeply that one seems to be sowing seeds upon icebergs. How can the warmth of one soul mellow and melt the frigid ignorance of a whole city? What is one among so many? Yet it is our obvious duty to obey the Master's command and push forward the Master's work, believing that the Master himself will give it lodging and growth in His own good time. Is he not able to turn the king's heart whithersoever he will? Has he not often in the past touched the secret springs of national life, and caused a nation to be born at once? Is not Jesus Christ the Sun of Righteousness, and are not His divine precepts those healing rays which are to prepare humanity for the great salvation? Is not the Holy Spirit the breath of the living God, and is He not able to cause life to spring up even in the bosom of death? Yes, certainly! and while these facts remain, faith and hope may abide.

The progress of Christianity amongst pagan nations, viewed in single decades, may not seem very great, but as we glance backward along the whole period since the birth of modern missions, scarcely a century as yet, we do see a marked change! The full tide of the spiritual summer has not come in, it is true. Nay, we cannot venture to hope that even the spring has fully dawned. But over the wastes of paganism we may see here and there greening patches which show that the God of the seasons is preparing the way for spring. Here and there flowers are appearing in the earth, and the voice of the singing bird may be heard. The change has begun. Undoubtedly our sight discerns this and so strengthens our faith. The frosts of winter are beginning to yield; the icy grip of paganism begins to relax; the sun of Christian love is slowly stealing beneath the surface of society, and congealed hearts are yielding to the genial warmth. The change has begun, and as surely as spring, when once its mighty forces have begun to awaken, shall move forward through whatever lapses, oscillations and discouragements, forward to the consummation of balmy May and regal June, so surely shall the nations that have once begun to yield beneath the power of Christ's Gospel stay not in their progress until the truth shall prevail. Then shall the handful of corn on the mountains wave like the forests of Lebanon. Then shall the hosts of God on earth and in heaven lift their rejoicing song to the skies, "the winter is past, the flowers appear on the earth, the time of the singing of birds is come!"

III. A third lesson which we may learn from the Spring is that the Change of a Spiritual Life from Evil to Good is often Gradual in its Nature and Manifestation.

In our climate at least, it is hard to tell where winter ends and spring begins. Who can tell just when Spring came? The sun gathered warmth and the earth gathered verdure. There were fitful days of sunshine and storm. The season oscillated through the months of March and early April, and appeared a score of times as though it would swing forward into the balmy days of May, but as the keen winds blew, swung back again, and reminded us that winter was still lingering. At last on the little patches of sward that look toward the south we seemed to see a growing tint of green. One morning we looked again and said to ourselves, "Surely the plots are brightening! They are looking very green to-day!" Then came a balmy day when we could swing the windows wide and let in the first breath of spring to course through chambers and hall and sweep out the lifeless furnace air from the corners and freshen the whole house. That was a day indeed to make our hearts glad, and fill us with hope of what soon should be. Another day we walked down the street and glanced over a railing, and there was a crocus peeping its face above the new grass. Another day when we looked there was a dandelion, the bright harbinger of May! Not a fragrant flower, indeed, nor a comely one to the common standard of human taste, but one whose cheerful face is filled with laughter and promise, and of all the flowers of our latitude is best worthy to be embalmed as the happy symbol of Nature's resurrection. Hark! there is the song of a bird! Not the chattering call of the sparrows whose dusky coats have been familiar on our streets throughout the winter days, but the sweet twitter of a robin, or the whistle of a vireo. Yes, the migratory birds have come back. They are here to stay—the vanguard of the coming host that by and by shall fill the trees and sing among the branches. It is spring! Spring has come! When did it come? We do not know. We cannot mark the day. Winter has so gradually shaded into Spring that we can only say that we know that Spring has come because we discern that Spring is here.

It is often so with that spiritual change which we call regeneration. It is hard to tell just when the old nature was put off and the new man was put on. Said Jesus, " As the wind bloweth where it listeth, and thou canst not tell whence it cometh or whither it goeth, so is every one that is born of the Spirit." Do you ask me what practical uses there can be to such a statement as this? I answer they are very great! For example, there are many Christians who make one of the most serious mistakes of their lives by erring upon this point. They have been long looking for a decided change somewhere in their spiritual life—a jumping straight out of ungodliness into Christian excellence. Because they cannot lay their finger upon such a time, nor fix with their thought the very day when and the place where the new birth came to them, they are full of sorrow;

they doubt their change of heart; they push aside the joy that Jesus lays at their lip, and refuse to join in the chorus with God's saints: "The winter is past, the rain is over and gone, the flowers appear on the earth, and the time of the singing of birds is come."

It is not well to push too closely into the kingdom of God's grace the analogies that are drawn from Nature, but I certainly do think that here at least God works in grace very much as he does in Nature. One need not deny that regeneration is instantaneous. It may indeed be so to the thought and act of God, but I am quite prepared to say that usually the manifestation of that change to the soul and upon the life is gradual. Why then should you hold yourselves back from the hopes, joys and privileges of Christ's household, because you cannot fix the date and place of your new birth unto God?

I recall the case of one dear old lady who during a number of years of my acquaintance gave constant and satisfactory evidence of a sweet and godly trust in her Holy Saviour. If in the household where she dwelt there was any Christian life at all, it was manifest in her. Those who had known her longest said that for many years, indeed, as it afterward proved, from the very days of her childhood, she had been the same loving, Christlike soul, humble in heart, walking with God and lovely in her conversation which was "fixed in heaven." Yet she would not come to the holy communion because she did not think herself a Christian. She would not solace herself with the hope of Heaven, with the consolation that she was God's child, because she thought this would be unbecoming in one who had no evidence of a change of heart! And why did she have no such evidence? Simply because she had been taught in her early childhood that regeneration would come to her through some mighty convulsion of soul. There would be a season of tempestuous sorrow for sin, and then, swift as lightning out of the thunder-cloud, would come to her the rapturous assurance of salvation, and out of the depths she would mount at once with strong wings to Pisgah heights, and sing with all saints, "Hallelujah to the Lamb!"

Have you any such belief or feeling as that? It is just as though you expected Winter to pass into Spring by a single convulsion of nature. One day of mountainous clouds, vocal with thunder and fearful with lightning flashes, followed by the clash and roar of all the elements, and then when the storm had swept by into the distant horizon, lo! the winter is gone! The snows have disappeared! The air is balmy with the breath of Spring! The earth is soft with the life of May. The meadows are green, the forests are filled with buds, the flowers appear, and the birds are singing, singing their sweet songs. There never was a season-change such as this, my friends! There are, indeed, differences, according to latitude and elevation, as to the degree of gradation in the progress of the coming Spring. To some lands and sections the season-change comes comparatively swiftly; to others it drags along through weary weeks and months. To-day,* while here on the banks of the Delaware and Schuylkill we are rejoicing beneath the blossoms, the tidings come to us from the forests of Maine and the Adirondacks of gathering floods from the masses of melting snow still packed beneath the trees. But in no land or latitude will you ever see a Spring-change such as this which our fancy has painted. One may venture to say that almost as rare as this in the history of redemption are the cases of souls who have passed from death unto life at such a sudden stroke. Some indeed, there have been. Others, there may be; but with the great mass of mankind whose experience is recorded in Scripture, and in the annals of the Church, and whose experience is known to us, the change has come as May comes—step by step, pushing away the old and bringing in the new. Ah! you who have been hesitating so long as to your standing before the Lord, stop and think of this! You, too, may be Christ's. You may be Christ's *now!* The Spring is already upon you. It has stolen in like the sweet May glory which enfolds hills and streams. Why are you yet waiting for her to come? Why do you fold about you the dry, dead leaves of winter, and sit mourning in the "sear and yellow

* May 5th, 1887.

leaf"? O soul, awake! Sing! Come and rejoice with us to-day! Raise these words of the ancient song, " The winter is past, the rain is over and gone, the time of singing birds is come."

Another class in whose behalf I would urge this truth is young converts. It is a most natural and beautiful step for one to take who turns from a life of unbelief to one of faith. And yet it is a great step, and it brings a soul into relations that are new and difficult. The difficulties are made greater by misunderstanding the possibilities of spiritual attainment and the obligations which Christ lays upon his children. There is no mistake more common than that he who publicly professes his faith in Christ thereby announces the fact that he has become a perfect saint. The young Christian finds himself oftentimes discouraged, because when his purpose is strongest to do good, evil is present with him. He goes forth to duty or pleasure in the morning having earnestly vowed to be faithful all that day to his new life and Lord; and that day will, perhaps, be one of humiliation. Before it has well begun he shall have occasion to mourn because of some lapse from the right way, some harsh word spoken, some thought or deed unworthy of his holy name and vocation. Then comes the thought, " I am no Christian at all! I am discouraged! I will give up trying to be better!" That would indeed be a most unchristian conclusion. One in such estate should not give up, but rather learn that such errors as his are to be expected.

One does not pass into perfection by a single stride, as he crosses the line from Germany to France, from the United States to Canada or Mexico. He passes as the world comes from winter to spring, from January to May. The progress of sanctification in the soul is gradual. The victory over sin is won by a long series of conflicts in which there are defeats, humiliations, but from and after which there is always an uplifting and regirding of the soul for conflict, and re-entering the lists to do new battle for righteousness and Christ. Make up your mind that to err is human, and that as you are human, you also will probably err. Purpose in your mind to sin as little as possible, but when the time of sinning has overtaken your soul, do not wonder as though some marvel had occurred, but, confessing your fault, turn with new devotion and vigor to the Christian life. Try to be better to-day than you were yesterday; to be better to-morrow than you are to-day, even a little better,—that will do,—and so day by day growing in grace and in the knowledge of Jesus Christ you shall find your soul gradually clothed upon with the beauty of holiness, and your life daily approaching the requirements of the Gospel.

Be sure of this, that the battle against sin in your heart will never end on earth. Even St. Paul could say: "But I see a different law in my members, warring against the law of my mind, and bringing me into captivity under the law of sin which is in my members. Oh! wretched man that I am! who shall deliver me out of the body of this death? I thank God through Jesus Christ our Lord." * Yes, through Jesus Christ your Lord, you too, as did St. Paul, shall overcome the law of sin that is within your members; but it will not be an immediate victory. It will be a life-conflict. You shall ripen into the Christian character, and when you become like St. Paul, the aged, you will be able to look back over the past, and with joyful spirit thank God for your sanctified being. Then you too may say and sing: "I have fought the good fight, I have finished the course, I have kept the faith: henceforth there is laid up for me the crown of righteousness, which the Lord, the righteous Judge, shall give me at that day."†

In truth, the work of perfecting shall never be ended within the human soul. There is but one absolutely perfect Being—God alone—who "is eternal and unchangeable, infinite in being, wisdom, power, holiness, justice, goodness and truth." If you shall be so happy as to attain immortality with God, there will be before you an eternity of attainment; there will be an infinity of divine gifts within your reach, and therefore all eternity cannot exhaust the possibilities of your acquisitions. Forever being perfected, and never being perfect! This is the destiny

---

* Rom. vii. 23-25. † II. Tim. iv. 7, 8.

which awaits you. Were it otherwise, you might conceive that even Heaven would grow monotonous. If
you could think that after ages and millenniums and
æons of time have rolled away, you should at last have
gathered to your expanded souls the whole treasures of
heavenly knowledge, love and grace, you might, even
with a whole eternity before you, still grow weary. The
soul of man is so constituted that progression is necessary to happiness, when once the mind has been set forward upon the path of attainment. It is a wise saying,
founded upon this philosophy of our constitution,

> "A little learning is a dangerous thing—
> Drink deep, or taste not the Pierian spring.

Man must drink deep when once he has tasted, and the
more he quaffs from the stream of knowledge, the more
eagerly does he long for deeper draughts. If he could
pause at the fountain-head and feel that the stream is dry,
that never more would it flow with fresh supplies for him;
that he had tasted all, that he had drunk every drop,
would there not then come to his soul that which would
throw a shadow even over heaven, a spirit of dissatis-
faction, a longing for something more? But we do not
cherish such a fear; for we know that the new life which
begins in regeneration here, flows on endlessly in the
hereafter. Progression is endless because God is infinite,
and the stores of knowledge which He has at command
can never be exhausted by the souls of angels and men.

I once stood in a cemetery laid out just above the
town of Huntingdon, Pa., and looked around upon a
beautiful mountain scene. The history of civilization in
its various stages westward lay within the compass of
my vision. "There," said my friend and guide, "is the
old Indian trail by which the red men threaded these
forests. Yonder is the bridle path by which the first
pioneers crossed towards the fertile fields of the west.
Yonder is the old road, wagon road, stage route, State
road over which the traffic of forty years ago rolled in
Conestoga wagons from Pittsburg to the sea. There is
the canal that succeeded the Conestogas in carrying
Philadelphia's freights to the foot of the Alleghenies;

and there is the track of the Pennsylvania Railroad with its scores of trains daily steaming to and fro bearing men and material from all ends of the world to all ends." A story of progress was outlined there as in a map— progress through conflict and cost, rising always toward something better.

We turned from this lovely and significant scene to read an inscription upon a neighboring grave-stone. The name carved thereon was that of an officer who fell during the civil war in defense of the Republic. The inscription contained these words: "His body lies in an unknown grave on the battle-field, but that God who gave him courage to die for his country will watch over it until reanimated by his noble spirit on that day when earth and sea shall give up their dead!"

Sweet hope! Death does not end man's progress in life and life's acquisitions. The old form of life ends, but the spirit survives and takes on a new semblance. The grave only closes the first stage of man's development; the trail through life's dark forest opens upon a wide road in the Eternity, and that in turn shall open into a wider, and with swifter growth and change as the ages go, man shall leave behind him the past and enter upon higher stages of progress. This is indeed an inspiring hope! Would that you all might receive it with unfaltering trust. Ah! the winter of Death would then cease to have dread for you, for you should know that there follows close upon it a celestial Spring that shall move forward into the perfect Summer with that fruitage whose seeds of blessedness are eternal within themselves.

> When even at last the solemn hour shall come,
> And wing my mystic flight to future worlds,
> I cheerful will obey; there, with new powers,
> Will rising wonders sing: I cannot go
> Where Universal Love not smiles around,
> Sustaining all yon orbs, and all their suns;
> From seeming evil still educing good,
> And better thence again, and better still,
> In infinite progression. But I lose
> Myself in Him, in Light ineffable!
> Come, then, expressive Silence, muse His praise.*

*JAMES THOMSON—"A Hymn on the Seasons."

The Birth of the Flowers.

"The flowers appear on the earth."— SONG OF SOLOMON ii. 12.

THE BIRTH OF THE FLOWERS.

WHAT beauty one sees covering the earth in mid-May! . The tender leaves, so far as the trees have put them forth, have all the freshness of Easter clothes. The meadows and lawn wear their brightest livery of emerald sward. The yellow, white and blue flowers spread their brilliant hues over all the landscape, and as they are the first show of the springtide their beauty has not palled upon our senses, and we welcome them with a thrill of pleasure.

The yellow flowers are not numerous, but there are some. The Buttercups nod in rich profusion. The Dandelion still lingers, although its sunny face, fresh with the icy breath of March, has been cheering us for weeks. Just now its stalks are tipped with those graceful globes which at one's touch dissolve into a score of seeds, every one tufted with a cluster of downy ciliæ that float it off upon the breeze over the meadow. A lovely English lady said to me, "I wonder that you Americans love the dandelion. We think it a rather nasty plant." Ah, but I do not wonder. Its flower glows with the first breath of spring; its seeds are veritable fairies in gracefulness, and its quaint notched leaves, that warrant its name of lion-tooth (*dent de lion*), mark it at once as noted among the common plants.

White flowers are more plentiful. The dog-eared petals of the Cornus (Dogwood) fairly cover the low tree, and show afar off through the woods like a white banner of ancient France. The Horse-chestnut, emblem of our "Buckeye State,"* lifts erect above its broad leaves tall clustered cones, that reminds one of the white pompon on a soldier's hat. The Locust trees have begun to show their pendent bunches of fragrant blossoms. There, too, is the Snowball bush, well deserving its name, for one might fancy a boy's fistful of

---

* The *Æsculus glabra* is Ohio's plant emblem.

(297)

snowballs had been stuck upon every twig. The Spiræa holds up branches flecked with woolly bloom. The Hawthorn's milk-white clusters "scent the evening gale." The Daisies are not yet plentiful, but you will find them with their star-white rays issuing from their hearts of gold; not the "wee modest crimson-tipped flower," of Burns' exquisite poem, but our own bold beauty who loves the sun and society. The wild Strawberry nestles close to the bosom of mother earth, with its delicate odor and dainty bloom. The creamy flower of the May Apple (Podophyllum) hangs on its wax-like stem beneath its broad leaves.

The blue flowers with their many shades of purple, lavender, violet, are in their glory. The Flag waves her banner at the edge of pond and brook, reminding us that the flowers appear on the water as well as on the earth. The Judas tree, with its pinkish blossoms, shows bright in the leafless clumps of shrubbery. The Polonia has put forth its huge clusters of heavy-scented cup-shaped blossoms, a strange sight indeed, a great forest tree decked from top to lowest bough with purple flowers. Yet the stately trunks of the grenadier Tulip Poplar will soon bear up even a nobler bloom.

Then there is the Lilac, sweet, old-fashioned flower, that loves the precinct of home, and rears its lavender blooms above its heart-shaped leaves, filling the air with a fragrance that calls up childhood's days. Shall we forget the Violet, the sweet social flower, whose beds and banks furnish exhaustless nosegays for the children's pink fingers? We must name at least one more, the majestic Wisteria (or shall we say Wistaria?), the queen of flowering vines, embowering the porch, draping the windows, swinging from the very eaves of the roof, hanging thick with purple bunches as big as grapes of Eshcol. It is a rare sight; worth crossing an ocean to see, as it grows here in our West Philadelphia, decked in its May glory!

Such a scene as this, even more brilliant with the lovely jewels of the field, must Solomon have witnessed when spring opened upon the valleys and hill-slopes of his native land. Flowers grow in great variety and abundance in Palestine, and from the month of January to May the groves and meadows are adorned with the blossoms of many different species of wild plants. There one finds the flora of the tropics, and there the sweeter familiar plants of our own temperate zones. Some of those flowers that appeared on the earth to Israel's king, and were marked by the eye of Him whose glory exceeded that of Solomon, are among the well-loved familiars of our own gardens. There were the anemone, crocus, tulip, hyacinth, wind-flower, narcissus, lily, violet, aster, pink, iris, daffodil, crow-foot, dragon wort, periwinkle, veronica, white clover, hollyhock, and a multitude of others which one need not stop to name, but which perfume the air to-day as in the days of the patriarchs and prophets, and give lovely prospect to the landscape.*

I. We learn first the Constancy of Divine Power in protecting and preserving the Beautiful and Good.

" The flowers appear on the earth." There is something inexpressibly touching in the thought that through the ages of the past, summer and winter have come and gone, and inevitably with the bursting forth of Spring have come back to us the old familiar faces of the sweet plants that our childhood knew. It was a part of the divine constitution of things, as we read in the book of Genesis, that the earth should bring forth grass, the herb yielding seed and the fruit tree yielding fruit after his kind, whose seed is in itself.† This primal law of plant life has never been broken. No one knows how long flowers have been appearing upon the earth in successive returns of the seasons, but we do know that as often as they may have come back, they came the same as when they left. Spring found them where Winter laid them. The sweet fancy of the poet is approved as a veritable fact in the clear light of science :—

> But cheerful and unchanged the while
> Your first and perfect form ye show,
> The same that won Eve's matron smile
> In the world's opening glow.‡

---

*McClintock & Strong—"Flowers." †Gen. i. 11. ‡Keble.

This is true within the historic period. The whole
world of Sunday-school teachers and scholars is now*
passing through a series of lessons which present to us
the life of the Pharaohs of Egypt and their oppressed
bondsmen, the Hebrews. We have been deeply interested in that triumph of modern archæology and photo-
graphic science which presents to us the figures of the
mummies of Seti I. and Rameses II., the Pharaohs during whose sovereignty the hapless babes of the Jews
were murdered, and the infant Moses was born and reared
to manhood. But there is a fact incidental to the discovery of these and other mummies with which few of
the public are acquainted, they have afforded botanists
an opportunity to compare the plant life of the Mosaic
period with the plant life of this day. Within the
mummy-wrappings have been found no less than fifty-
nine species.† Some of these are represented by the
fruits employed as offerings to the dead, others by the
flowers and leaves made into garlands, and the remainder
by the branches on which the body was laid out during
or after embalmment, and which were enclosed with the
offerings within the linen wrappings that enveloped the
mummy. These plant remains were hermetically sealed
within the wrappings, and thus, according to Mr. William
Carruthers of the British Museum, have been preserved
with scarcely any change.‡ By placing the plants in warm
water a series of specimens was obtained which, although
gathered four thousand years ago, are as satisfactory for
the purposes of science as any collected at the present
day. These specimens consequently supply means for the
closest examination and comparison with their living representatives. The colors of the flowers are still present,
even the most evanescent, such as the violet of the lark-
spur and knap-weed and the scarlet of the poppy. The
chlorophyl remains in the leaves, and the sugar in the
pulp of the raisins. It is difficult, says Mr. Carruthers,
without actual inspection of the specimens of plants

---

* May, 1887. † Determined by Dr. Schweinfurth. ‡ Address to
the Biological Section of the British Association, Birmingham,
1886, by William Carruthers, President of the Section, Pres. Lin-
næan Society, &c.

employed as garlands, to realize the wonderful condition of preservation in which they are. These specimens consequently supply means for the closest examination and comparison with their living representatives. Thus examined and compared, their absolute identity with the present indigenous forms of the species represented is demonstrated in the clearest manner. With scarce an exception the most learned botanists have not been able to detect any peculiarity in the living plants which is absent in those obtained from the tombs. Thus through four thousand years, since Seti I. decreed the slaughter of the Hebrew babes, and the daughter of Pharaoh, Thermuthis, preserved the infant Moses from the waters of the Nile, these flowers and vines, trees and plants of Egypt have fallen with every winter's decay, and at the coming of Spring have appeared on the earth again bearing the same form, features and color that they carried to their season-sleep.

Nor is this all. The hand of geology has turned over the pages of Natural History far back of the period of Seti, Rameses and Moses, so far back that one may scarcely venture to estimate the age. Reading from these uncovered pages the paleo-botanist declares that since the glacial epoch at least, say a quarter-million years, no appreciable change has taken place. It is still an established axiom with botanists that "species must be dealt with as fixed quantities." * In our own country we are enabled to read the story of plant life from a period of the Tertiary as far back at least as the Oligocene. Lequereux identifies as among the plants found in the fossil-yielding strata, hickories, oaks, birches, poplars, willows, elms, cedars, wild roses, sumac, alders, ferns, catalpa and bignonia. These grew in the woods of that ancient period precisely as they do in our own forests; and in the lagoons and ponds of the Tertiary the blooms of water lilies and the blossoms of grasses, reeds and iris showed precisely as they do to-day in the ponds of New Jersey and the lagoons of the South.† Thus the

---

* CARRUTHERS. † LEQUEREUX—"U. S. Geological Survey of the Territories, Vol. VII., 1878; Tertiary Flora." See for illustrations the Coal Flora Atlas of the Second Geological Survey of Pennsylvania.

law impressed by the Creator's hand upon plant life, to
"bring forth seed after its kind," is proved to have been
in all these years in active operation.   The plants and
flowers have appeared and disappeared with the season-
changes, while the ages have come and gone.   There is
an obvious bearing of these facts upon the theory of
evolution, but we are now looking to them for illustrations of spiritual truths.

What lesson do they suggest ?   Surely we will not
forget that the Lord himself has compared the holy influences of the gospel to the seed which is cast into the
ground.   He who scatters that seed may be assured that
the hand of God will care for his influence and works
throughout all ages.   Good deeds are the flowers of
human life.   The law of heredity is operative upon
them also.   Seasons shall come and go, the years shall
wax and wane, centuries and generations shall pass, but
the good that men have done shall spring up anew with
the new-coming lives of the new ages, and shall perpetuate for good man's work in this world, aye, and in the
next.   The power of an endless life is in every honest
effort for good.   This is an immortality which all may
covet,—the immortality of holy living and useful deeds.
With what hope and joy should we commit our labors,
wrought in love and fear of God, to the keeping of the
future, knowing that He who "is the same yesterday,
to-day and forever," will see to it that the holy seed
shall never cease to find a lodgment and growth among
the children of the earth.   The frosts of winter, the fret
of time, the storms, floods and convulsions of earth,—
all social changes and all assaults of Satan shall vainly
seek to quench this influence from the world.   For a
little while indeed adverse forces may seem to succeed;
for a little while winter may hide away the seeds, may
cut down the stalks to the very bulb or root; but God's
hands shall wheel on the course of time, and when the
ages shall have ripened, the old Song of Solomon shall
be heard again upon the air of spring; "The winter is
past, the rain is over and gone, the flowers appear on the
earth!"   "In the morning sow thy seed, and in the
evening withhold not thine hand, for thou knowest not

which shall prosper, whether this or that."* "In due season ye shall reap if ye faint not."†

"Sow thy seed." Yes, remember that it is SEED that you are sowing, and that it is the seed which contains the principle of life, by virtue of which the flowers appear on the earth. Diamonds are beautiful, certainly. Diamonds are valuable, certainly; but, Christian friends, we sow seeds—not diamonds—that which is to grow and bear fruit it may be an hundred fold. The glitter and polish of rhetoric may not be out of place in pulpit and Sunday-school, but he who comes to these spots where furrows of virgin soil await the sower, with no seed, fails utterly. A jeweled hand may scatter seeds. But a hand that scatters jewels without the seeds has no place in the Lord's vineyard.

II. Nor let it be forgotten that there are other seeds scattered through this world of ours than seeds of holiness and faith. Evil as well as good is a constant quantity.

Our blessed Saviour has taught us how the enemy comes while we sleep, and sows "tares" among the "wheat."‡ As far back as the thought of science can go upon the sure roadway of observation, it declares it to be true that the tares and goodly grain have sprung up and grown together. The same weeds that trouble tillers of the soil in Egypt to-day were the pests of their ancestors in those old times of which we have been speaking, forty and fifty centuries ago. Grains of barley and wheat are of frequent occurrence in the tombs. M. Mariette found barley in a grave of the fifth dynasty, at Sakhara, five thousand four hundred years old. The fields of barley then were infested by a weed known as the Spiny Medick.§ Another of the Egyptian tares found among the mummies is the Charlock,‖ better known among us as the wild mustard. It infests the flax crop, and there is scarce a field in Egypt where it may not be found to-day, and often in such quantity that its yellow

---

*Eccl. xi. 6. †Gal. vi. 9. ‡Matt. xiii. 25. §*Medicago denticulata.* ‖ *Sinapis arvensis*, var. *allionii.*

flowers, just before the flax comes into bloom, present the appearance of a crop of mustard.* Thus the vigor of evil, tested by its endurance, is quite equal to that of the good.

That vigor is also seen in the power of weeds to disseminate themselves with great rapidity under adverse circumstances. Sir Joseph Hooker found the familiar English weed known as Shepherd's Purse, itself a colonist from Central Asia, growing abundantly on a solitary Antarctic islet.† Wondering greatly how it could have gotten there, he traced it finally to the grave of a sailor, around which the intrusive little plant flourished luxuriously, and from which, as a centre, it had evidently distributed itself over the island. How came the plant within the soil of that English sailor's grave? The spade with which the grave was dug had been used to dig in English soil, and a single seed of Shepherd's Purse, clinging to particles of earth upon the spade, dropped off and mingled with the Antarctic soil of that burial mound, and grew and spread until the all-encompassing sea checked its career of conquest.

It is not a pleasant reflection for us that evil influences, like these tares of ancient Egypt and the weeds that grow among our garden plants, have staying qualities quite as vigorous as those of lovely flowers and useful plants. But it is a wholesome thought, and one which never should drop away from our minds; for it points to a fact which we are daily called upon to face, and upon which, in all our efforts to overcome evil in our own hearts and subdue sin in the world, we should calculate with unfailing accuracy. The evil and the good, the tares and the wheat, the flowers and the weeds shall grow together until the day of judgment. So our Saviour teaches, and it will not do for us to forget the teaching lest we relax our vigilance in watching and our diligence in laboring to preserve the world from the incoming and growth of those hurtful principles which thwart all holy effort, and must surely destroy those over whom they obtain the power.

* CARRUTHERS—"Address to Biological Section Brit. Assn."
† GRANT ALLEN—"Collin Clout's Callendar," page 12.

III. We have thus far been drawing comfort and instruction from the fact that God shall preserve our influence and works. Let us remember that this includes the Source of Work and Influence—Ourselves.

One of the most familiar of the lessons which Jesus taught the world is the duty of absolute trust in God as drawn from the flowers. "Consider the lilies," He said, "how they grow: they toil not, neither do they spin; yet I say unto you, Even Solomon in all his glory was not arrayed like one of these. But if God doth so clothe the grass in the field, which to-day is, and to-morrow is cast into the oven; how much more shall he clothe you, O ye of little faith? * * * Fear not, little flock; for it is your Father's good pleasure to give you the kingdom." *

One day the well-known missionary Fidelia Fisk was instructing a class of pagan women. She was compelled by the customs of the country to occupy a sitting posture on the floor without that support of body and back so grateful to women afforded by our comfortable chairs. A heathen convert present, noticing that her teacher was greatly fatigued by the day's hard work, left the circle of hearers and sat down behind her, placing her back to Miss Fisk's back. The missionary lady recognized the kindness and timeliness of the act, and leaned gently against her dusky friend; but this did not satisfy.

"No! No!" said the convert, "if you love me, lean hard, lean hard."

I think I can hear the voice as of our Heavenly Redeemer saying to every weak and weary soul, timid, doubting, fearful, and longing, "if you love Me, lean hard." "Cast thy burden on the Lord." Cast thyself on the Lord. Do not fear to rest thyself fully upon Him!

> He will comfort and keep thee,
> He will carry thee through.

This lesson of untroubled trust in God every opened flower of Spring teaches human hearts. If God lavishes such ceaseless wealth of care upon a flower, what may He not, what will He not do for His own immortal children?

---

* Luke xii. 27-33.

Sweet nurslings of the vernal skies,
  Bathed in soft airs, and fed with dew,
What more than magic in you lies,
  To fill the heart's fond view?
In childhood's sports, companions gay,
In sorrow, on Life's downward way,
How soothing ! in our last decay
  Memorials prompt and true.

*   *   *   *   *   *

Ye felt your Maker's smile that hour,
  As when he paused and owned you good ;
His blessing on earth's primal bower,
  Ye felt it all renewed.
What care ye now, if winter's storm
Sweep ruthless o'er each silken form ?
Christ's blessing at your heart is warm,
  Ye fear no vexing mood.

Alas ! of thousand bosoms kind,
  That daily court you and caress,
How few the happy secret find
  Of your calm loveliness !
Live for to-day ! to-morrow's light
To-morrow's care shall bring to sight,
Go sleep like closing flowers at night,
  And Heaven thy morn will bless.*

Consider the lilies, *how they grow !* We have considered, and have learned that back in those far ages of the Tertiary, the lilies were growing in ponds and lagoons just as they do now; that therefore their life and the lives of their companion flowers of fields, forests and waters have been held here countless ages in perpetual life by the hand of God. Frail, perishing things of a day! Yet thus has God carried their life unquenched amidst the convulsions of ages and birth-throes of continents. He promises thus to carry you, O soul of man! Surely he will fulfill his promise. Trust Him, trust Him implicitly! Trust Him and doubt not, but keep with you through life and to the very portals of opening eternity the joyful confidence that He will hold your soul securely and perpetuate it with the immortality of the blessed in the gardens of your God. The flower of our mortal form shall indeed decay, but the life of the spirit runs on with an immortality far outlasting that of forest growth or garden bloom. God has

.* KEBLE—"The Christian Year."   15th Sunday after Trinity.

guaranteed this, and His word shall be made good. "The grass withereth, the flower fadeth, but the word of our God shall stand forever."*

I was driving once along the margin of a flooded stream and was stopped at a point where the road for many rods was overflowed. "Can we go on?" I asked of a neighbor. "Yes, drive forward, it is not deep. The road is safe!" And though no road was in sight, nothing but the broad expanse of turgid water, I drove on and reached the other side in safety. A good lesson, I said; and bethought me of Whittier's lines,

> Nothing before, nothing behind;
> .The steps of Faith
> Fall on the seeming void, and find
> The rock beneath.†

Thus is it often in the affairs of this life. Thus is it always when our footsteps draw near the brink of that river of death which divides between us and the shore of the Heavenly Canaan. Pathless, dark, intangible, shoreless seems the stream, and the waters cold as winter; but the Rock of Ages bridges the way, and beyond the Flowers appear!

---

* Isa. xi. 8.   † "My Soul and I."

LECTURE XVII.

Beautiful Flowers and Tender Grapes.

"Whose glorious beauty is a fading flower."—
ISAIAH xxviii. 1.

"The flowers appear on the earth;
*   *   *   *   *
The fig tree ripeneth her green figs,
And the vines are in blossom,
They give forth their fragrance."
SONG OF SOLOMON ii. 12, 13.

BEAUTIFUL FLOWERS AND TENDER GRAPES.

FLOWERS have always been associated in the human mind with beauty. They are emblems and expressions of a sense of the beautiful, not only in man, but in the universe. We have an apt illustration of this in our Saviour's remark concerning the lilies of the field, "that even Solomon in all his glory was not arrayed like one of these." * He who looks upon Nature with a careful eye, and observes such constant regard to that harmony and arrangement of form, color and function which results in what we call beauty, is compelled to find some reason for this effect. Jesus, in the passage just quoted, plainly asserts that the beautiful clothing of the flowers is wrought by God, and clearly implies that this beauty " which to-day is, and to-morrow is cast into the oven," has some cause higher than can be explained by their limited life and ephemeral destiny.

Mr. Darwin, and many others following him, have been able to trace some relation between beauty and utility. They have attempted to show that the beauty of animals and plants performs a very important part in securing protection to the individual or propagation of the species, and that it has probably been developed through such usefulness. We need not scruple to allow at least a modicum of truth within these speculations. But there must always remain the conclusion that the fact of beauty in the creature implies a sense of beauty in the creative Force; and further, the sense of beauty implies a Personal Force, a Mind, as the source of such sentiment. It is foreign to our present purpose to consider the argument for the being and personality of God which is readily deducible, along this line of reasoning, from the beautiful flowers and all other lovely things in

---

* Matt. vi. 29.

this world of ours. We must be content simply to present the thought, and express the conviction that beauty in flowers or elsewhere is an inevitable expression of the character of the Creator, reflecting that Taste which dwells in infinite perfection within the Divine; and moreover, that apart from all bare utility, it has a higher purpose within itself, namely, to contribute to the happiness and holiness of men.

> God might have bade the earth bring forth
>   Enough for great and small,
> The oak tree and the cedar tree,
>   Without a flower at all.
> We might have had enough, enough,
>   For every want of ours,
> For luxury, medicine, and toil,
>   And yet have had no flowers.
>
> Then wherefore, wherefore were they made,
>   All dyed with rainbow-light,
> All fashioned with supremest grace,
>   Upspringing day and night :—
> Springing in valleys green and low,
>   And on the mountains high,
> And in the silent wilderness
>   Where no man passes by ?
>
> Our outward life requires them not,—
>   Then wherefore had they birth ?—
> To minister delight to man,
>   To beautify the earth.*

I. The first lesson which invites your attention is that the spirit of Christianity compels Alliance between all Physical and Moral Beauty.

Of the two splendid columns that stood at the gateway of Solomon's temple named Jachin and Boaz it is written that on the tops of the pillars was lily-work.† This was the objective presentation of a fact elsewhere declared that "Strength and beauty are in his sanctuary."‡ And again, "Out of Zion, the perfection of beauty, God hath shined."§ The beauty and strength of the Church has always been and ever must be its holiness. The familiar phrase "the beauty of holiness"

* MARY HOWITT—"The Use of Flowers." † I. Kings vii. 22.
‡ Ps. xcvi. 6. § Ps. l. 2.

well expresses this conviction as it has dwelt in the heart of the Catholic Church.

There is profound need in this age that these ideas should be kept closely associated. Every one who has followed the trend of some of the leading minds and philosophic speculations of our time must have seen how strong is the tendency to a wide breach between the two. Beauty, say these thinkers, is a matter by itself; holiness or personal purity or morals have no necessary connection therewith.

There is a strain in modern thought as foul as any in ancient Athens, Pompeii or Rome. Men conceal it from view or smother it under the name "Æstheticism." By whatever name, its odor is quite as ill. Modern æstheticism may be described as demanding from art, literature, architecture only a perfect form without regard to the inner life of the heart,—its spiritual purpose and thought. It declares that no matter how false and unclean may be the thought of the poem or painting if it be only artistically perfect, and true to nature, it has fulfilled its destiny. It exalts beauty of mode irrespective of morals. It makes the beauty of form perfect and chief, and the beauty of holiness it belittles or denies. I do not say that this is all of modern æstheticism, but it is much of it, and the evil is more widely spread and deeply rooted than you suppose. Shall it prevail? Not if the Church and the world will bend a serious ear to the heavenly message. The whole thinking of Christianity has in the past gained victories most conspicuous. In the future it shall not deceive our hopes. It triumphed over the art and architecture of paganism.

I say nothing of the positively immoral, but speak of the negative features thereof. The sculpture of Rome and Greece was a glorification and expression of form, the utterance of mere beauty of the body, female loveliness, manly strength. The Venus de Medici, Apollo Belvidere, and the Dying Gladiator are the best examples of pagan art. And what is the underlying purpose of Christian art? Americans cross the ocean in multitudes to behold the gothic temples of Europe.

They gaze upon carvings in stone, paintings upon glass, creations of the brush that adorn church walls, and see everywhere the ideas of true Holiness which were brought by the Gospel of Christ into the world. The lives of the apostles, prophets, and holy martyrs are celebrated therein, and above all, the life of Christ Himself. It is man that is glorified, but not physical man,—it is man the spiritual being, who by attainments in holy living and by service of humanity rises above the attractions of the world, the temptations of avarice and ambition, the lusts of the flesh. Thus art in painting and in its sublimest forms, architecture and sculpture, speaks throughout Christendom of the glory of the New Life, the exalted thoughts of Jesus, the blessedness which He brought to man. There are excrescences upon this art, survivals of paganism, monstrosities that belonged to the ignorance and superstitions of the times, but the ideas are there, and they are worthy, grand, soul-uplifting, man-transforming, Christ-honoring. Holiness dominated the thinking of men and triumphed over mere sensualism, however accurately expressed. Thus the æstheticism of ancient paganism yielded before Christian thought as it was expressed in art. May it ever be so!

Let me quote here for its close bearing upon our subject from the last words publicly uttered by the late Sidney Lanier. "Wherever there is contest, as between artistic and moral beauty, unless the moral side prevail, all is lost. Let any sculptor hew us out the most ravishing combination of tender curves and spheric softness that ever stood for woman, yet if the lip have a certain fullness that hints of the flesh, if the brow be insincere, if, in the minutest particular, the physical beauty suggest a moral ugliness, that sculptor, unless he be portraying moral ugliness for a moral purpose, may as well give over his marble for paving stones. Time, whose judgments are inexorably moral, will not accept this work. For, indeed, we may say that he who has not yet perceived how artistic beauty and moral beauty are convergent lines, which run back into a common ideal origin, and who, therefore, is not afire with moral beauty just as with artistic beauty; that he, in short, who has not come to that stage of quiet and eternal frenzy in which the beauty of holiness and the holiness of beauty mean one thing, burn as one fire, shine as one light, within him is not yet the great Artist."*

In reply to the saying that art is the work of man, Nature the work of God, Hegel says that God reveals Himself in man, and therefore the best of man's works are the best of God's. This is true. The holy life, the sublime strength, the patient endurance, when they are objects for the subjective appreciation, do show the possibilities of God rather than nature. Art does not reach this height, and mere genius cannot realize these in art with perfect understanding and self-consistency. No mere artistic work could draw such a character as Jesus Christ, and there is more in the saint than in any picture of him in colors or words.†

It was the concrete exhibition of ideal human loveliness in Jesus Christ which gave men a deeper sense of sin, taught them their imperfections and the conditions for their ultimate well-being, which clarified and corrected their conception of the highest, which caused the new ideal of their own possible advancement to shine gloriously out of the mists, and gave them an undoubting assurance that the ultimate hope of human thought had been reached, and the riddle of existence solved.

II. There is another point which may be considered in this connection. We have been thinking that the graces of life represented by the flowers are developed by the spirit of our holy religion. Is it in contradiction of this that we see so many Graces in the Lives of Heathen?

1. We admit the fact. No child of God should have a disposition to derogate from, but rather exalt and applaud all that is good among the pagan nations, and thank God that so much of the original bloom has survived the frosts of sin. We must allow that Confucius, Buddha, Zoroaster and Mohammed may bring forth and

---

* Lecture delivered before John Hopkins University in April, 1881. † HEGEL's "Æsthetics." By Professor KEDNEY. Page 51.

preserve upon the life of their disciples the graces of artificial culture; but only Christ Jesus can cover the world with the flowers of a spiritual springtide. Hothouse flowers are comely, but their loveliness is in spite of their surroundings, not because of them. Surely, the systems out of which the natural graces of non-Christian nations have grown are not suited to develop graces in the whole race. What we see in China or India is not the bloom of the earth under a spring sun, but simply a conservatory bloom. Like the flowers and buds which the florist fastens upon wire stems in building his floral emblems and bouquets, the graces of philosophy and natural religion have no vital stalk to rest upon. But Christianity brings blossoms whose stems are united to a living Vine, to the Rose of Sharon and the Lily of the Valley; these have in them the power of an endless life; transplanted to another sphere, the garden of God, they will root and grow and bloom forever.

2. This seeming contradiction may be observed in Christian communities. There are some unregenerate people who have very many graces. Some ungodly men are delightful companions. They have natures rich in attributes which exalt humanity, and manners that adorn their behavior as flowers do the garden. But we must not forget that much of this beauty is due to heredity, to the reflex influence of Christians, and the direct influence of Christian institutions. Christ has left his impress upon all society. The distinction has been made, and in some measure is just, that the Church of Jesus includes the regenerate of God, but the kingdom of Christ embraces all within those nations wherein the Church has been established. In this sense these lovely men and women, though unregenerate, have caught and retain upon their sensitive natures the reflection, aye, the impress of Christian graces. Yet at the best, it must be said that these graces are artificial; their loveliness is like that of the painter's canvas laid upon the surface by an external force, not like that of the flower, a product and expression of an inward personal life-force. One may find a most perfect exposition of this truth in

the thirteenth chapter of the First Epistle to the Corinthians. There we are taught that one may have outer
adornment of the goodliest and most gracious behavior,
may bestow ail his goods to feed the poor, may even
give his body to be burned, yet lacking Agape, grace,
charity, love, all else profiteth nothing. Here we see the
difference between the graces of polite society and true
Christian loveliness. It is precisely the difference between natural flowers, the growth of spring, and artificial
flowers, the product of human skill.

3. There is this other point to be noted. The philosophy of heathenism, the ethics of modern unbelief, the
graces of society, the culture of art, science, and literature are impracticable as forces taken by themselves for
the elevation of the masses. One might as well undertake to adorn the whole surface of the earth with hot-
house plants, or decorate it with vases of artificial flowers,
as to open up upon the entire life of humanity the graces
of a Christian civilization simply by the forces known
generally under the word culture. There is but one
force known among men that is practicable for the rescue
of our race from the unloveliness and misery of sin. It
is the force of the Holy Spirit breathing through the
religion of Jesus Christ. If ever the fairest graces of
humanity are to mantle the whole earth it shall only be
when the Sun of Divine righteousness and love has girdled the race with quickening rays to give Divine kindling within every human heart and vitality to the Gospel
truth which comes to it. Nothing but Christianity can
accomplish this result, and this result I believe Christianity will accomplish.

4. We pass from these general to individual reflections, to your own experience and life. The heart which
is renewed in the image of Christ must set forth upon
the behavior some flowers of Christian loveliness. The
true Christian has in him necessarily the elements of a
true gentleman. Read some of the precepts of our
holy faith. Begin with the Golden Rule. "All things,
therefore, whatsoever ye would that men should do unto

you, even so do ye also unto them."* "In honor preferring one another."† "Be pitiful, be courteous."‡
"Being reviled we bless."§ "Thou shalt love thy neighbor as thyself." ‖ "Rejoice with them that rejoice;
weep with them that weep." ¶ "Give to him that asketh
thee." ** "If thine enemy hunger, feed him." †† "Using hospitality one towards another."‡‡ "Forget not
to show love unto strangers."§§ "Love suffereth long,
and is kind; love envieth not; love vaunteth not itself, is not puffed up, doth not behave itself unseemly,
seeketh not its own, is not provoked, taketh not account
of evil; rejoiceth not in unrighteousness, but rejoiceth
with the truth; beareth all things, believeth all things,
endureth all things."‖‖ "If a brother or sister be naked,
and in lack of daily food, and any one of you say unto
them, Go in peace, be ye warmed and filled; and yet
give them not the things needful to the body; what doth
it profit?"¶¶ Let us sum up these matchless precepts.
"Finally, brethren, whatsoever things are true, whatsoever things are honorable, whatsoever things are just,
whatsoever things are pure, whatsoever things are lovely, whatsoever things are of good report; if there be
any virtue, and if there be any praise, think on these
things."***

These are some of the precepts of our divine Lord and
his inspired apostles intended to regulate the believer's
faith. The very reading of them is a powerful enforce-
ment of their claim to emanate from a Divine Source.
Can you find such rules of true gentility anywhere in
literature, independent of the influence of the Holy
Scriptures? I dare assert that such cannot be found.
These are flowers that appear on the earth when regenerated by the influence of the Spirit of our faith. The
tendency of Christianity is always to develop these
flowers of courtesy, politeness, genuine goodness, and
unselfishness. When one is born again there will be
some show of these graces. No matter how small the

---

* Matt. vii. 12. † Rom. xii. 10. ‡ I. Pet. iii. 8. § I. Cor. iv.
12. ‖ Matt. xix. 20. ¶ Rom. xii. 15. ** Matt. v. 42. †† Rom.
xii. 20. ‡‡ I. Pet. iv. 9. §§ Heb. xiii. 2. ‖‖ I. Cor. xiii. 4-7.
¶¶ James ii. 15, 16. *** Phil. iv. 8.

degree of faith may be, no matter how recent the change,—the flowers will certainly appear as soon as the winter is past. Up among the glaciers of the Alps, where the snow-line verges upon the spring, laying their bright faces against the very borders of the eternal snows, one sees the flowers. Yes, there they are, gentians, veronicas, forget-me-nots lifting their blue corols against the very ice. I have seen the like on the Rocky Mountains, where the flowers creep to the border of the snows that hang upon the summits throughout the spring, and linger even in the heats of August. There they always will be, wherever there is the faintest stirring of vegetable life.

> Everywhere about us are they glowing—
>   Some, like stars, to tell us Spring is born;
> Others, their blue eyes with tears o'erflowing,
>   Stand, like Ruth, amid the golden corn.
>
> Not alone in Spring's armorial bearing,
>   And in Summer's green-emblazoned field,
> But in arms of brave old Autumn's wearing,
>   In the centre of his brazen shield;
>
> Not alone in meadows and green alleys,
>   On the mountain-top, and by the brink
> Of sequestered pools in woodland valleys,
>   Where the slaves of Nature stoop to drink;
>
> Not alone in her vast dome of glory,
>   Not on graves of bird and beast alone,
> But in old cathedrals, high and hoary,
>   On the tombs of heroes, carved in stone.
>
> In the cottage of the rudest peasant;
>   In ancestral homes, whose crumbling towers,
> Speaking of the Past unto the Present,
>   Tell us of the ancient Games of Flowers.*

So it is with the soul renewed. If it be changed at all there will be a blossoming out of virtues and graces. One would as soon think of May without flowers as a genuine conversion without softening of the manners, sweetening of look and tone and action. The remark of Mr. Whitfield, I believe it was, is only another way of

---

* HENRY WADSWORTH LONGFELLOW—"Flowers."

putting the same truth : " I have little confidence in the religion of a man who is not made thereby more kindly even to his cat." I fear that some persons who profess and call themselves Christians, and who, it may be hoped, are indeed such, are fighting against the very power that is seeking to beautify their lives because they have mistaken upon this point. The flowers do appear in their lives, but they deliberately pluck them up and cast them away as altogether contrary to a manly character and true Christian walk.

" I am a very blunt man!" You have more than once, doubtless, heard that utterance as a sort of proud, satisfactory and sufficient excuse for riding rough-shod over one's sensibilities. Or you have heard it said, " I must be faithful!" as the sufficient reason for breaking into the garden of one's heart and trampling upon every tenderest sentiment and honorable impulse. Now, I am free to say for myself, that I do not like such "blunt" people, and I am not pleased to be the subject of such so-called faithfulness.

Never was there a more faithful man to the souls of men than St. Paul, and yet a spirit of courtesy and tender persuasion is everywhere manifest in his words and actions. Who was so faithful—who can be—as the Son of Man himself? Yet gentleness and sweetness, the very flowers of gentility, goodness, charity and compassion, marked his earthly career. You may be sure that men will not tolerate your so-called bluntness and faithfulness when they show conspicuously the absence of kindness, consideration and good manners. Seek therefore to prove by the beauty of your character and dealing, that Christianity makes men better in every respect. The man who becomes a Christian becomes more truly a gentleman; the woman who becomes a Christian becomes more certainly a gentlewoman. How can it be otherwise? When the winter is past the flowers *must* appear in the earth !

I do not forget that all soils are not equally and naturally adapted to flowers. Some have to be made over with fresh material, and worked carefully and long before the sweet blossoms that we love to see in our beds and borders, can be made to grow within them. Such differences appear also among men. Some natures are more rugged than others, less adapted to the graces of life and better fitted for the rougher work which sometimes has to be done in a hard and wicked world. Yet, even so thinking, I do not recall what has been spoken, but declare that, as I read the Gospels of Christ, the result is well worth the labor, and that no matter how rugged the natural disposition, if it once receive the Gospel with a true spiritual faith it will inevitably blossom forth with some graces of a Christian gentility. Of this one may be well assured, there is no life so poor that the flowers of grace will shun it, just as there is no spot of earth wherein the flowers of the field may not be made to appear.

III. A third lesson which we may learn from the appearing of the flowers is that the best Test of a Change of Heart is a Change of Life.

We count the winter months to be December, January and February, and the months of spring we name March, April and May. That division may be true of other lands and certain sections of our own land, but it is not true of the northern part of these United States. Often the dreariest form of winter prevails during March, which the almanac makers have declared to be a Spring month. But every one knows that the almanac is not infallible, and that the seasons have a way of their own of hastening and retarding their coming, and shortening and prolonging their stay, with utter indifference to the fixed proprieties of our artificial appointments. You may label March "Spring time," but if the fields are snowbound and the temperature below freezing point, you will know it to be winter quite the same. The thermometer and the flowers are better tests of Spring than the almanac.

The first class in whose behalf I would apply our metaphor is the children. They have often been the victims of that error which hedges about the period of regeneration with arbitrary bounds. You doubtless know some excellent people who are very sceptical about God's ability to convert a little child. Although the Saviour said, " Of such is the kingdom of Heaven," they hold very firmly to the notion that the kingdom ought to be barred against " such." In other words, if a child wishes to make profession of his faith in Jesus Christ they say he has not yet reached the proper age— he is too young! Pray, what is the proper age? When may the young people say, " The May day of my soul has come; the winter is past!" When? You do not name the exact date perhaps, but in your minds you have fixed a boundary and have said, on this side of youth it may be spring, on that I hardly believe it is. Therefore you hold the dear children back from professing their Lord and keeping the Paschal feast in memory of his dying love. What shall we say to you? If April gives three weeks of spring weather shall we refuse to call it Spring because it is not the First of May? If leaves are fully opened upon the trees in squares and parks, forests and fields, and the grass is almost ready for its first cutting, and the flowers have been peeping their blue eyes above the sward for weeks, and the spring birds have been chirping, whistling, piping, twittering, and caroling from house-tops and trees, will you point your finger to the almanac and say: This is not spring, and we will not suffer ourselves or others the comfort of a belief that so it is? Yet, thus acting you would be no wiser than you are in that unfortunate policy which excludes children from the public privileges and private enjoyments of full membership in Christ's Church.

No man may limit the operations of the Holy Spirit. There are diversities of gifts, we are told, but the same Spirit.* Regeneration has its own laws. No man can say how early in life the quickening of the soul may come, and no man ought to fix bounds in any case, and say that it cannot be come until the years have thus far advanced, or until body and brain shall thus far have grown. The point for all to consider is simply—has this child the experience that befits a Christian child? Does he love his Saviour? Does he wish to confess Him? Does he understand the mystery of the Holy

---

* I. Cor. xii. 4.

Communion of his body and blood? Does he enjoy the services of God's house, and the fellowship of God's people? Is it his desire to remember the Lord's death until he come? Have the flowers of religious Faith and Hope appeared? I endorse cordially the direction of that venerable communion in whose ministry I serve, concerning children born within the pale of the visible Church and dedicated to God in baptism: " When they come to years of discretion, if they be free from scandal, appear sober and steady, and to have sufficient knowledge to discern the Lord's body, they ought to be informed it is their duty and their privilege to come to the Lord's supper.

" The years of discretion, in young Christians, cannot be precisely fixed. This must be left to the prudence of the eldership. The officers of the Church are the judges of the qualifications of those to be admitted to sealing ordinances; and of the time when it is proper to admit young Christians to them."*

The flowers of the vine as spoken of in the text well illustrate this truth for us. " The fig tree putteth forth her green figs, and the vines with tender grapes give a good smell."† The figs, you observe, are " green figs," the grapes are " tender grapes." It is rather in the promise than in its realization that the Christian character and life are here presented. The fruits are immature. The ripening is yet to be; but that does not alter the fact that the change from winter to spring, from death to life, has really taken place. Are there not those who seem to think that in the Lord's vineyard the harvest should come in the time of sowing, and the vintage in the time of bloom? Children may be Christians, but they will be Christian children. It is not fitting in the economy of nature, or in the economy of grace that the child should be anything but a child. The blossoms of the True Vine will be simply—blossoms.

We do, indeed, sometimes find children who are prematurely old. They seem never to have been children. But this condition is the result either of misfortune or of

---

* Westminster Confession of Faith, Directory for Worship, chapter ix. † Authorized version.

sin. The bloom of childhood has been nipped by con-
genital disease, or destroyed by hereditary taint and
environment of sin, or by cruel, foolish society. Oh, it
is both a sorrow and a shame—a child life on which no
flowers of childhood are blooming! What folly, nay, I
will add, what wickedness to seek to perpetuate a condition and character like this in the Church of the living
God. Let children be Christians, but let them be Christian children! Remember that even "green figs" and
"tender grapes" tell the story of a present spring. Says
the inspired writer, "Man cometh forth as a flower."*
But the flower cometh forth as a bud. Children are the
Buds of Humanity. Would it not be a strange garden
without buds in spring time? Would it be a garden at
all? No, indeed! Then bring in these Household
Buds, our children dear, to adorn the garden of the
Master and glorify by their sweetness the grace which
calls them into life, and which in due time will cause
them to open into full beauty, and develop the seeds of
a holy maturity.

2. Again, that quality in the act of regeneration and
the work of sanctification which I have been pleading in
the children's behalf needs also to be mentioned for the
encouragement and vindication of many adult believers.
I need not repeat what was said in a former lecture upon
the progressive character of the religious life; but I wish
here to emphasize the difference between regeneration
and conversion for the sake of a lesson which I am sure
many need to learn. Regeneration, which is the new
birth, is a gift once for all time; conversion, which is the
turning again to God, is a gift and duty for every act of
sin. Thus the questions emerge: Does regeneration
leave man's heart perfect, sinless; or can one be a Christian and sin at all? It must be remembered, in answer
to this, that in the act of regeneration the habit is
changed, its general drift and bent are turned toward
God. There may be variations from the right line—they
are sinful. They should be sorrowed for; should be

* Job xiv. 2.

shunned; they are not to be justified, nor repeated; but the soul should not despond because of them, nor do they necessarily prove that one is not a Christian The mind and manner in the outcome of the whole life journey may be heavenward, and in the child of God it will be so in spite of those lapses into which he may fall. The Spring does not at once cover and clear away all the marks of Winter. The stubble stands in the wheat-field, the corn-stalks on the prairie, the spears of withered grass upon the meadow, the dry leaves in the forest. Nevertheless, around all debris and decay of the season past Spring slowly weaves her emerald mantle, and amidst the living green appear the flowers.

I know an apple tree that stands almost the last survivor in an old orchard. Its sturdy trunk is covered with parasitic fungi and knotty warts; its limbs are partly gnarled and decayed; but look up into its branches on a May morning! The twigs are white with blossoms; the air is fragrant with their odor. For five-and-twenty years the old tree has yearly made that promise of fruitage, and for five-and-twenty years has fulfilled it. It has sheltered and fed the children of the cottage over which it spreads its boughs. It feeds and shelters the children still, and the gray-haired sire who bends upon his staff as he looks into the blossoming top and thinks of the spring time of his life. One may regret the roughness, excrescences, knots, and twists of the old tree, but is it not a *tree?* Aye, has it not in the main been a good tree? Dare you, will you forget the genuine service of the past, the blessings still whitening upon it, because of its gnarled form? At least, God will not forget. He is not only merciful, but just. He knoweth our frame; He remembereth that we are dust. He will treasure up our deeds and deal in tenderness with " the worm Jacob."

I am not pleading that the trees in the Lord's garden should grow gnarled and wart-covered with sin. Nay, it is better that they should grow from youth up tall and shapely as well as fruitful. But I do insist that a tree upon which year by year the flowers appear, and whose flowers year by year develop into fruit, is and ought to be accounted *a tree!* " By their *fruit* ye shall know them." That is the Master's test; let it also be ours.

IV. Let us notice as we lay aside our theme that the flowers are associated with the Brevity of human Life and the Blessedness of Immortality in Heaven.

The Hebrew prophets give little notice to the flowers compared to what one would naturally expect from the abundance and beauty of these objects of Nature, as well as from the usual sensitiveness of the writers themselves to the influences of Nature. For the most part, Scripture references are confined to mournful reflection upon the decay of the flowers, which are alluded to under the general name of " grass." This fact is made a parable of the uncertain tenure of human life. Of man Job says, " He cometh forth as a flower and is cut down."* The Psalmist David repeats the mournful refrain, " As for man, his days are as grass; as a flower of the field, so he flourisheth."† Isaiah represents the pride of Ephraim as the " glorious beauty of a fading flower."‡ Again, that voice which the prophet heard sounding in the wilderness the note of preparation for the coming of the Lord, is tuned to the same minor key: " All flesh is grass, and the goodliness thereof is as the flower of the field: the grass withereth, the flower fadeth."§ The same spirit largely pervades the New Testament allusions to flowers. St. James exhorts the rich to rejoice " in that he is made low: because as the flower of the grass he shall pass away. For the sun riseth with the scorching wind, and withereth the grass; and the flower thereof falleth, and the grace of the fashion of it perisheth: so shall the rich man fade away in his going."∥

Even our Saviour in his well-known allusion to the lilies, although He does indeed emphasize their glorious beauty, yet seems to be touched quite as deeply with the sense of their swift decay in the words, " If God so clothe the grass which to-day is, and to-morrow is cast into the oven." These expressions remind us of kindred

---

* Job xvi. 2.   † Ps. ciii. 15.   ‡ Isa. xxviii. 1.   § Isa. xl. 6–7.
∥ James i. 10–11.

thoughts associated with flowers in the tender words of
two of our best known American poets :—

> Gorgeous flowers in the sunlight shining,
>   Blossoms flaunting in the eye of day,
> Tremulous leaves, with soft and silver lining,
>   Buds that open only to decay ;
>
> Brilliant hopes, all woven in gorgeous tissues,
>   Flaunting gayly in the golden light ;
> Large desires, with most uncertain issues,
>   Tender wishes, blossoming at night.*

The wind-flower and the violet, they perished long ago,
And the brier-rose and the orchis died amid the summer glow ;
But on the hill the golden-rod, and the aster in the wood,
And the yellow sunflower by the brook, in autumn beauty stood,
Till fell the frost from the clear cold heaven, as falls the plague on
    men,
And the brightness of their smile was gone from upland, glade and
    glen.

And then I think of one who in her youthful beauty died,
The fair meek blossom that grew up and faded by my side.
In the cold moist earth we laid her when the forest cast the leaf,
And we wept that one so lovely should have a life so brief;
Yet not unmeet it was that one, like that young friend of ours,
So gentle and so beautiful, should perish with the flowers.†

There is another quotation from Scripture which I
make because it introduces to us in the way of contrast
a more cheerful lesson.   St. Peter‡ quotes from Isaiah
these words,

> All flesh is as grass,
> And all the glory thereof as the flower of grass.
> The grass withereth, and the flower falleth :
> But the word of the Lord abideth for ever.§

"And this is the word of good tidings," he continues,
"which was preached unto you."   Thus we are led
through the sad reflection of man's sure and early perishing, like the flower, to joyful confidence in the word of
God which assures him of immortal blessedness in
Heaven.

---

* HENRY WADSWORTH LONGFELLOW—"Flowers."   † WILLIAM
CULLEN BRYANT—"The Death of the Flowers."   ‡ I. Pet. i. 24.
§ Isa. xl. 8.

Our sacred poets have been quick to catch this cheerful association. It is not strange, inasmuch as the earthly Canaan is a land of flowers, that hymnologists should have clothed the heavenly Caanan with kindred beauty. Who of us has not rejoiced in Isaac Watts' picture of the heavenly country?

> There is a land of pure delight
>   Where saints immortal reign ;
> Infinite day excludes the night,
>   And pleasures banish pain.
>
> There everlasting spring abides,
>   And never-withering flowers ;
> Death, like a narrow sea, divides
>   This heavenly land from ours.
>
> Sweet fields beyond the swelling flood
>   Stand dressed in living green ;
> So to the Jews old Canaan stood,
>   While Jordan rolled between.

The sweet hymn of Tappan, beginning "There is an hour of peaceful rest," has made us think of heaven as a land of immortal bloom :—

> There fragrant flowers immortal bloom,
>   And joys supreme are given ;
> There rays divine disperse the gloom ;
> Beyond the dark and narrow tomb
>   Appears the dawn of heaven. *

To my mind this is something more than a poetic figure. I confidently expect, if I am so happy as to reach Heaven, to behold it decked with flowers—I was about to say, but will not,—lovelier even than those which beautify this world. I would fain hope to see there some of the familiar plants whose forms and fragrance are associated in memory with the holiest thoughts of parents and kindred, home and sanctuary ; that have carried to me expressions of the sweetest loves of life ; that have borne to me in sickness and trial tender remembrances of kind friends; that have been laid by mourning hearts and trembling hands upon the graves of the dear and dead. But of that one need not

---

*WILLIAM B. TAPPAN.

be too confident. Enough for us to think and believe that the heavenly country will be made a fitting place for us, and that doubtless our Father, who knows us as we are, will not forget our pure and lawful tastes, and in some wise, that shall minister to our unalloyed happiness, will deck the plains of Heaven with a beauty that must be perfect since it is the consummate work of Him who is "altogether lovely." Yet, whatever remains uncertain, this at least we know, that the highest joy of heaven will be to gaze forever upon the unfading Beauty and inhale forever the holy Fragrance of that Life which when on earth was sweetly symbolized by flowers,—the Rose of Sharon, the Lily of the Valleys, the true Vine "with the tender grapes."

LECTURE XVIII.

The Salt of the Earth.

"Ye are the salt of the earth."—MATTHEW v. 13.

THE SALT OF THE EARTH.

THE sense in which a saying is to be taken often depends quite as much on the spirit of the utterance, the character of the speaker and the circumstances under which the words were spoken, as upon the exact phrasing itself. Here is an illustration. Had this sentence, " Ye are the salt of the earth," been spoken by a Pharisaic rabbi, how differently the world would regard it! We might well conceive a Jewish doctor reiterating,— in the village synagogue, or the Sanhedrim room on Mount Moriah, in just such figures as Jesus used in this Sermon on the Mount,—the old boast of Jewish superiority, Ye, children of Abraham, are the salt of the earth! Ye, Hebrews, are the light of the world! Ye, Jews, are a city set on a hill. The only sentiment produced in our minds would be indignation, or perhaps, if the grace of God and charity prevailed, pity. To be sure, there is a standpoint from which our supposed rabbi would be quite correct. " What advantage then hath the Jew?" cried the inspired apostle.* "Much every way: first of all, that they were intrusted with the oracles of God." That was a fact of Providence which justly placed them far above other nations in point of spiritual condition and privilege. What then was the error of our supposed rabbi? The answer brings us to our first thought, namely:—

I. Christianity is a Religion for the whole Human Race. The duty, responsibilities and endeavors of Christianity embrace the world.

The Jew looked at his position not from the high ground of duty, but from the low standpoint of pride. The catholic responsibilities which had been laid upon

---

* Rom. iii. 1-2.

(333)

him he perverted into odious caste. He had, indeed, been made the conservator of the oracles of God. But for what? He was salt, but salt of the *earth*. He was light, but light of the world. God honored him that thereby the universal brotherhood might be blessed. The treasures of Heaven were committed to him that mankind might be enriched. Like Joseph in Egypt he was exalted to spiritual lordship among men that he might garner the bread of life, and spread it among the perishing sons and daughters of Adam.

It was a terrible sin, it was the one unpardonable sin of that nation that this duty, responsibility and catholic love were permitted to degenerate into a religious and ethnic caste. Yet, let us not judge too harshly! Perhaps the proportion of Israelites who knew the time of their visitation and rose to the height of its noble vocation was as great as is to-day the proportion of like spirits in our own land of infinite possibilities. At least, thank God!—there were Jews enough, though a mere remnant according to the election of grace, to open their hearts to their real divine mission, and carry a catholic faith into the whole world.

"Ye are the salt of the earth." The words fell from the lips of Jesus of Nazareth as he sat on the Mount of Beatitudes, with his disciples gathered around him. He was organizing redemption for the race,—not for the Jews alone. He was drilling, instructing, disciplining men who should be conservators of the Gospel, that full fruitage of the old faith of Israel. He was not organizing a new religious caste; he was not building up one more barrier between the already too much riven and separated elements of humanity. He came not to destroy, but to save; not to divide in a sectarian sense, but to unite. To save the world from further corruption and decay; to lift anew the standard of the old, simple faith of the patriarchs; to fling forth once more the banner of universal love; to rally by his Good-news the nations to his standard, and cement them into one kingdom and family by the blood of his cross,—such were the great purposes of the Teacher who sat upon that mountain top in Galilee.

The broad sky was above him. No walls of earthly or sectarian temple shut him in. The vaulted dome of the universal Father's dwelling-place raised its azure heights around him. The grass and flowers brightened the face of mother earth, the floor of the temple wherein He taught. It is an inspiring picture that rises upon our imagination; and how incalculable the issues of that hour! From that hill-top has flowed down upon the world unto the remotest ages a stream of blessing. In that sermon was a fountain of salvation, and like another Elisha the Master's hand had cast into it the salt of healing and preservation. "Ye are the salt of the earth" —not for Judea and Galilee, but for the world I commission you. Not for the lordship of earthly ambition such as, in the dreams of modern Popes, might bring abject rulers and peoples to bow before the sceptre of a universal Bishop, but the field is the world to plow, and plant, and till;—a harvest-field in which to gather sheaves for the glory of Christ and the weal of souls.

Has there not always remained in the world the temptation to fall into substantially the error of the ancient Jewish rabbi and make Christianity a caste? Has there not often been manifest a spirit of pride in our religion, as lifting the nations which possess it above other nations such as the Japanese, the Chinese, the Hindoo, the Negro, the Indian? Has there not been thus wrought out a spirit of caste so strong as to tempt Christian nations to tyranny, selfishness, inhumanity, cruelty in dealing with nations of an alien faith? Nay! within the very bosom of Christianity how often is the same spirit developed? We have seen one denomination looking contemptuously upon another; one calling itself "The Church," and all others "the sects," "the dissenters;" saying "We are THE people; depart from us because we are holier than thou!"

It should not be so! The Christian is a true cosmopolitan—a citizen of the world. The spirit of primitive Christianity overleaped natural and political boundaries; oceans, rivers, mountain chains; Alps, Apennines, Pyrenees; Danube, Rhone or Rhine; channels, seas and oceans. Over these all ran and leaped and flew the spirit of universal love and consecration, and the earth was made one. Race, nationality, language, denomination were barriers that dropped down at the presence of this spirit, and hearts of Christians mingled in their devotions around the throne of the one Lord of the Church and the earth. Shall it ever be thus again? Yes, it shall thus be. The Church is not yet ripe, but is ripening for that day. It will come! It is coming! Above the horizon of the future I see the dim outlines rising.

The third Millennial of Christianity will greet its full glory. Hark! It is the grand chorus of the universal kingdom of our Lord, chanting as with one voice those articles of our venerable creed, " I believe in the Holy Catholic Church—the communion of saints." "Glory to God in the highest, and on earth—Peace!"

Of the Divine Father it is said, "For God so loved the *world*." * Of Jesus Christ it is said, "And he is the propitiation for our sins ; and not for ours only, but also for *the whole world*."† Of the Holy Ghost it is said, " And he, when he is come, will convict *the world* in respect of sin, and of righteousness, and of judgment."‡ To the Apostles and Christian ministry it is said, " Go ye into all the world, and preach the gospel to every creature." § Of the Saints it is said, " Ye are the salt of the earth."|| Our love is to be like the Father's, our spirit of self-sacrifice and bestowment like the Saviour's, our labors and spiritual influence like the Comforter's— for *the world;* our commission is like that of the apostles, to all mankind—" Ye are the salt of the earth."

Herein is one of the essential elements of Christianity. It expands the mental horizon of man. It lifts him upon a high mountain-top and shows him all the kingdoms of the world; not in the spirit of the old tempter, to have and hold for selfish pleasure, for it is Mount Calvary whereto Christ leads the Christian, and earthly ambitions can find no place thereon. Christianity gives to man a larger, broader, higher, deeper nature. It teaches and compels him to love, duty and

---

* John iii. 16. † I. John ii. 2. ‡ John xvi. 8. § Luke xvi. 15.
|| Matt. v. 13.

sacrifice for the race. Glorious truth! How dimly apprehended even now!

Perhaps some despondent Christian heart is saying to-day, "Alas! but the earth is not the Lord's. Who has believed our report? How few there be that be saved! Salt is but a sparingly distributed mineral after all. I fear that the figure of your text holds good, and that Christianity is no more widely distributed than salt." Doubting and timid fellow-believer, is it so? Whence are the supplies of salt? Here and there salt springs bubble up from the bowels of the earth, and human industry converts the saline waters into the pungent preservative crystals. Here and there, again, we see immense deposits of this mineral within the earth, as along the shores of the Dead Sea, in Louisiana, and in Germany, and these are mined by human industry. These are our chief sources of supply, but there is another, older, and more primitive source. Go stand upon the seashore. Dip up in your hand from yon retiring wave a portion of the waters. Place it to your tongue. It is salt! Yes, the great sea is there spreading from equator to poles. It holds its sovereignty over three-fourths of the earth's surface.

Assuming as a basis of calculation that each gallon of sea water contains about a quarter of a pound of salt,* and allowing an average density of 2.24 for rock salt, it has been computed that the entire ocean, if dried, would yield no less than four and a half millions (4,419,360) of *cubic miles* of rock salt! That would make a mass about fourteen and one-half times the bulk of the entire continent of Europe above high-water mark, mountain chains and all. Salt is not in such narrow diffusion, therefore, as you had supposed. It is everywhere,—as universal as ocean.

It is written† that in the days of the peaceful kingdom of the Messiah "The earth shall be full of the knowledge of the Lord, as the waters cover the sea." Or, to put it in other words, they who are the salt of the earth shall fill the earth. Has the promise not been fulfilled? In a measure, yes! The salt of the faith has

---

* 0.2547 pound. † Isa. xi. 9.

been cast everywhere in our days. The great salt ocean
of Christian love and truth skirts and laves the shores
of every continent. It engirdles islands. It runs up
and pierces the hearts of nations as the tide waters of
the Atlantic push back along the Delaware almost to
our city gates. We have been singing many years
Bishop Heber's noble missionary hymn :—

> Waft, waft, ye winds ! his story,
>   And you, ye waters ! roll,
> Till, like a sea of glory,
>   It spreads from pole to pole.

We might change the sentiment from supplication with
its outlook into the future, to one of realization and
thankful retrospect of work accomplished, and say :—

> The winds have borne the story :
>   The healing waters roll,
> And like a sea of glory,
>   They spread from pole to pole.

Certainly, much remains to be accomplished, but on
the contrary much has been done towards the accomplishment of the sublime and difficult commission committed to the Church by Jesus Christ eighteen centuries
ago. More will be done, much more than ever our most
sanguine visions depicted, when the Church shall rise to
fully conceive and undertake the work that Christ has
laid before her, the healing of the whole world, as " the
salt of *the earth.*"

II. In the second place we are here taught the Value
of Individual Effort and Character.

This truth comes to light when we read our text with
the emphasis on the first word. " YE are the salt of the
world." Not Christianity simply, but Christians ! "YE"
—not alone the doctrines which ye preach—" are the salt
of the earth."

Truth. doctrine, dogma must not be undervalued, but
it ought to be a prominent thought in your minds that
Ye are personally an element in the great work of saving
the earth,—not your creed simply, but yourselves ! Not
your system, but yourselves ! Not your Church, but
yourselves !

"Do I not support the Church?" you ask. "Do I not pay the minister to preach the faith? Do I not contribute to send missionaries to the ends of the earth, to carry the Gospel to the heathens? Do I not contribute to publication societies and religious journals to print and distribute the Gospel?" Yes! all that you do. You ought to do a great deal more of that! But were you to do your utmost, still the truth remains, "YE are the salt of the earth." The world will not be saved without the personal influence and direct labor of Christian men and women. Your own individual duty can never be done by proxy.

Our Lord once said to Peter, "Thou art Peter, and upon this rock I will build my Church."* There has been a vast amount of discussion over the intent and effect of this saying. On the one hand it is said, "Thou art Peter, and upon this rock"—on thee, Peter, the apostle—"I will build my Church." On the other hand it is claimed that Jesus meant to say: "Thou art Peter, and upon this rock"—that is, the confession that I am the true Messiah which you have made—"I will build my Church." To me it seems that both parties have the truth. On the rock-truth and the rock-truth bearers, on the true confession and the true confessors, on Peter's creed and Peter's self alike Christ has built and ever will build his Church. In other words, while Christian doctrine must be proclaimed and defended as forming the thought and so controlling the life of men, we must emphasize equally the fact that Christian individuals are required to give force and vitality to the truth which is embraced. However pure the doctrine may be, if the Church professing it be dead, indifferent, inactive, or if its life be contradictory of its precepts, the truth shall have little sway upon the minds and consciences of mankind.

"Ye are the salt of the earth," said Jesus; "but if the salt hath lost its savor"—what then? This expression is an indication to us that under the imperfect conditions of transportation in Christ's era, salt frequently reached the consumer in a very impure state, being largely mixed

* Matt. xvi. 18.

with earth. Salt which has lost its savor is simply the earthy residuum of such impure salt after the sodium chloride has been washed out. What a striking image this presents of a character from which has been taken away all those elements of spiritual health and saving which mark a true child of God. What is such a Christian? He is but a lump of common earth from which every heavenly element has been absorbed, and there is no place for him, and no use for him but to mingle with the earthy elements to which he belongs, or as our Lord expresses it—" to be cast out and trampled under foot of men."

Let all who put the chief emphasis upon the Church as an organization simply; upon the ministry as simply an apostolic succession, the recipients and vehicles of the grace of Christ to men,—let them remember this!—the Church without the true Christian is but the earth without pure salt. A Church organization whose members have lost their spiritual pungency and saving power is no better, indeed I sometimes fear it is even worse than any other simple human and earthly organization around it. Oh! beloved friends, our only safety for ourselves, our only security for the preservation of the Church, our only hope that we shall be the saving element in the world is that we ourselves should retain the savor of a holy faith and holy life, keeping us in communion with our Holy Lord. Ye! Ye! Keep the emphasis upon this word, "Ye are the salt of the earth."

III. A third lesson which we may learn from this natural symbol concerns the Method of Christian Saving.

How does salt fulfill its office of savoring and preserving? It is laid upon the object, it dissolves into the animal fluids, it melts away out of sight and pervades the whole tissues with its curative, preservative qualities. Put a few grains of table salt into a dish of broth. It is distributed silently and swiftly throughout the whole. It reaches every drop of the fluid mass. It cannot be seen, but it can be tasted.

It is often thus that Christianity operates in benefiting human life and preserving the health of society. It is a hidden power, working not in the broad glare of observation, but silently entering the hidden openings and disseminating itself secretly. There are some Christians at least who find comfort in such a reflection. They know that their work is not lost to the world, not forgotten of God because it is not wrought in the eye of day. When Joshua had led the tribes of Israel across the river Jordan he gave commandment that a stone memorial should be erected upon the bed of the stream, each tribe contributing its portion to the monument. Then the waves of the Jordan flowed back and covered it out of sight. The stream rolled on and rolls on. What good could such a memorial as that do? Who could see it there buried under Jordan's wave? And yet it was there. There it was known to be. There God could see it. No matter though Jordan might flow with so muddy a flood as to justify Naaman's sneer when comparing it with the limpid streams of Damascus. No matter how fiercely and high its waves might roll when the freshets of spring swept down its overflowing channel. The eye of God beheld the hidden memorial, and knowing the purpose of his people's hearts in placing it there, He accepted the offering and was well pleased.

Why should the Holy of holies in the Jewish temple, that most sacred part of the sanctuary, have been decorated and well nigh covered with gold? Nobody ever saw it except the high priest who entered it for a brief moment or two once a year. But it was there in the presence of God. Its beauty and value were offerings unto Him; and was it not enough for the devout spirits who made the offerings to know that God did see, and was satisfied with the honor paid Him?

We look at our own beautiful sanctuary and admire its graceful proportions and stately architecture. Our eyes run along the line of visible blocks of hewn granite and carved limestone with well-pleased glance. But these exterior blocks form but a little part of the temple. True, they are all that we see, but behind them within the walls, and beneath them in the mighty foundations, hidden out of sight and never to be seen, are those humble rocks that make up the body of both foundation and walls. Why should any one think that because he is out of sight, his influence counts for nothing? God has compared all Christian souls to "living stones" in the temple of His salvation. If you be among those living stones that lie in the foundations and form the very kernel and heart of the wall, are you any less the Lord's? Are you any the less serving the Lord?

Why, also we may ask, should any one think because he happens to have his place in the outer and visible arrangement of these living stones, that he is better or more useful than those who are not seen and known of men? Nay, Christian friends, let us remember always that he who works in silence and retirement, who faithfully does his duty as in the sight of God, without fear or favor of men, counts as much as any other in the kingdom of Christ for the glory of God. At all events it is ours to drop where the Master puts us, and there abide while He bids us, using all the power He gives and diffusing our influence silently, savingly, continually. Thus, in the method as well as the quality of our savoring, we shall be as "the salt of the earth."

IV. A fourth lesson from the salt points to the Saving and Savoring Influence of Christianity.

It is quite as true of material saving as of spiritual salvation that Christians are the salt of the earth. Had there been ten righteous men in Sodom the Lord would have spared that city for the ten's sake. No doubt the condition which could not then be met has often since been the ground for preserving communities and cities. We shall never know, until eternity uncovers the fact to us, how greatly the presence of God's people has been the means of diverting judgments and calamities from men. At the origin of Christianity the world was in a peculiar condition. The nations which had theretofore dominated the race were in a condition of decay. The then known world was embraced within the Roman Empire, and the outlying nations, although subdued by the iron hand of their Roman masters, were tied in loose affinity to the central government. Rome itself was undergoing a decline which was rapidly accelerating with each decade of time. The received religions of the old world were fast losing their hold upon human faith. The minds of men were completely unsettled as to the nature and obligation of religion and the verity of immortality. Then came Christianity with its positive truths, its conditions of absolute obedience and surrender, its untroubled outlook into the future, and unquenchable confidence in God's love for the miserable and gift of a happy immortality to the believing. It formed a rallying centre for the best elements of mankind in every nation of the Roman Empire. In the crash and convulsions of the ensuing ages, when everything good seemed buried under the general ruin and the race appeared lost, Christianity saved society from total wreckage. Around it as a principle of life gathered all the salvable elements of the world, and out of the ruins there rose slowly, steadily, and at last with mightily accelerated vigor that colossal power, the Church of Jesus, which ever since has maintained a dominating influence within the circles of civilized men. Thus Christianity saved society in the primitive centuries of our era.

There was a period when the Latin Church saved society. Perhaps it may be said with too much of truth, that it was largely responsible for that condition which demanded a saving. Be that as it may, during the Middle Ages kings and nobles, inflated with their idea of rulership by divine right, utterly ignored the common people and used them like the stones before their castle gates, or the bridge over the castle moat, as mere stepping stones and approaches to their own selfish ambition, pleasures, and enrichment. In that period the power of the Pope and the clergy interposed between the people and their oppressors and saved society from the destruction which threatened from the abuses of the feudal system. It was well for the world to know that there was a power greater even than tyrant kings and cruel barons. It was well for society to feel the force of a spiritual influence, to listen to a voice that claimed to be of God, and learn to recognize the rulership of conscience and heaven. It was well for society, yes, its very salvation—that this strong influence speaking in the name of God was exercised in behalf of the masses of mankind. It is true, that oftentimes this was done not through a gentle ruth and holy love, but simply from an ambitious policy which sided with the commons in order to play them as a check against nobles and kings. But God overruled the wrath of man to his praise, and even with many unlawful ambitions, selfish policies, and corrupt administrations, the Church of Rome became a savoring element, and rescued the race from a destruction into which titled tyrants were riding it under whip and spur.

Soon the tide turned. Christianity became a government not a Gospel, a ritual not a Voice, a system not a Salvation, a policy not a Religion, a party not a Catholic Faith. The Church lost its grip upon conscience, and held men by their fears. Its rulers became corrupt,— the salt had lost its savor, and once more general decay seemed to threaten the human raee. Again Christianity interposed. Luther the monk of Erfurth came forth from his Augustinian monastery; touched with one hand the throne of Omnipotence, and with the other the heart of that "invisible Church" which ever survives amidst the visible Kingdom of Christ. Once more the saving salt was thrown into the fountains of learning and of common life, and the healing streams of the Reformation rolled through the earth bearing upon their broad, health-giving currents the hopes, thoughts, faiths, forces that have made this new Christendom that now reigns in the midst of a rediscovered world.

Thus it has always been, and thus it is to-day. The religion of Jesus Christ is the salt of the earth. It has sweetened and purified the fountains of human life and caused the lands through which it flows to put forth beauty and fruitfulness. This is the truth which inspires the efforts of the Church to send the Gospel to the uttermost bounds of earth. We believe that the world needs Christianity, that there is nothing to take its place —nothing that can savor society and stay the progress of decay except that holy faith which has made our own lives sweet with holy obedience and bright with the hope of Heaven.

Stop! Do not let your thought concerning the aggregate divert you from the individual. You need saving also, do you not? Yes, that is a real necessity with every soul. Did not Jesus always deal with souls from that viewpoint? Yes! He ever took it for granted; He often declared it; He put it within the very texture of all his speech and conduct as an awful fact not to be questioned, never to be concealed. "The Son of man came to seek and save that which is lost." The lost sheep of the shepherd, the lost coin of the housewife, the lost son of the good father, the lost soul of the rich man—these are facts which Jesus dealt with in serious, loving, pitying faithfulness. What did He mean? I do not know. You are lost! You need saving! I know that; I know that Christ is here to-day to save you. Do you ask, "What shall I do to be saved?" "Believe in the Lord Jesus Christ and thou shalt be saved!" This is the one answer for all time, for all souls, for *you!*

V. Finally, we may learn from our text the Saving Power of Christ.

A considerable portion of the salt of commerce is prepared by evaporation of sea-water through artificial means. But the more primitive method was wholly dependent upon the fervor of the sun's rays. That primitive method indeed has provided for us the chief supplies which furnish the salt of commerce. The rock salt found imbedded within the earth, and which is so extensively mined for domestic use, bears evidence of having been formed by the evaporation of lakes or seas at former and perhaps remote geological periods. The character of the crystals themselves, the stratified nature of the deposits with their interposed beds of clay, and the marine shells often occurring abundantly in the surrounding rocks of contemporary periods, all point to this simple solution of the presence of such vast quantities of rock salt. The ancient convulsions of the soil that shut off great bays or arms of the sea from the general ocean, and left their waters in vast natural salt-pans to evaporate beneath the rays of the sun and the action of the winds, have produced for us the masses of mineral salt.

Thus we have one more blessing to add to the sum of indebtedness due to that venerable friend of man, the sun. You already discern the trend of our metaphor. Who is the Sun of Righteousness who rises upon this earth of ours with healing in his wings? It is the Lord Jesus! Well we know that it is by the power of Jesus Christ alone that they who are of the faith are separated from an unbelieving world and thus become in truth, as Christ has called them, the salt of the earth. "By the grace of God," said St. Paul, "I am what I am."* So every Christian says. Not unto us, O Lord! not unto us, but unto thy Name be all the glory.

> Sinners! whose love can ne'er forget
> The wormwood and the gall,
> Go spread your trophies at His feet,
> And crown him Lord of All!

Still shines that Sun of Love upon this ocean of humanity seething and rolling in sin and death. Still the power of Christ is exerted to separate you, and all who will yield to the power of his grace, from the elements of destruction, that you may become not only one of the saved, but one of those who, as true salt of the earth, shall savor others.

A religious significance was very early attached to salt, a substance so highly prized and often obtained with so much difficulty. Homer called salt "divine." Plato named it a "substance dear to the gods." As covenants were ordinarily made over a sacrificial meal in which salt was a necessary element, the expression "a covenant of salt"† meant an agreement consecrated by sacrifice and therefore sacred. The preservative qualities of salt were held to make it a peculiar and fitting symbol of an enduring compact, and influenced the choice of this particular element of the covenant meal as that which was regarded as sealing an obligation to fidelity. Among the ancients and among the Orientals at the present day, every meal that included salt had a

---

* I. Cor. xv. 10.   † Num. xviii. 19.

certain sacred character, and created a bond of piety and guest friendship between the participants.

Christians who are the salt of the earth are witnesses to that sacrifice of Calvary by which God's covenant love was established and completed for the redemption of a lost world. Every Church of Jesus abiding under this covenant, proclaims God's faithfulness in Christ's sacrifice. Every believer who hopes that he has been saved by divine grace bears testimony before all who know him of the power of that Sacrifice, the endurance of that covenant, and the unbroken fidelity of that promise by which salvation is brought to men. Oh impenitent souls, receive this testimony! Listen to the voice of this witnessing. Let every believing soul rescued from the power of sin, be an encouragement and call to yield to the separating Force of the Sun of Righteousness and Love, and ally yourselves with those who shall be among the saved, and will join with the saved to be " the salt of the earth."

LECTURE XIX.

———

A Man's Natural Right
to Own Land.

"And thou hast said unto me, O Lord God, Buy thee the field for money and call witnesses."—JERE-MIAH xxxii. 25.

A MAN'S NATURAL RIGHT TO OWN LAND.

SIMPLE truth and justice require me to dispel from
your minds at the very outset the confusion which
exists as to the relative character and standing of An-
archists and Communists. With the theories of Anarch-
ists we can have no measure of sympathy. Their
banner cry is the destruction of all government, the
annihilation of all the old sacred faiths, laws and customs of society. But this is not true of all communists.
There is a philosophy of Communism which is worthy
at least of our respect. It has had many forms which
have illustrated the law, the power and spirit of our
divine Lord;—many advocates whose characters have
been beautiful and whose lives have been holy and useful.
It is a most ancient philosophy and, as we shall presently
see, has characterized a most ancient form of government. The common right of the people to the land,
and the common usage thereof by the people, are as old
as the patriarchs of Bible story; and some of those who
urge this principle and policy of government, as it seems
to me, are simply desirous of remanding humanity to
the estate of the patriarchs. Their ideal government is
the patriarchal government, a tribal government, and no
one can truthfully or seriously affirm, certainly no believer in the Bible can do so, that such a policy and such
advocates are necessarily mischievous, unchristian and
wrong.

Moreover, it ought to be a matter of sincere satisfaction and congratulation instead of the contrary, on the
part of those who believe that Communism even in its
purest form is impolitic and destructive of modern civilization, that the discussion of the underlying principles
at issue has passed from the lips of ignorant men, de-
signing and self-seeking charlatans and demagogues, to
men whose character for purity, honesty and sincerity

of purpose and desire to benefit mankind are beyond question. I hail with pleasure, and not with regret, the fact that there has recently stood amongst us as an advocate of these views a learned gentleman, a clergyman of a venerable communion, whose character and career have heretofore highly illustrated the virtues of the man and the minister. While the leaders of Communism are men such as he, we may all be inspired with the hope that the issue shall be remanded from the sphere of mere brute conflict, to the loftier and nobler arena of intellectual discussion and moral truth. There let us seek to keep it. The question must be met. We cannot put down by the strong hand of cruelty the men who hold to Communism in land, even though they be mistaken. Mere dogmatism, threats, assertion and reassertion will not prevail. We must convince the judgment, if not of those already enlisted, at least of the multitude who are turning now an open ear to the witchery of their enticing theories. Under a profound conviction that this is the duty of the leaders of thought, I have purposed this day to consider the subject of the right of individuals to own land.

The fundamental principle of Communism is that land belongs to the people, and that it should be held by the government of the people for the people's use and behoof without distribution to individuals to be held by them in fee. In other words, that the ownership of land is a natural and common right, like the ownership of sunlight, air and water.

To justify the opinion expressed that those who hold such views are entitled to consideration, I would simply call attention to the fact that in one form or another the doctrine forms the basis of many of our laws regarding the tenure of land. In our own country a vast quantity of the land, "the public domain," belongs to the Government, and the greater portion of that now held by individuals was originally distributed by the Government. The Homestead Law grants in severalty to every actual settler one hundred and sixty acres of this common domain. The first settlers in New England carried with them the idea of the village commune. They decreed a grant of land to each householder to the extent of twenty acres. Of the rest of the land a portion was to be held in common. The right of "eminent domain" pertains to the General Government, and indeed, to the local State Government, by which any property may be seized and set apart for common use. We hold in Philadelphia a large portion of the land in common, for the streets belong to the people for egress and ingress from and to their own homes, and for carrying out the common purposes of human life. The city may legally and often does condemn lands, burial places, houses, churches to the common use in order to establish roadways. Our squares and parks are held in common for the use, entertainment and invigoration of all the people.

We recognize this idea in those laws that prohibit or limit the right of entailing property, the law against accumulations, the law forbidding perpetuities. In Great Britain this principle is very strongly exhibited in the land laws. In fact, it is an undisputed maxim of English as well as of Scottish law that the sovereign is supreme lord of all the land. It is an unquestionable legal rule that there is no such thing in the British system as an absolute private right of property in land, but that the State alone is vested with that right, and concedes to the individual possessor only a strictly defined subordinate right subject to conditions from time to time imposed by the community. The nearest approach to private property permitted by the laws of Scotland is that by which "subordinate vassals" may convey themselves into "direct vassals" of the crown. Among the Celtic tribes of Ireland and the Scottish clans, even down to modern times, land was the possession of the tribe or the clan. The chief was the leader, but not the owner. In our own day and country this nation has recognized time and again this principle of village or tribal communes in its treaties with the various Indian nations. So that this law is a part of our legal system in so far as it applies to the aborigines of the soil. In view of such facts we must recognize the truth that there is much in history and law to be said for the fundamental principle of modern communism. Thus much being granted, let us turn to the question whether it be contrary to natural justice for the individual to become possessor of land in fee, that is as his property, to be held and handed down to his heirs?

I. First, then, it may be claimed that natural justice bears at least as strongly in favor of individual as of communal tenure of land, and that in the controversy human and Divine law must settle the question of right.

It is affirmed that individual right in property is contrary to natural justice. It is affirmed with the same breath that the community, village, state or nation may and should parcel out the land to its citizens according to the various necessities of the same; these homes and lands to be held simply at the will of the Government. In short, individual citizens become tenants-at-will of the aggregate of citizens, which is the State. But it seems to me that natural justice is as surely violated by communal as by individual land ownership. It simply changes the scale, not the essential principle, to vest the tenure in a village or state commune. For Nature is not communistic, but cosmopolitan. Does not natural justice declare, with equal force, that when a government of American citizens shall have thus adjusted the communal property, there may come from across the sea a million of exiled Englishmen and Irishmen and assert their right to share with those already in possession? Why should not natural justice give them a share? for they, too, are men, and Nature includes all men. When our English and Irish friends are thus settled, what again shall hinder an irruption of the peoples of Northern Europe, the Germanic nations that flocked of old to Italy, from crossing the sea and making the same claim of partition of property on the ground of natural justice? For, are they not men? And Nature is as broad as humanity. Still further, what is to hinder the hordes of China from flocking across the Pacific Sea through the Golden Gate and over the Transcontinental Railways, and making a like

demand of Irish, English, German, and American occupants of the soil? If our standard be so-called natural
justice, interpreted by the canons of communism, is it
not manifest that the laws controlling property must be
made as broad as Nature, and so take in the whole race?
Is it not manifest to the least logical mind that a law
which limits the partition of land for usage and occupa-
tion to the citizens of any nation, State, or community
has just as clearly violated the law of "natural justice"
as have those nations and people who dispose of their
sovereignty in the land for a consideration to families or
individuals, to be held as theirs in fee? If Citizen
Smith may not justly own a house or farm for himself,
his family and heirs, with what color of natural justice
may forty Citizens Smith form a corporation or commune and own houses and lands for themselves, their
families and heirs, as against all the rest of the human
race?

In a case such as we have supposed where shall the
limit come? Would not the inevitable result of such a
reign of communism be to remand man to the savage estate where the law of the mightiest and the most numerous prevails? Would it not give strong nations and
the most populous nations the right to unsettle and destroy from the face of the earth the weak or sparse peoples?

There is a law of natural justice which is sanctioned
also by the law of the Holy God, that reads thus, "He
that provideth not for his own, especially those of his
own household, has denied the faith and is worse than
an infidel."* Nature in man compels him to secure for
himself, his wife and offspring a retreat that shall be indeed a refuge against the injustice, selfishness, aggres-
sions, the ignorance or misfortunes of their fellows.
There is nothing in this law when rightly used and not
abused that hinders him from the largest charity and
consideration for his fellow-men. For the same Divine
Spirit that gave this law, based upon Nature, gave also
another law, "As ye would that men should do to you,
do ye also to them likewise."†

---

* I. Tim. v. 8.   † Luke vi. 31.

II. Second, we find this right strongly implied, at least, in the Original Constitution bestowed on man by his Creator when he was placed in possession of the earth. "And God blessed them; and God said unto them, be fruitful and multiply, and replenish the earth, and subdue it; and have dominion over the fish of the sea, and over the fowl of the air, and over every living thing that moveth upon the earth." *

There is no question, so far as I am aware, of the right of men to individual property in the beasts, the only limitation being those conditions which Nature has imposed. For example, personal ownership of the horse, ox, sheep, dog, camel, chicken, goose, duck and other creatures classed as domestic animals has never been questioned. Is there any living man to-day who would venture to rise in the midst of this or any other community to question the absolute right of the carter or drayman to his horse, or the farmer to his herds and flocks, to dispose of them and their products according to his will? Who would challenge the laws that secure men in their ownership of these creatures? The wild animals and wild fowls, it is true, are not protected by law as property except when they are killed in lawful chase and in those lands where parks and preserves for game are maintained. We exercise and claim no owership of the wasp, the mosquito or the spider, for these have never yet been utilized by man for his service, but among insects the bee and silk moth become property, because they have been made useful servants of the human race.

Now it seems to me that the analogy here holds good.

If we can claim rightfully that the divine constitution, by which man was made natural lord of the beasts of forest and field, and the fowls of the air, gave him personal ownership of those creatures, by parity of reasoning the same constitution gives him like property rights in the earth, which these creatures inhabit, and which at the same time was bestowed upon him to subdue and rule. The only limitation must be the power of man to subdue beneath his law and hand. If we be told that the land is a natural gift of God, like the ocean highways, the

* Gen. i. 28.

air and sunlight, we answer that man cannot subdue and portion the great seas, the air of heaven, and the sunlight, but he can subdue, and parcel, and possess the land. Just as Natural Justice, and the instincts of human nature, and the outcome of human nature in its long experience, justify him in casting the ægis of ownership over those creatures who can be subdued to domestic use, while those who cannot be are left as outlawed, so land which can be held and possessed by him, may lawfully, justly and naturally become his for individual holding and use.

But we do not stop with this reasoning, strong as it is, by analogy and inference from the original natural conditions of man's inauguration as chief magistrate of the earth. We pass on to show that the divine constitution was early recognized by the patriarchs and fathers of the faith, and has the fullest sanction of the Holy Spirit speaking in the word of God.

III. We find individual ownership of land at the very Beginning of Commercial Life as recorded by the Scriptures.

The first account of an actual purchase and sale recorded in the Scripture is the purchase of a plot of ground by Abraham. "And Abraham hearkened unto Ephron; and Abraham weighed to Ephron the silver, which he had named in the audience of the children of Heth, four hundred shekels of silver, current money with the merchant. So the field of Ephron, which was in Machpelah, which was before Mamre, the field and the cave which was therein, and all the trees that were in the field, that were in all the border thereof roundabout, were made sure unto Abraham for a possession in the presence of the children of Heth, before all that went in at the gate of his city."* In this glance at the condition of land tenure in primitive times we observe two facts: the first, that the common possession of land evidently obtained amongst the children of Heth; second, that this did not prevent them from absolute sale of a portion to Abraham to be held by him and his successors for the uses to which it was devoted.

* Gen. xxiii. 16–18.

It is a touching and significant expression of a natural sentiment which has dominated men in every age, that the first example of barter and ownership in land should have been that of a sepulchre for the beloved dead. Are we prepared at this date to raise the question, Has a man a right to own a grave?

IV. Again, a study of the Agrarian Laws of Moses clearly shows as a part of Hebrew jurisprudence the principle of individual ownership of land.

After a long period of bondage in Egypt Moses was commissioned by God to lead out the Israelites from their land of bondage to the land of promise. When the land had been conquered by Joshua it was divided among the people by allotment. An enumeration of the Hebrew yeomen showed that there were six hundred and one thousand seven hundred and thirty persons who were entitled to an allotment. "And the Lord spake unto Moses, saying, Unto these the land shall be divided for an inheritance according to the number of names. To the more thou shalt give the more inheritance, and to the fewer thou shalt give the less inheritance; to every one according to those that were numbered of him shall his inheritance be given."* This land the people held independent of all temporal superiors by direct tenure from Jehovah their Sovereign.

This right was established and secured in perpetuity by a remarkable law known popularly as the law of the year of Jubilee. On every Sabbatic year, if the land had been alienated from the possessor, it was to revert to the families which originally possessed it. "Then shalt thou send abroad the loud trumpet on the tenth day of the seventh month, in the day of atonement shall ye send abroad the trumpet throughout your land. And ye shall hallow the fiftieth year, and proclaim liberty throughout the land unto all the inhabitants thereof: it shall be a jubilee unto you; and ye shall return every man unto his possession, and ye shall return every man unto his family. A jubilee shall that fiftieth year be unto you; ye shall not sow, neither reap that which

---

* Num. xxvi. 52–54.

groweth of itself in it, nor gather the grapes in it of the undressed vines."*

The purpose of this law doubtless was to maintain the perpetuity of land in small holdings among the people. It was a guard against monopoly; a law in favor of equality in land tenure. To render this equality solid and lasting the tenure was made inalienable, and the estates thus originally settled upon every family were to descend by an indefeasible entail in perpetual succession. Certainly it had the tendency to equalize possessions among the people, making extreme poverty and overgrown riches alike impossible.† It gave to every member of the body politic an interest in the soil, and so also in the maintenance of public order and the supremacy of law,—an interest which he had not even the power to part with permanently. It made the virtues of industry and frugality necessary elements in every man's character, so that labor was as honorable amongst the Hebrews as it has ever been in America,—a sentiment which is expressed by St. Paul in his well-known saying, "If any man will not work, neither shall he eat."‡ Under such a polity as this it was impossible that a few could revel in the enjoyment of immense fortunes, while the multitudes suffered lack of the common necessities of life. Entailed misery became well nigh impossible, for the power of heredity was broken by the return of the year of jubilee before it could fix upon the children of the alienated landholder the impress and stamp of pauperism. The hand of this Hebrew government was laid with equal beneficence upon all.

No doubt this law, independent of considerations of individual happiness, had regard to the maintenance of religion and the perpetuity of the Hebrew commonwealth. The possession of property fixed the people to the soil. The devotion to agriculture separated them from the ambition of war. Seated among their mountain heights, like the thrifty citizens of the Swiss republic in our own day, on the great highway between Egypt to the south, and Nineveh and Babylon and Syria to the

---

* Lev. xxv. 8–11. † WINES—"Laws of the Ancient Hebrews," page 403. ‡ II. Thess. iii. 10.

east and north of them, they had the strongest induce-
ment to maintain their independence. Every individual
was bound by law to do military duty. No standing
army was required, but, like our own militia laws, the
Hebrew code required every yeoman, at the summons
of the head of the government, to rally under his own
legitimate chiefs and leaders to defend his altars, his
hearthstone and his little farm. In short, the policy
seems to have been just the reverse of that which, as we
learn from Cæsar,* prevailed amongst the ancient Germans, who discouraged agriculture, permitted no fixed
quantity of land in severalty, or boundaries of property,
but assigned to communities and families at frequent
periods such spots for homes as were thought suitable,
in order to weaken their hold upon domestic life, and
nurture and maintain within them the habit and love of
war. Whatever may have been the purpose, the fact remains that under sanctions of Jehovah, Moses, the great
lawgiver of the Hebrews, bestowed upon individuals
property in land.

An interesting exception was made under the general
law of Jubilee as to houses in towns, which if not redeemed within one year were alienated forever.†. The
purpose, or at least the tendency of such a provision
would be to discourage an abnormal development of
city life, and to maintain the advantage of rural and agricultural habits. A sort of quit-rent was required of all
landholders, to be paid to the divine proprietor in tithes,
or the tenths, which was used to maintain the governing, literary, pedagogic, and priestly class, the whole
tribe of Levi being set apart to these special functions,
and being debarred from the general allotment and ownership of land which fell to the other tribes.

This provision of the Mosaic code strikes us as the
more significant in view of the fact that the Israelites in
Egypt must have been accustomed to an entirely different law and mode. A glance at the administration of
Joseph when he was premier of Egypt, will show us that
individual ownership of lands largely prevailed among
the Egyptians, but during the years of famine of which

* De Bell. Gal., chapter VI. † Lev. xxv. 29, 30.

we have a record in the book of Genesis, the lands were sold to the sovereign for corn, and thus became the property of the state. This common tenure largely prevailed, so far as we can learn, among the Egyptians, and it would seem that in the land of Goshen the Israelites maintained their position as tenants-at-will of the government, or if you please of the Pharaoh, the head of the government. They had, in short, the full benefit of communism during the friendly dynasty under which they had been introduced into Egypt, and all the terrible disadvantages of the system under the administration of a king "which knew not Joseph." With these four centuries or more experience of communism, and under the leadership of Moses, a man who was learned in all the wisdom of the Egyptians, it certainly is significant, and casts an immense fullness of side-light upon the question we are considering, that these liberated bondmen received from Jehovah their Lord a constitution based on individual ownership of land, and maintained it through all the following generations.

Is not this this the inevitable tendency of races as they rise in civilization? Among our own populations the principle of land communism is well illustrated in the customs of the American Indians. But those who best know the necessities of the red men, see the only hope for their assured future in the rejection of tribal possessions of land, and acceptance of the practice of ownership in severalty, as it exists among white men. Surely, we shall not be persuaded to take up and wear the " cast-off clothes " which our national wards, as they mount into a higher civilization, are leaving behind them with other trammels of a savage estate?

V. The views of the Holy Scripture concerning Landmarks is an evidence that the Divine law sanctions and protects the individual tenure of land.

In the book of Job, we read condemnation of those who remove the landmarks.* " Thou shalt not remove thy neighbor's landmark, which they of old time have set, in thine inheritance which thou shalt inherit, in

* Job xxiv. 2.

the land that the Lord thy God giveth thee to possess it," * was one of the statutes of the Israelites. This was surrounded by the sanctions of religion. On that day when the people were placed one half upon the slopes of Mount Gerizim to bless the people, and the other upon Mount Ebal to curse the people, among the very first of those violators of the law upon whom the awful maledictions of Jehovah were invoked, we find those who destroy the boundary marks. " Cursed be he that removeth his neighbor's landmark. And all the people shall say, Amen."† This idea of the religious sanction of the boundary lines of the people we see preserved in the mythology of ancient Greece and Rome. The god Hermes or Mercury being himself messenger of the gods, it became his office to aid messengers and travelers, and to this end it was he who inspired the idea of erecting sign-posts at cross-roads with directions as to whither each road led. These sign-posts took the form of statues, if they may be so called, consisting of pillars running narrower towards the foot and surmounted by the head of Hermes, and were called Hermæ. This name Hermæ or Terminii, belonged also to the field boundaries, which were under the protection of the same deity, Mercury.‡

VI. Moreover, we know that this law of possession and inheritance was not of Transitory Life. It did not become a dead letter upon the statutes of Israel. It received the sanction of prophets, priests, legislators, and rulers in the succeeding ages of the nation.

An illustration of this occurred in the reign of Ahab. This sovereign had a fancy for landscape gardening, and desired a vineyard belonging to a neighbor named Naboth to piece out his own property and add to the beauty of his park. Naboth refused to sell or exchange his vineyard on the ground that it was contrary to the law for him to alienate the inheritance of his fathers. The sovereign could not conceal his disappointment, and his wife Jezebel the queen, less scrupulous than

---

* Deut. xix. 14.   † Deut. xxvii. 17.   ‡ MURRAY—"Manual Mythology," 126.

Ahab, and indignant that the king should be thwarted by a common citizen, concocted a scheme by which under false charges Naboth was condemned, slain and his vineyard escheated to the state. When the sturdy citizen was stoned to death Ahab rounded out his pleasure park with the stolen vineyard.

But the matter was not so to end. The Eternal Justice, Sovereign of Israel as of all lands, had somewhat to say in this case. "And the word of the Lord came to Elijah the Tishbite, saying, Arise, go down to meet Ahab the king of Israel. Behold, he is in the vineyard of Naboth, whither he has gone down to take possession of it." I will not repeat the story. You may read it for yourselves in the twenty-first chapter of the first Book of Kings. I have simply to call your attention to the fact that the prophet of God, in obedience to the divine command, found Ahab on his stolen possession; declared to him the wickedness of his course and predicted his violent death, adding, with a striking sense of the eternal fitness, that "in the place where dogs licked the blood of Naboth, shall the dogs lick thy blood, even thine." There can be no question that in this case Naboth did right, that the law of Israel maintained him in possession of his property; that that right was so sacred and secured that not even the sovereign on his throne could overcome it, and dispossess the humble citizen of his property; and finally, that the Almighty God here also gave the sanction of His authority to the act of Naboth and the principle upon which he stood.

We take another case to show the vitality of this law and the fact that the individual possession and purchase of property were sanctioned by God. Our illustration carries us to a late period in the history of the Hebrew monarchy, under the reign of Zedekiah, nearly six hundred years before the era of Christ. The sacred city of Jerusalem was besieged by the army of Nebuchadnezzar, king of Babylon. The prophet Jeremiah was a prisoner in the house of the king of Judah, having been shut up because he had predicted the capture of the city and the captivity of the people. In such condition anything like a transaction in real estate, one would think, would have been the last thought to enter the prophet's mind. Yet we have such a record as this: "And Jeremiah said, The word of the Lord came unto me, saying, Behold, Hanamel, the son of Shallum thine uncle shall come unto thee, saying, Buy thee my field that is in Anathoth: for the right of redemption is thine to buy it. So Hanamel mine uncle's son came to me in the court of the guard according to the word of the Lord, and said unto me, Buy my field, I pray thee, that is in Anathoth, which is in the land of Benjamin: for the right of inheritance is thine, and the redemption is thine; buy it for thyself. Then I knew that this was the word of the Lord. And I bought the field that was in Anathoth of Hanamel mine uncle's son, and weighed him the money, even seventeen shekels of silver. And I subscribed the deed, and sealed it, and called witnesses, and weighed him the money in the balances. So I took the deed of the purchase, both that which was sealed, according to the law and custom, and that which was open: and I delivered up the deed of the purchase unto Baruch the son of Neriah, the son of Mahseiah, in the presence of Hanamel mine uncle's son, and in the presence of the witnesses that subscribed to the deed of the purchase, before all the Jews that sat in the court of the guard. And I charged Baruch before them, saying, Thus saith the Lord of hosts, the God of Israel: Take these deeds, this deed of the purchase, both that which is sealed, and this deed which is open, and put them in an earthen vessel; for they may continue many days. For thus saith the Lord of hosts, the God of Israel: Houses and fields and vineyards shall yet again be bought in this land."[*]

I have cited the entire passage, as it has such a clear bearing upon the question at issue that he may read who runs, and a wayfaring man though a fool need not err therein. Now this passage has always been regarded as one of the sublimest acts of faith on the part of God's ancient servant. The prophet was a prisoner. The country was overrun by an invading foe. Hostile armies were thundering at the gates of the capital, and Jeremiah knew that the city would surely be captured and

---

[*] Jer. xxxii. 6-15.

the people scattered as captives. Yet he so trusted the word of his God that he believed that, notwithstanding the circumstances surrounding him, in some after day the promise would be redeemed and once more there should be that token of prosperity, peace, and religious revival expressed in the closing verse of the section quoted: "For thus saith the Lord of hosts, the God of Israel: Houses and fields and vineyards shall yet again be bought in this land."

The theologian who takes the ground that the purchase and possession of land as property by the individual is wrong—contrary to natural justice and so also contrary to the word of God, is bound to explain this section. He is under obligation to show how the prophet could have acted as he did. He is bound to explain why the Church in all ages has esteemed this conduct one of the sublimest acts of faith, that esteem being based, as is alleged, upon behavior contrary to natural righteousness.

Further and above all, he is bound to explain how, in accordance with his theory, the Almighty God should make such a command to Jeremiah. That he did make the command is asserted directly again and again, both in the narrative and in that touching and wonderful prayer of the prophet which follows the completion of the business transaction. We find the fact put in these words: "And thou hast said unto me, O Lord God, buy thee the field for money and call witnesses, whereas the city is given into the hand of the Chaldeans." * You observe that Jeremiah felt in his heart that the Lord owed to him some explanation of this strange command under such apparently unreasonable circumstances, and the Almighty vouchsafed the explanation. We read further in the chapter and in the course of the communication given to the prophet, this divine assurance: "Fields shall be bought in this land whereof we say it is desolate without man or beast; it is given into the hands of the Chaldeans. Men shall buy fields for money and subscribe deeds and seal them and call witnesses in the land of Benjamin, and in the places about Jerusalem and in the cities about Judah, and in

---

* Verse 25.

the cities of the hill country, and in the cities of the low-
land and in the cities of the south, for I will cause their
capitivity to return, saith the Lord."*   Now, can any
theologian, can any clear-minded reader of the Holy
Scriptures explain how, in face of such divine sanctions,
it becomes contrary to righteousness and justice for men
to do like things in these days in the cities and vineyards,
in the hill countries and valleys of America or any
other land?

---

* Verses 43, 44.

May a Christian Own Land?

"Whiles it remained, was it not thine own?"—
ACTS v. 4.

MAY A CHRISTIAN OWN LAND?

WE are to examine in this lecture what may be regarded the crucial point in the discussion of a man's right to own land. It may be said, it has often been said, all the regulations heretofore considered belong to the Old Testament dispensation. "The old things are passed away; behold, they are become new."* Whatever may have been lawful for the Jew (it is asserted), it is not permitted a Christian to own land. The spirit of Christ and the deeds and decrees of the apostles and Primitive Church sanctioned land communism, and on that ground we may advocate it to-day.

I may be permitted to say, first, that there are some old things that in the sense of the saying quoted never will become new; or rather let me change the expression and assert that there are old things which are forever new by the spirit of eternal life that lodges within them. Nature is one of those old things—old! no one knows how old. New! every one who will seek her smiling face upon a bright May morning, or consult her mysteries in the midst of winter snows and storms, will find how sweetly or how keenly fresh she is to-day, as she has always been. Human nature is old, but human nature is new also, as new to-day as when it fell a virgin creature from the Creator's hand. What human nature was in the garden of Eden, in the desert of Sinai, among the hills of Palestine, in the vineyard of Naboth, in the prison of Zedekiah's palace, it is to-day and always will be. That justice which belongs to human nature, and which is natural justice, is unchangeable, and whatever laws and principles based thereupon have been established as of God by reasonable inference are binding to-day with a force as fresh as when first they were laid within the constitutions of the human mind.

*II. Cor. v. 17.

But we accept the challenge, and turn now to that period of the New Testament Church from which nearly all Christian communes have obtained their supposed authority for their organization and regulation. In the fourth chapter of the Acts of the Apostles, at the thirty-second verse we thus read: "And the multitude of them that believed were of one heart and soul, and not one of them said that aught of the things he possessed was his own, but they had all things in common." "And with great power gave the apostles their witness of the resurrection of the Lord Jesus: and great grace was upon them all. For neither was there among them any that lacked: for as many as were possessors of lands or houses sold them, and brought the prices of the things that were sold, and laid them at the apostles' feet: and distribution was made unto each, according as any one had need."*

Here now is an undoubted case of communism. This is the ideal communistic society, a holy company of believers so dedicated to the service of God, and the dissemination of their new faith, and the welfare of humanity, that they voluntarily resigned all possessions and made a common fund. Does not this constitute a repeal of all the laws and usages of the past? Does not this give the sanction of the Primitive Church to a state and organization like that which is advocated by many modern communists? We must meet the question.

1. Undoubtedly the Church, particularly in the Latin and Greek communions, has always extended the sanction of its great authority to the existence of such communities, but you will observe first of all, that they were simply forms of Christian fellowship, not of civil government; they were integral portions of the Church, not of the State. The very foundation principle of the State, the *family*, was wanting, for they almost invariably took the form of communes of one sex, the result being communities of monks on the one hand and nuns on the other. Sometimes, as in the case of our modern Shakers,

---

*Acts iv. 33–35.

Economites, and similar communistic families, the sexes wrought, fed, and worshiped together as a common family of brothers and sisters, but in the practice of celibacy.

2. My second answer is that there is not a word in the positive precepts of our Lord Jesus Christ or of any of the New Testament writers ordaining the existence of such communities or such state of general society. The attitude of our Lord Jesus Christ on this subject is worthy of remark. He raised no contention with the old order of things. He announced no principle that by necessary and logical inference would overthrow that order. He mingled continually with those who possessed landed property, and although he was free to denounce oppressors of the poor and despoilers of the widow, no word fell from his lips censuring owners of land.

It would seem from the Gospels that among his closest friends and sincerest disciples were those who occupied homes of their own. He accepted the hospitality of these and other householders with the utmost freedom, and with never a suggestion of disfavor or rebuke. His favorite retreat when at Jerusalem was the beautiful home of Lazarus and his sisters Martha and Mary on Mount Olivet. To this delightful suburban retreat he continually and lovingly resorted after the wearying toils and vexing contentions of a day's teaching in the Holy City. Can we suppose that these beloved Bethany friends were guilty of wrong or impropriety in their ownership of their Bethany home, and that our blessed Lord received therein from them the sweets and solace of hospitality without a word or seemingly a thought of protest or rebuke? We cannot think it.

Among the apostles of Jesus was John, a friend of the High Priest, who owned " his own house." * The original expression† need not imply that John had a house in Jerusalem, but certainly does show that his usual habitation was fixed, and *was his own.*‡ When the

---

*John xix. 27. † εἰς τὰ ἴδια. ‡ *Vide* Alford's Greek Testament *in loc.*

Master hung upon the cross in the agonies of dissolution it was to this disciple, the beloved John, that he committed the care of his mother. It would almost appear that the fact of John's ownership of a home in which that venerated mother might fittingly be sheltered, was the one which decided the choice and action of Jesus in committing the Virgin Mary to this disciple's care.

Can we permit ourselves the thought that He who in the last moments of his life wrought such a work as this, could have known that the house in which his mother should find a safe retreat for the closing days of her life, was held by a law and tenure contrary to natural justice and Divine right? The thought is utterly inadmissible! It is true indeed that this evidence concerning our Lord's attitude towards the question of personal ownership of land is largely of a negative character; and yet there are circumstances under which such testimony has all the weight of the most positive witnessing. At all events, it is clearly manifest that the teaching and example of Jesus Christ cannot be quoted against the right of individual ownership of land.

3. In the third place, the action of the primitive Christians was voluntary. It has the force of example, it is true, but that is no further authority than the reasonableness of the example under similar circumstances may bestow. There are other actions of the apostles and primitive Christians, many of them, indeed, which we study with interest for the sake of their underlying principles, but which no one has ever thought to have the sanction of Divine authority, or to be of moral obligation to the people of these days.

4. But in the fourth place, and this is conclusive, we find in the direct utterance of St. Peter, the first of the Apostles, a clear renunciation of any purpose to annul the laws of property. In the fifth chapter of the Acts of the Apostles occurs the well-known incident of the punishment which fell upon Ananias and Sapphira

for a breach of faith, good-fellowship and truth. The incident briefly is this: Ananias and his wife sold a possession, that is a field, as the Greek indicates, claiming to have given the proceeds to the common fund, but they privily kept back a part of the money. When they brought this to the apostles their hypocritical conduct was uncovered by St. Peter, who addressed the false Ananias in these words, "Why hath Satan filled thy heart to lie to the Holy Ghost and keep back part of the price of the land? Whiles it remained did it not remain thine own? and after it was sold was it not in thy power?"

Do you discern the force of these words of St. Peter? Here is the most undoubted recognition and assertion by the apostle of the fact that while the field of Ananias was unsold *it was his own!* Even after the price of the land had been paid, and before it was given to the apostles, still, says Peter, "it was in thy power." The right of property only ceased when it was given into the treasury of the Church. The hypocrisy and falsehood of the man and woman were the sins punished. It was the claim on their part, before God and His Church, to a virtue which they did not possess, that excited the indignation of St. Peter, and brought down upon them discipline and the judgment of Heaven, not the violation of a communal law. It is inconceivable under the circumstances, as related, that the law of the Primitive Church required every member to dispossess himself of his property in land. On the contrary we here have the very highest authority, namely, the apostle Peter, speaking by the Holy Ghost, for the belief that Christians could lawfully retain lands, even as before their conversion. To those theologians who recognize St. Peter as the first Pope and head of the Church, it seems to me that this assertion ought to come with all the force of an ex-cathedra, and therefore an infallible utterance of the Church of Jesus Christ sanctioning the right of the individual believer to own land. "Whiles it remained was it not thine own?"

It is perhaps well to answer the question, Then why did the apostles encourage this community of goods?

The answer is obvious. The majority of the first believers in Jerusalem were poor; though many, like Nicodemus and Joseph of Arimathea, and the family at Bethany, and Mary the mother of Mark, and St. John himself, were possessors of more or less property. This Christian community was established in the very heart of the Jewish capital, under the shadow of the temple and within the environing prejudice, bigotry and hatred excited by sanhedrists and priests against the sect of the Nazarene. Those who know to what extent this spirit of caste was carried will understand at once that the condition of the poor and humble believers must have been a sad one indeed. They would have been utterly cut off from the means of support; so entirely tabooed or "boycotted," to use the modern well-known phrase, that no one would buy from them, or sell to them, or employ them, or even greet them upon the streets. It was therefore necessary that those who had aught should contribute to the support of those who for the sake of the faith were thus cut off from a livelihood. In short, it was Christian love waging its first battle against caste. It was the spirit of Christian brotherhood rising supreme over selfishness, and making willing sacrifice in behalf of the brethren of the faith.

The same state of things has existed frequently in history, and as often the Church has been fostered by the same triumphant exhibition of brotherly love. In modern times Christian missions among the Hindoos have been compelled to face a condition similar to that which met the Primitive Church in Jerusalem. Hindoo caste is so strongly intrenched in the minds and customs of the people that our first missionaries were compelled to organize their converts into Christian villages in order to preserve life. Conversion to Christianity meant outlawry in India. The native believer was expelled from the very bosom of his family, cut off from wife, family, parents, from all men,—remorselessly separated from every kind of social, commercial, and communal contact.

It is not strange, therefore, that in order to meet exigencies of a special time and condition the apostles should have encouraged a community of goods; but in so doing they no more sanctioned the doctrine of modern communism, or condemned the individual holding of land than do our American missionaries in India today, and it would be just as reasonable to attribute these principles to the latter Christian apostles as to the primitive ones.

5. But in the fifth place we are enabled to show by subsequent records that the interpretation of the apostle's principles and action here given is the true one. After the deliverance of St. Peter from prison by the interposition of an angel, we find this record: "When he had considered the thing he came to the house of Mary, the mother of John whose surname was Mark, where many were gathered together praying."* Here then is the inspired record of the fact that in that city of Jerusalem and among those primitive people, the mother of one of the evangelists, a lady of such importance that her house was the centre of the community for private devotion, to which St. Peter inevitably turned in his time of need, had retained her own house in her own hands. Obviously there was no compulsion in the primitive society resting upon any member to dispose of property; and those who chose to reserve their estates or any part thereof did not lose standing among the primitive Christians. Nor is this case of Mary alone in the sacred records. We read of St. Peter as dwelling in the house of Simon the tanner, apparently one of the brotherhood, at the time when the heavenly vision came to him, bidding him go to the house of Cornelius the centurion to convert him to the Holy faith.† The first convert to Christianity in Europe was Lydia of Thyatira, whose heart the Lord opened at the preaching of Paul, and who upon her conversion and baptism said, "If ye have judged me to be faithful unto the Lord, come unto my house and abide there."‡ When Paul was prohibited the use of the synagogue at Corinth for the propagation of the new faith we are told that he established his headquarters in "the house of a certain man named Titus Justus, one that worshiped God, whose house joined hard to the synagogue."§ There

---

*Acts xii. 12. † Acts x. 32. ‡ Acts xvi. 15. § Acts xviii. 7.

is one name which has been embalmed in the beautiful allegory of Bunyan as a type of Christian Hospitality in all ages, of whom John speaks as the "beloved Gaius,"* and whom Paul calls, Gaius mine host, and the host of the whole Church.† Paul when imprisoned at Rome joins with Timothy in greeting Philemon, and adds his salutation "to the church in thy house."‡ It is useless to multiply these references. True, we cannot be positive that all these householders to whom the sacred writers allude were owners of the properties in which they dwelt, but in consideration of the circumstances surrounding the various persons quoted, it is unreasonable to think that all of them were simply tenants, as was Paul when he "dwelt two whole years in his own hired house"§ at Rome. Indeed the evidence of the context and the associations as they appear therein seems to place all the individuals to whom I have referred among the number of those who possessed their own homes, and ample means besides, as well as disposition to make them centres of Christian influence and the seats of a holy hospitality. In this view they show that the whole spirit and practice of the early Church, as it was gradually distributed from Jerusalem throughout the surrounding nations, was quite in accordance with the ancient and prevailing customs, and with that which so universally obtains among Christians and civilized people to-day. The primitive Christians dwelt upon their own land and under their own roof-trees, and were sanctioned by the holy apostles and by their Lord. I do not hesitate to affirm that under such a light of testimony from so many independent quarters, extending over so great a period, and embracing such varied sources, it is absolutely impossible for any theologian to justify by the word of God the claim that an individual tenure of land and house is contrary to righteousness, natural justice, Christian charity, and the law of God.

I have yet one further point which I will not urge as an argument, but which seems to me to have the force at least of an indication, and a very sweet and sacred one.

---

* III. John i. † Rom. xvi. 23. ‡ Philemon, verse ii. § Acts xxviii. 30.

Before our blessed Saviour left the world he gave his disciples assurance and some degree of insight of that immortal habitation which it was his holy mission to procure and prepare for them that love and trust Him. "In my Father's house," he said, "are many mansions. If it were not so I would have told you. I go to prepare a place for you. And if I go to prepare a place for you I will come again and receive you unto myself, that where I am there ye may be also." * Does it not impress one who reads these words of Jesus that it was evidently his purpose to stir up within the disciples' minds a sense of holy longing and eager anticipation of the reward of heaven by appealing to that sense of personal possession and security therein which is so strong in the nature of man?

Those disciples were called upon to wander like their Master through many lands without homes—oftentimes having not where to lay their heads. For his sake they had forsaken houses and brethren, sisters, father, mother, wife, children, lands. They had the promise that they should receive an hundred-fold and inherit everlasting life. That receiving was not to be for them on this earth, but in another and better country; and as I read these beautiful words of the Master I seem to hear Him say: "Toil on! bear the sacrifice here! House you may not have on earth, but there is for you a mansion in the heavens. Here you may have no land that you call your own, but in that 'land of pure delight where saints immortal reign' there shall be for you, yes an hundred-fold, a possession, inheritance, and portion in the land of Heavenly Promise, which shall be yours forever and forever."

For myself I can hardly conceive of the Heavenly city and the Heavenly country independent of some place or mansion which shall be my own, where I may retire from the great crowd—no less a crowd because they are of the redeemed—and with my friends and kindred spirits enjoy under my own vine and fig tree, and under my own roof, the double joy of Home and Heaven. I do not think there is anything contrary, but much in accord both with human nature and theology in the suppo-

---

* John xiv. 2, 3.

sition that the Lord appealed to a like feeling in the breasts of his disciples when he encouraged them to endure all loss and sacrifice on earth in view of their own promised place in one of the many mansions in the Father's house in Heaven. If so, that very appeal throws upon the principle on which it is based the great authority of our Saviour's sanction. He recognizes as praiseworthy the hope to hold one's own mansion in the Heavenly city; he acknowledges its lawfulness by building thereupon the aspirations after the rewards and joys of immortality with God. It is surely a fair inference that the legal fact and human sentiment which Jesus made the groundwork of a metaphor that holds out to man the promise of an infinitely holy home, could not have been believed by Him to be unnatural and unholy. No! nor can we for a moment justify such a conclusion!

If this conception have in it aught of verity it gives the semblance of something more substantial than poetic imagery to those hymns of the Church that express the sentiment of a personal home in heaven. Some of these hymns are among the most familiar and best beloved by the people. Such for example is the one beginning

> When I can read *my title clear*
> *To mansions in the skies*, .
> I bid farewell to every fear,
> And wipe my weeping eyes. *

Such also is the hymn,

> On Jordan's stormy banks I stand,
> And cast a wishful eye
> To Canaan's fair and happy land,
> Where *my possessions lie*. †

And now as we bring these meditations to a close, will it not be well for you all to ask, have I through faith in Jesus Christ and the holiness which comes from faith, been made meet to be one of the "partakers of the inheritance of the saints in light"? ‡ Have I secured for myself "a title clear" to that heavenly home which the Divine Lord has gone to prepare for those who love him?

---

* ISAAC WATTS.   † SAMUEL STENNETT.   ‡ Col. i. 12.

The thirst for land is not unnatural, at least the desire for so much of land as shall constitute a home on earth is natural and praiseworthy. But how many there are who in the fevered ambition to add acre to acre, farm to farm, house to house on earth, are sacrificing their interest in that immortal Home without which all earthly possessions can be of little value! "For what shall it profit a man, if he shall gain the whole world, and lose his own soul? * Vain, vain shall man be secure in the possession of an earthly inheritance, if when the last hour comes, which surely and swiftly draws near to all, he shall fall on death without assurance that he shall pass into the heavenly country and the sweet possession of a heavenly mansion! Better, better far to be landless here than Homeless in the Hereafter? Yet there is no reason why in the exercise of a good faith and good conscience, you may not be " true to the kindred points of HEAVEN and HOME."

* Mark viii. 36.

THE END.

Lightning Source UK Ltd.
Milton Keynes UK
UKHW01f1359130718
325661UK00006B/317/P